Transforming Health Care

Virginia Mason Medical Center's
Pursuit of the Perfect
Patient Experience

Advanced Praise for *Transforming Health Care: Virginia Mason Medical Center's Pursuit of the Perfect Patient Experience*

This remarkable story of Virginia Mason's journey to Lean offers hope that America can achieve the high-quality, affordable care we all deserve.

— **Ceci Connolly**, Senior Adviser, McKinsey Center on Health Reform

A comprehensive and insightful book that chronicles an arduous journey to achieve an exceptional patient-centered culture using a management system only now recognized as relevant to health care. This is a story of how Virginia Mason became the benchmark against which other health care systems must judge themselves, and a beacon in a field that has resisted change for far too long.

— **David M. Lawrence**, MD, MPH, Chairman and CEO (retired),
Kaiser Foundation Health Plan and Hospitals, Inc.

The challenges to our U.S. health care system have never been greater. We are challenged by the high cost of care and less than optimal quality and safety. Virginia Mason Medical Center has been on a ten year journey to demonstrate just what is possible and the results have been profound. What is equally amazing, and must reading for health care leaders, is the story of their journey. It is possible to improve quality and safety while simultaneously reducing cost!

— **John Kitzhaber**, MD, Governor of Oregon 1995-2003

U.S. health care is replete with stories of failed attempts to improve quality and control soaring costs, only to succumb to perverse incentives, infighting and an entrenched *status quo*. Virginia Mason offers a different path forward, by showing what happens when all of health care's stakeholders—doctors, employers, insurers—align themselves behind pursuing the best care for the patient. It's a potential model precisely because its leadership medical staff had to overcome the same challenges that affect hospitals and clinicians across the country today.

— **Vanessa Fuhrmans,** *The Wall Street Journal*

Congratulations to the Virginia Mason team for being another great example of committing to a compelling vision and to continuous quality improvement … . Thank You!

— **Alan Mulally,** former President and CEO, Boeing Commercial Airplanes;
current President and CEO, Ford Motor Company

If you work in the health and medical care field and you believe you and your institution are as good as it is possible to be, you should read this book. It will reset your standards and show you how to produce more value for your patients at a lower cost. This is a front line story, not a pie in the sky theory or project of the month. It is a story about real people dedicated to the pursuit of habitual excellence.

— **Paul O'Neill**, 72nd Secretary of the U.S. Treasury, former Chairman and CEO of Alcoa

Health care transformation is a process not an event. This book richly describes this process at Virginia Mason—not just the principles but all the challenges along the way and how they were overcome. It is a textured account of an ongoing journey and as such is an invaluable aid to anyone serious about transforming their own organization.

— **Richard Bohmer**, MBChB, MPH Professor of Management Practice, Harvard Business School

This is the story of a journey. It's a journey that began almost a decade ago, that continues today, and that will likely continue for the foreseeable future. Through a number of powerful case studies, this book illustrates how Virginia Mason Medical Center has steadily improved the safety, quality, and efficiency of its patient care—one process at a time. But more importantly, it is a study in leadership and cultural transformation in one of our nation's most important industries—health care. That transformation has made patient-centered care much more than a slogan at Virginia Mason; it has become a way of doing business, each and every day.

The beneficiaries of that transformation, first and foremost, are the patients Virginia Mason serves. But of equal importance is the new-found sense of accomplishment and satisfaction that these changes have engendered among the Medical Center's physicians, management team and employees. This book is inspiring must reading for anyone who leads, or aspires to lead, any health care organization.

— **William F. Jessee**, MD, FACMPE, President and CEO, Medical Group Management Association

If you want to understand what health care can become, you need to know about Virginia Mason Medical Center. This book gives you the complete story. It is essential reading.

— **David Cutler**, former Senior Health Care Advisor, Obama Presidential Campaign

An inspiring tale of leadership, discipline, and persistence by an organization committed to excellence in patient care. VMMC has redefined patient-centeredness as the core of process change. By so doing, not only has it transformed its culture and dramatically improved outcomes, it has set new standards for quality and efficiency. Must reading for all health care leaders who are serious about quality.

— **Lucian L. Leape**, MD, Harvard School of Public Health

How does a hospital change the very culture of medicine? By abandoning the philosophy that says *This is the way we've always done it!* That's the essence of the amazing story of true change told by Charles Kenney in **Transforming Health Care: Virginia Mason Medical Center's Pursuit of the Perfect Patient Experience**. But hold on: This is *not* a cold chronicle of good people moving deck chairs around on the deck of the Titanic. This is genuine course-changing, history-changing work born of steely determination to stop hurting patients by finding ways of practicing medicine that tradition never taught.

How does one transform to an idyllic hospital where errors never hurt patients and people are happy? By breaking the molds and infusing a common vision and by starting down the path Dr. Gary Kaplan and Virginia Mason were courageous enough to blaze ten years ago—when no one else was even peeking outside the box.

If you intend to keep your patients safe—if you intend to improve the working environment, the bottom line, and the camaraderie of your hospital—you cannot ignore this story! This book isn't about Lean, Toyota, or any single methodology as much as it's about a refusal to maintain the terrible *status quo* documented by the Institute of Medicine in 1999. This book is the foundational element of understanding what it takes to really change a moribund culture.

— **John J. Nance**, author, *Why Hospitals Should Fly*

Virginia Mason Medical Center is widely recognized as the pioneer in applying the disciplines of the Toyota Production Systems to improve the delivery of health care. Now, with the publication of **Transforming Health Care**, we have a first-hand account of what they did and what they learned: the steps they took to make the concept of Team Medicine a reality; the struggles and successes in moving from physician-centric to patient-centered care; and the projects they have undertaken to redesign clinical pathways to eliminate waste and error, reduce scientific uncertainty, and promote patient preferences. An easy read, but also an in-depth account of Virginia Mason's effort to transform itself. This book is a must for students of organizational behavior as well as for those who aspire to improve health care.

— **John E. Wennberg**, MD, MPH, Peggy Y. Thomson Professor Emeritus (Chair)
in the Evaluative Clinical Sciences & Founder and Director Emeritus,
The Dartmouth Institute for Health Policy and Clinical Practice

This inspiring book tells the story of how Gary Kaplan and his team (and Board) at Virginia Mason Medical Center overcame the myriad barriers that stifle most transformational journeys in American health care before they begin. Virginia Mason has shown itself and its teachable processes to be the kind of shining examples which we desperately need other health care providers to embrace and emulate. The main lesson that's applicable to health reform? We *can* make health care better, more patient-centered, and less costly, *if* we combine the proper sense of urgency with patience and faith that we can all learn to focus on what really matters, together, every single day.

— **Len M. Nichols**, Ph.D., Director of the Center for Health Policy Research and Ethics,
George Mason University.

Transforming Health Care

Virginia Mason Medical Center's Pursuit of the Perfect Patient Experience

Charles Kenney

Foreword by Donald M. Berwick, MD, MPP

CRC Press
Taylor & Francis Group
Boca Raton   London   New York

CRC Press is an imprint of the
Taylor & Francis Group, an **informa** business

A PRODUCTIVITY PRESS BOOK

Productivity Press
Taylor & Francis Group
711 Third Avenue
New York, NY 10017

© 2011 by Virginia Mason Medical Center
Productivity Press is an imprint of Taylor & Francis Group, an Informa business

No claim to original U.S. Government works

Printed in the United States of America on acid-free paper
10 9 8 7

International Standard Book Number: 978-1-56327-375-9 (Hardback)

Library of Congress Cataloging-in-Publication Data

Kenney, Charles.
    Transforming health care : Virginia Mason Medical Center's pursuit of the perfect patient experience / Charles Kenney.
        p. ; cm.
    Includes bibliographical references and index.
    Summary: "A chronicle of one of the most unusual series of events in the history of medicine, this book tells the story a group of men and women clinicians, administrators, frontline workers, trustees, and leaders blessed with vision, courage, and a relentless determination to improve. It is the story of a medical center transformed. Ultimately, it is the story of a new and possibly better way to take on the challenge we face in the United States today to provide superb medical care to our people while at the same time controlling costs"--Provided by publisher.
    ISBN 978-1-56327-375-9 (hardcover : alk. paper)
    1. Health services administration--United States. 2. Health facilities--Administration--Standards--United States. 3. Medical care--United States. 4. Virginia Mason Medical Center. I. Title.
    [DNLM: 1. Virginia Mason Medical Center. 2. Health Facilities--organization & administration--Washington. 3. Cost Control--methods--Washington. 4. Delivery of Health Care--organization & administration--Washington. 5. Efficiency, Organizational--Washington. 6. Patient Satisfaction--Washington. 7. Quality Assurance, Health Care--methods--Washington. WX 28 AA1]

RA971.K4393 2011
362.12068--dc22   2010040400

Visit the Taylor & Francis Web site at
http://www.taylorandfrancis.com

and the Productivity Press Web site at
http://www.productivitypress.com

Contents

Foreword xi

Note About This Book xv

Preface: A Surprising Visit xvii

1 A New Idea 1
Change or Die 3
Physician-Centric 8
Germ of a New Idea 10
Toyota Mantra: Eliminate Waste 11

2 Journey to Japan 13
A Daring New Path 13
Skepticism 16
The First Trip 17
An Industrial Symphony 20
"Aren't You Ashamed?" 22
The Missing Piece 23
"This Is Ludicrous" 27
No Going Back 29

3 The Blue Yarn 33
A Revealing Value Stream 34
The Patient's Voice 37
New Space, New Process 39
Continuous Improvement 41
Standard Work 44
A Singular Success 46

4 Safety Crusade 49
Patient Safety Alerts™ 50
A Nurse's Courage 53

A Doctor's Courage 53
Why Shouldn't *Everybody* Get a Flu Shot? 55
Mrs. Mary McClinton 58
Mistake Proofing 61
A Culture of Safety 61
Evolution of the PSA System.. 63

5   Ambulatory Care Breakthrough **69**
Stress on Primary Care 69
Moving the Mountain of Waits 70
Mistake-Proofing Care: Early Steps 73
Creating a New Tool.. 75
Inventing the Flow Station.. 77
Breakthrough... 79
Skill–Task Alignment 80
Primary Care Transformed 83
Going to *Jidoka*... 85
External Setup 87
Biggest Room in the House 90

6   Transforming Procedural Care **93**
Creating a New Ambulatory Surgical Experience 93
Design Challenge... 94
Listening to Patients 96
Setup Reduction 98
Breakthrough... 100
Center for Hyperbaric Medicine 103
Ask Why.. 105
Patient Focused... 106

7   Transforming Inpatient Care **111**
Geographic Cells 112
Report/Handoff 114
In-Room Documentation 116
Visual Work Environment 116
Medical Emergency Teams 118
Hourly Rounding: From Reactive to Proactive 120
Knowing the Frontline Work... 122
Dramatic Change in Nurse Culture... 123
Shorter Length of Stay 126

8   Better, Faster, More Affordable 129
Identifying The Customer... 131
"We Can Do Better"... 133
Value Stream Reveals Huge Waste................................... 135
Same-Day Access 137
Marketplace Defines Quality... 139
Home Run... 143
Financial Conundrum 144
Perverse Incentives 146

9   Management Method 149
Seeing Virginia Mason with Fresh Eyes 149
Structure and Discipline 152
Training within Industry 153
Standard Work: Hand Hygiene 154
World-Class Management 155
Daily Management 156
"The State of the Union Every Tuesday Morning" 159
"Everybody Can Be a Leader".. 161
Leadership 163

10   The Journey Continues.. 165
Will You Teach Us?.. 165
If You Build It 167
Role Model 168
The Virginia Mason Institute.. 170
"Accountable Outside Our Own Walls" 172
The Obstacle of Arrogance.. 174
A Nonsystem 176
A Sense of Hope.. 178
The Journey Continues 179
"We're Just Getting Started".. 181

Source Notes... 183
Preface 183
Chapter One.. 184
Chapter Two.. 184
Chapter Three.. 185
Chapter Four 185
Chapter Five 185
Chapter Six.. 185

Chapter Seven.. 186
Chapter Eight 186
Chapter Nine... 186
Chapter Ten... 186
Appendix 187

Glossary... **189**

Appendix **193**
Applying VMPS to Business Functions 193
Relentless Attack on Waste 194
Bringing Flow Stations to Specialty Department 196
General Internal Medicine: Spreading Innovation in Ambulatory Care... 199
Breaking Down Silos 200
Skill–Task Alignment 201
Uphill Battle 203
Restructuring...204
Introducing Flow Stations...205
The New GIM 207

Acknowledgments **211**

Index **215**

About the Author **223**

Foreword

Donald M. Berwick, MD, MPP

Administrator of the Centers for Medicare and Medicaid Services

The word *transformation* is much used in the stratosphere of quality improvement, but its meaning varies. The big idea, underlying all uses of the term, is that harvesting the full promise of modern system improvement methods requires much more than a mere catalog of projects. Piecemeal redesign of the elements of health care, in particular, can certainly benefit patients; if I have a heart attack, I would like to know that my hospital can give me the right drugs at the right time. But, a hospital, let alone health care as a total system, is a monstrously complex organism—hundreds or thousands of processes ticking away all the time with thousands or tens of thousands of staff interacting among themselves and with equipment, patients, software, and the relevant environment. To assure excellence in *everything* that affects patients and families is only a dream, self-evidently out of reach, if all we can do is to lengthen the list of targets. How many projects could possibly be enough?

And so, we, who are ambitious about excellence, invoke "transformation" as the key to systemic, pervasive improvement. We imagine, somehow, a new organization, in which continual change through scientific design and redesign is in its very nature, everywhere, all the time, and in which excellence is the result.

Health care is not yet that; it is not yet transformed. Ask the staff. Most doctors, nurses, technicians, managers, and others—even executives and boards of directors—will not describe their workplaces as anything like new, refreshed, learning organizations. More likely they will describe days filled not with continual improvement but rather with continual fights to stabilize, to get through the latest storm, or to simply survive the day's work. Of course, they care about what they do—most care deeply—but they lack leverage, optimism, and opportunity to change their work. Instead, they just *do* their work. When they do find a chance to make an improvement, it will likely be local, personal, and, too often, evanescent. The status quo system is the default.

To change that—to make the continual, positive evolution of health care as a system not just possible but native—what "transformation" do we need? The answer historically tends to come in packages with names like "TQM," "Reengineering," "Six Sigma," and "Lean Production." Each of these, and many more, have contributed to progress, but they usually come and go with disappointing regularity.

Health care is hungry for something truly new—less a fad than a new way to be. We are staggering under the burden of too many defects, too much cost, and too much variation in care, all described with scientific rigor and social commitment a decade ago in the landmark Institute of Medicine reports *To Err Is Human* (1999) and *Crossing the Quality Chasm* (2001). Even one convincing example of a major health care organization that crossed the chasm might be enough to give us both the confidence and the template we need. Transformation, in that regard, isn't vague at all; it refers to *results,* unprecedented performance in all important dimensions of care, at a cost we can embrace as sustainable.

Virginia Mason Medical Center (VMMC) is not yet quite that beacon, but it has a better shot at becoming one than almost any other large health care organization in America today. This book recounts a journey that offers an enormous dose of hope that VMMC can demonstrate the transformed results that we so badly need. Why? Because of the degree of commitment and investment of VMMC's senior leaders and Board to a method of management that is scientific, pervasive, conceptually powerful, and, for health care, new. These leaders had the curiosity to look far from traditional health care methods, into the depths of the Toyota Production System (TPS), the energy to study the approach deeply over time and with literally hundreds of the key clinicians and managers in their organization, the courage to declare the new way unblinkingly to themselves and the world ("This will be our management method"), and the persistence to execute the new approach relentlessly over nearly a decade, so far, of execution of the approach. Best of all, they can now report strong signals of the kind of results that will make all of this effort worthwhile.

What is their secret? If the answer fit into a sound byte, I wouldn't believe it. The type of transformation in method that VMMC is now defining is hard, hard work. The guiding theorist behind the approach they are adopting, Taiichi Ohno, was the genius behind the TPS that took several decades to take form. The TPS became, and remains, the most powerful collection of concepts of leadership, management, and engineering of production since Frederick Taylor's.

(Toyota's recent quality problems are anomalies of great importance, but have more to do with migration from TPS principles than with the principles themselves.) As hard as the disciplines of TPS are, it is even more challenging to adapt them to the health care context—as they must be adapted—to make them credible and salable to the entire health care workforce, and to continue to shape and refine them into health care's breed—aptly named and credited now as the Virginia Mason Production System. Gary Kaplan and his colleagues have spent years of full-time effort to nurture these methods and embed them into every function and detail of their complex organization. They need not be told what Dr. W. Edwards Deming often reminded would-be improvement leaders: "There is no instant pudding."

I cannot resist the temptation, nonetheless, to select one keystone idea as, perhaps, the heart of the matter. It is repeated several times in different ways in this book: "Management must be on the *genba.*" For me, no concept is more crucial to the transformation we need in results. *Genba* means, more or less, the shop floor. It is the place where the needs of the customer—patient—meet the work of the system—the front line—the coal face—the place of actual value creation. In my view, health care overall today suffers from enormous and costly distance between those who establish the context of health care—payers, policymakers, regulators, and even educators, on the one hand—and those who give the care, day-to-day at the front line, on the other hand. As a result, context can become insensitive to the texture of the needs of the people who give and receive care, and the *genba* can become unhelpful and disconnected from the social and economic imperatives that shape the context. The result is waste, disarray, misunderstanding, and loss of pride and joy in work. This is a chasm of its own, and bridging it with sound leadership and design is a precondition to systemic success.

By any reasonable definition, VMMC is en route, and in small company, to authentic transformation—transformation of approach, of theory, of capacity, and, I have every confidence, ultimately, of results. Neither they nor I would claim that they have found a direct or easy route (nor, importantly, the only plausible route) to the future they want to build. However, their hard work, scientific integrity, deep curiosity, and commitment to mission offer hope and optimism to the many who join me in cheering them on to unparalleled success.

Note About This Book

The Virginia Mason Production System is based on the Toyota Production System, a manufacturing approach Toyota has used for more than 50 years. Like Toyota, Virginia Mason's experience is truly a journey in continuous improvement. This book represents a snapshot in time describing Virginia Mason's place on that path. Applying the manufacturing methodology to health care is difficult and, by its nature, evolves on a daily basis. Today, a visitor to Virginia Mason may see processes or work flows that are different than what is described in this book. Some improvements, in fact, have not been spread to all corners of the organization. Other improvements may not have been sustained simply because change is hard, and it takes people to ensure it is maintained. However, through a culture characterized by the rigorous and consistent application of the tools and methods of VMPS, all processes and work flows ultimately will be more efficient, resulting in higher quality care and improved patient safety.

Preface: A Surprising Visit

In November 2009, an eight-person delegation from one of Japan's leading hospitals flew to Seattle, Washington, to see how Virginia Mason Medical Center (VMMC) has applied the essential principles of the Toyota Production System (TPS) to health care. Prominent Japanese businessman Yutaka Aso led the delegation from Aso Iisuka Hospital, which his family founded and has owned for decades.

Mr. Aso and his colleagues had heard a great deal about how Virginia Mason had adapted the TPS to health care—the model that is now known as the Virginia Mason Production System™. The Japanese delegation wanted to see the transformation that had moved Virginia Mason into the front ranks of American health care in quality, safety, and efficiency. After a three-day visit, Mr. Aso and his team returned to Japan and indicated that they would like to send teams to Seattle from their hospital and likely others from across Japan. The teams would visit on an ongoing basis to explore how they might apply the Virginia Mason approach in Japanese hospitals.

This was richly ironic. The system, after all, had been created and perfected in Japan and Virginia Mason contingents had been traveling there since 2002 to learn the Toyota techniques on the factory floor. Given the success of the model at Virginia Mason, however, the Aso delegation's visit made perfect sense. Chihiro Nakao, one of only two living *senseis* to study directly with TPS founder Taiichi Ohno, stated emphatically that Virginia Mason leads the world in applying these methods to health care.

Since Virginia Mason began its transformation, hundreds of doctors, nurses, trustees, administrators, and CEOs from thirty-one states and eight nations have made their way to Seattle to see the work firsthand. Some have come for a day, others for a week or more, and still others have made a half-dozen repeat visits. Virtually every week someone from the world of health care is actively learning at Virginia Mason, and the number of requests for visits continues to increase.

Initially, some visitors were drawn by the novelty of a Japanese manufacturing system's application to a major American medical center. Even after the novelty wore off, however, the number of visitors increased dramatically for one reason: to see if it really worked.

The leadership at Virginia Mason adapted the TPS philosophies and practices out of a conviction that the health care industry lacked an effective management method that would enable Virginia Mason to achieve its goals: to always put the patient first; to provide the highest quality, safest care; to foster and maintain patient and staff satisfaction; and to achieve financial success.

The foundation of the method is *kaizen*—continuous, incremental improvement to eliminate the waste, inefficiency, and variation that plagues so many processes essential to the health care experience. Initially at Virginia Mason, *kaizen* was a theory or a tool. Now it is a way of life. *Kaizen* has helped Virginia Mason achieve huge advances in streamlining repetitive and low-touch aspects of care delivery, which in turn enables providers to focus on value-added work—all to the direct benefit of the patient.

Results speak for themselves. A Patient Safety Alert system instituted by Virginia Mason in 2002 was inspired by the Toyota stop-the-line practice empowering any worker to halt the assembly line to prevent a defect. Every one of Virginia Mason's 5,000 employees is now empowered to stop the line whenever a threat to a patient is perceived. Since the program's inception more than 15,000 Patient Safety Alerts have been called, resulting in countless cases where harm was prevented—in some cases fatal harm. More important, data from these alerts has identified broader systemic problems and threats to safety that have resulted in wholesale improvements. Virginia Mason now has some of the lowest rates anywhere of central line infections, falls with injury, surgical site infections, and ventilator-associated pneumonia.

Another notable result of the safety work is that Virginia Mason professional liability insurance expenses declined 26 percent from 2007 to 2008 and then dropped an additional 12 percent the following year. Insurers have asked Virginia Mason to teach its safety methods to other medical centers. (If medical groups nationwide reduced their malpractice premiums similarly, they would save $3.2 billion.)

Much of the work has occurred on the clinical frontlines. For example, measurements at Virginia Mason revealed that nurses were spending barely one third of their time connecting directly with patients. After a series of foundational changes, nurses now focus on patient work 90 percent of the time.

After rigorous application of the Virginia Mason Production System methods, an innovation team created a computerized module that sorts through electronic medical charts and automatically identifies disease management and preventive testing that is due or overdue. The primary care team at the Virginia Mason Kirkland clinic standardized planned care for diabetes, which provides patients with quality levels rarely seen in national statistics: 82 percent have an A1C

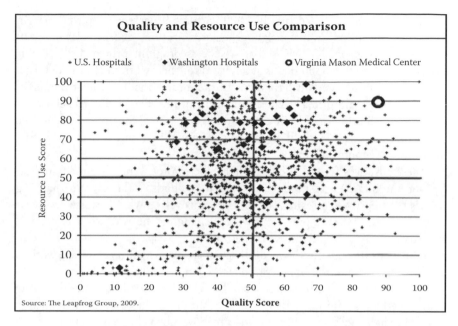

Quality and Resource Use Comparison

◆ U.S. Hospitals ◆ Washington Hospitals ○ Virginia Mason Medical Center

Resource Use Score / Quality Score

Source: The Leapfrog Group, 2009.

under 8 and 68 percent have an LDL cholesterol below the target of 100. LDL is at target in 78 percent of high-risk patients. Fewer than 7% have poorly controlled diabetes.

In 2009, for the fourth consecutive year, Virginia Mason was selected as one of the top hospitals in the United States for quality outcomes by The Leapfrog Group—the only hospital in the Pacific Northwest to make the list. (Leapfrog is made up of some of the largest health care purchasers in the country, including Boeing, FedEx, IBM, Intel, Motorola, and others.) The 2009 award was even more meaningful, however: It was the first time The Leapfrog Group measured and compared American hospitals on their level of efficiency, defined as "the intersection of quality and cost." This is a defining metric, for it goes to the heart of the U.S. health care challenge to provide high-quality care while controlling costs. When compared with 1,165 hospitals in forty-one states, Virginia Mason finished in the top 1 percent on the combination of quality and cost.

The Virginia Mason Production System has made the medical center an order of magnitude more efficient than ever before and this efficiency, in turn, has improved countless safety, quality, and financial metrics. From losing money two consecutive years (1998 and 1999) for the first time in its history, Virginia Mason has achieved positive margins every year since applying these methods. Although VMMC is a nonprofit, positive margins are essential for reinvestment in facilities and equipment. In 2008 the medical center achieved its strongest financial performance ever with a $28 million gain and a 3.6 percent operating margin, and then exceeded that in 2009 with a 5.9 percent operating margin totaling $47 million. While neighboring organizations chose to lay off staff during the recession, VMMC's shared success program provided all eligible frontline staff up to a $500 bonus as a reward for their work to eliminate waste.

Financial improvements have come in the most difficult areas of the medical center. The main primary care clinic (General Internal Medicine) achieved a positive contribution margin in 2008 after losing money for three decades. The medical center saved $11 million in planned capital investment over eight years by using space more efficiently.

These advances were made possible by the rigorous and sustained application of Virginia Mason Production System methods. Value stream mapping reveals the step-by-step reality of a process, uncovering what is waste and what is value-added. Mistake-proofing involves changing the way work is done to reduce or eliminate the chances of an error.

Clinicians throughout the medical center aspire to identify standard work in care processes to improve quality, reduce variation, and to prevent mistakes in the belief that medical errors often result from lack of discipline in standardizing work. In the beginning of their journey, Virginia Mason leaders frequently heard the challenge that standard work somehow robs a clinician of freedom and creativity. But the team has persisted and shown that standard work improves quality, reduces safety hazards, and frees up time for the staff to take better care of patients—and actually use their creativity more fully.

Very little of this work has been easy and a great deal of it has been exceptionally difficult. Applying the Toyota principles requires a degree of leadership and teamwork infrequently found in health care. It requires taking on a medical culture instinctively rooted in silos, resistant to teamwork, standard work, and, quite often, evidence-based care; a culture that by its nature is much more often provider-centric than patient-focused. It requires the creation of a shared vision for an organization, leadership throughout the ranks, and a sustained sense of urgency.

None of that happens automatically, nor is it necessarily something that is obvious at the start of a journey. Virginia Mason leaders have learned and adapted countless times as they have forged ahead. A critical lesson came when they saw that leaders at all levels had to get to the front lines to teach, coach, and monitor; to make sure that waste was eliminated, and standard work was identified and followed. This was not easy. Over time, some important gains slipped, requiring a redoubling of management efforts to lead with greater rigor, accountability, and discipline. Virginia Mason leaders knew that vision and innovation were important, but they learned along the way that structure and discipline were even more critical. Thus they have imbued their system with structure and discipline, with accountability and rigor. These are the elements that enabled them to push back and sustain their impressive gains. Virginia Mason leaders believe they now have a system that is sturdy and enduring enough to reach far beyond any individual or group of individuals. They are confident it will live on well after the current leaders have moved on.

Consultant John Black, a former leader at Boeing, emphasizes the critical nature of leadership, telling health care CEOs: "You can do it if you lead it yourself; otherwise, forget it." Black has written and consulted widely on the Toyota process (including advising Virginia Mason), and he believes there are three elements essential to success: personal commitment of the CEO, hiring a master *sensei,* and committing to a "long-term 'slog' through the swamp of waste and defects that lies hidden beneath the surface of your daily operations."

Inherent in the work is a nettlesome paradox. Within health care, there is a growing—and entirely appropriate—impatience for change to improve quality and control costs. Although a sense of urgency and impatience is appropriate to leading change using the Virginia Mason Production System, another essential element is patience. Hopes that this work will result in a quick fix will almost certainly be dashed. Urgency combined with patience along with faith that deep change will come with time strikes the right balance. This notion is unappealing to many in health care who say that their CEO or their board expects results *now.* In this sense, the culture obstructs opportunity for improvement.

Dr. Gary S. Kaplan, the Virginia Mason CEO, was awarded the 2009 John M. Eisenberg Patient Safety and Quality Award for Individual Achievement from the National Quality Forum and The Joint Commission. The award recognizes individuals who have made significant and lasting contributions to improving patient safety and health-care quality—and Dr. Kaplan has certainly done that. Although Dr. Kaplan was the individual recipient, the award served as a much broader recognition of the relentless work accomplished by Virginia Mason clinicians, administrators, and staff since 2001.

"This is a powerful method that we have applied with rigor and worked to align it throughout our organization," he says. "It has required in-depth training and leadership constancy over several years. It's been difficult and there have been times of frustration and disappointment. But we have improved. Our patients are safer, and we provide better quality care than before—much better care. Our patients have never been as well-served at Virginia Mason as they are now."

In 2008, the Virginia Mason Institute was formed to enable the men and women of the medical center to share what they have learned with others; to provide teaching and guidance on the methods. Dr. Stephen Singleton, medical director of the National Health Service in the Northeast Region of England, is working closely with Virginia Mason and has thus far sent 160 of his colleagues to Seattle to learn. Early in 2010, six other organizations—from North Dakota to Florida—were engaged with the Virginia Mason Institute in similar teaching relationships. "It's working very well," says Dr. Singleton. "They've shown that they can teach others how to do the Virginia Mason Production System."

This book tells the story of one of the most unusual journeys in the history of American medicine. It is the story of a group of men and women—clinicians, administrators, frontline workers, trustees, and leaders—blessed with vision, courage, and a relentless determination to improve. It is the story of a medical center transformed. Ultimately, it is the story of a new and possibly better way to take on the challenge we face in the United States today to provide superb medical care to our people while controlling costs.

Chapter One

A New Idea

They journeyed west in 1920, six physicians from the Mayo Clinic and the University of Virginia, seeking to create something special in the practice of medicine. They believed in the heretical idea of *team* medicine; they believed that working together—pooling their resources and, more importantly, their thinking—they could break down silos and work collaboratively as teachers, researchers, and providers of the finest quality care. "They were considered radicals for their time because they actually wanted to work together, modeling their approach after the Mayo Clinic, the first big group practice," says Gary S. Kaplan, MD, Chairman and CEO of Virginia Mason Medical Center (VMMC). "So we have these innovative, revolutionary genes."

Over the course of eight decades the practice grew exponentially as it evolved into a world-class medical facility. On the cusp of the twenty-first century, however, Virginia Mason was in trouble. In 1998, for the first time ever, Virginia Mason lost money for the year and then suffered an additional loss the following year. This trend was disturbing enough by itself, but in the context of the sharply competitive medical marketplace in Seattle, the results were alarming. Virginia Mason was a not-for-profit system with a 336-bed acute care hospital, 445 doctors, and multiple clinics located throughout the Puget Sound area. In a city with two larger competitors, Virginia Mason was medium-sized and relatively undercapitalized. The fact that many medical centers throughout the country were facing similar financial difficulties—in part due to the siege of ill-conceived forms of managed care—was little consolation.

For in addition to the financial woes, something deeper and more profound was roiling Virginia Mason. As the medical center grappled with harsh financial realities, a group of leaders within Virginia Mason—doctors and senior administrators—were engaged in assessing the most fundamental of all issues in medicine—the quality of care. Two landmark reports from the Institute of Medicine (IOM) of the National Academies—*To Err Is Human* (1999) and *Crossing the Quality Chasm* (2001)—painted a disturbing portrait of American medicine as a system that wasted tens of billions of dollars annually even as it provided care that was far too often inadequate and even harmful. The IOM found that perhaps as many as 98,000 preventable deaths occurred annually in U.S. hospitals and that many other patients were subjected to medication errors. Perhaps most shocking, however, was the finding by the IOM that in the United States, "health care harms too frequently and *routinely* fails to deliver its potential benefits."

This notion that the system *routinely* failed to deliver its potential benefits did nothing less than contradict the bedrock belief that Americans enjoyed the finest health care in the world. To Virginia Mason doctors passionately committed to the highest quality care for their patients, the IOM reports were deeply unsettling. Although the reports caught many medical centers throughout the country by surprise, Virginia Mason was not among them. In fact, it could be argued that at the start of the new millennium it was one of a relative handful of pioneers actively pursuing a quality improvement agenda. Years before those reports were published, Virginia Mason had embarked on a serious quality improvement effort, but the work failed to stick, in part because it lacked the consistent attention of clinicians and the medical center leadership at the time.

It was abundantly clear by 2000 that Virginia Mason needed to change. Dr. Kaplan had practiced internal medicine at Virginia Mason for many years, and he possessed an intimate understanding of the institution. After taking over as CEO, Kaplan quickly recognized that a "sense of crisis" had settled over the medical center. On the surface, that crisis concerned finances, but just beneath the surface, intense conversations were taking place throughout the medical center about clinical quality. The quality issue was less quantifiable than finance, of course, but for Kaplan and other doctors, it was more urgent because it struck at the heart of their mission.

Dr. Robert Caplan, who played a pivotal role in the Virginia Mason work to improve safety, says he and his colleagues took a very hard look at reality. "We just began to look at each other and say, 'Everybody says they're great. We say we're great, our competitors say they're great. *Where's the proof?*' We knew people weren't really as great as they said because we read reports from the Rand Corporation, the IOM, and Dartmouth, and we knew there was variation in cost and variation in outcome. But I think it was a group of people looking around and being honest—that's what really energized us."

Where's the proof? Dr. Caplan's question was as brave as it was vexing, for it raised the possibility that perhaps the proof might *not* be there; perhaps Virginia Mason clinicians were not providing the level of quality they had always assumed they were. "We had always believed in the quality of the medicine we practiced," says Caplan. "And we were all really committed to safety, committed to quality, and as we have this conversation we think we're doing a good job. It's why we get up in the morning, but we just can't *prove* it."

Sarah Patterson, then Virginia Mason senior vice president, shared Dr. Caplan's concerns. "We realized around 2000 that just because we brought ourselves together in one building and we had what we called 'team medicine' didn't mean that on any given day in any given interaction we were actually optimizing care for our patients," says Patterson. She and her colleagues read about the epidemic of medical errors in the United States and wondered aloud whether that was happening at Virginia Mason. "And I remember there were people on our team who said, 'I believe it's happening, but I don't believe it's happening at Virginia Mason.' And then there were others who said, 'I believe it's happening, and I don't know why we *wouldn't* believe it's happening at Virginia Mason. Why would we be different?'"

Change or Die

When he took over as CEO, Dr. Kaplan recognized the urgent need for change and innovation. But change *what,* exactly? Innovate *how,* exactly? It was not at all clear what direction made the most sense. Kaplan had been part of the informal, ongoing discussions about quality, of course, and under the guidance of the Virginia Mason board the quality discussions quickly morphed into a formal project to create a new strategic plan for the medical center. It was that plan, developed over about a year's time and completed in late 2001, that defined the Virginia Mason mission as being all about the patient. In retrospect, this could hardly seem more obvious, yet the reality in American health care in 2001—and to a significant extent even today—was that medicine was anything but patient-focused. And, initially, when Kaplan met with his board, he assured them that the medical center was patient-centered. This was a reflexive reaction, for he had always believed this, but board members pressed him to look more closely. When Kaplan did so, he saw quite clearly that Virginia Mason was organized not around patients but around the doctors. As he thought more about it, he knew from personal experience this was true. For years, Kaplan had invariably promoted Virginia Mason to other doctors as a physician-driven, physician-led place. "Everything was designed around us," he says.

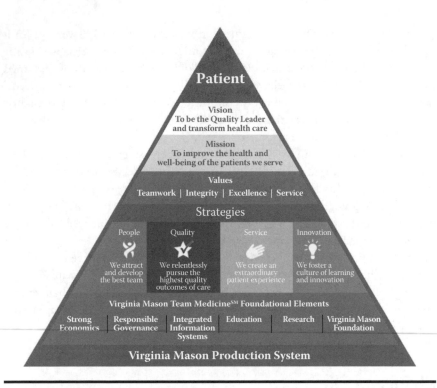

Patient

Vision
To be the Quality Leader
and transform health care

Mission
To improve the health and
well-being of the patients we serve

Values
Teamwork | Integrity | Excellence | Service

Strategies

People	Quality	Service	Innovation
We attract and develop the best team	We relentlessly pursue the highest quality outcomes of care	We create an extraordinary patient experience	We foster a culture of learning and innovation

Virginia Mason Team Medicine℠ Foundational Elements

Strong Economics	Responsible Governance	Integrated Information Systems	Education	Research	Virginia Mason Foundation

Virginia Mason Production System

©2009 Virginia Mason Medical Center

That had to change. "We need to be a great place for doctors, and we need to have physicians in leadership roles," says Kaplan, "but we need to keep in front of us all of the time that it is all about the patient."

The strategic plan, completed in late 2001, yielded a visual reminder of this—a pyramid with the patient at the top—above doctors, nurses, administrators, board members, budget considerations—above *everything and everyone.* This was pivotal. It was emphatically clear that change at Virginia Mason would focus on quality rather than finances. Kaplan believed providing high-quality care would solve the financial issue, and he was supported in this belief by the clinical and administrative leadership as well as the board of directors. Many medical centers would have focused more energy and time on a dollars-and-cents solution to their financial problem, but Virginia Mason's leaders believed that if it was truly all about the patient, then the solution had to focus on quality care. Yes, governance changes would be required, budgets trimmed, and personnel shifted. But at its core, the journey Virginia Mason would embark on was not about any of those things; it was not to be a conventional journey. Yet, it would have a straightforward goal: to become the finest provider of health care anywhere.

Organizational goals and visions—in health care and other sectors—have a long and distinguished history of being ten parts rhetoric and one part reality. Gary Kaplan was well aware of this, and he believed the way to avoid that trap was to identify a tangible method—a *management framework*—to achieve the vision. Neither Kaplan nor any member of his team knew what that method would be, but he believed the right approach existed out there somewhere in the health care universe. They just had to find it. The search was aided by Kaplan's active involvement in a variety of medical organizations throughout the country including the Medical Group Management Association, the largest group practice association in the nation, where he served as board chair. He was also a member of the executive committee of the American Medical Group Association, representing 95,000 doctors nationwide, and Chair of the AMA Group Practice Advisory Committee. In these capacities, he traveled extensively and had come to know scores of physicians and administrators at other hospitals, universities, physician groups, think tanks, and medical associations. With contacts nationwide, Kaplan embarked on a search to find an organization that had cracked the code and figured out how to transform itself into an entity capable of providing the finest possible patient-centered care.

"I was convinced that somebody must have this figured out," Kaplan recalls. He visited numerous organizations from the Mayo Clinic to Johns Hopkins, from Massachusetts General Hospital to the University of Michigan, where he had gone to medical school. Although many of these organizations were doing great work in particular areas, he found none that had transformed itself into the kind of patient-centered entity he and his team aspired to lead. Kaplan heard some thoughtful observations about the quality and cost challenges, about safety issues, but he did not hear or see a *method* to get to zero defects.

"We were looking for ideas around innovation, around quality, safety and economics," he says. "I wanted ideas that we could steal, shamelessly, that would help us. But what I found was that there was no method to get there. We realized that nobody had a management method in health care to achieve this."

How was this possible? How was it that in an industry with literally millions of the finest minds in the world—an industry comprising more than 16 percent of the U.S. economy—no one had figured it out?

"I think a lot of factors come into play in trying to understand it," he says. "The natural trajectory of the profession and the industry, first of all, was not one to look outside of itself. Health care professionals have always felt that we had a noble calling, that we were serving the communities and our patients, and with that sometimes comes, I think, a certain amount of elitism. Some might call it arrogance and an unwillingness to look outside. So one construct is all we really had was ourselves to benchmark against and when you don't look outside, you don't necessarily see what's possible. Also the industry had grown up around the caregiver, not the patient.

"And I think another factor—no matter where you sat in health care organizations, and I'll speak for myself as well—there is a surprising lack of understanding of the work at a granular level. What is the value stream of work? And if you don't understand the current state and, even worse, you *don't know* that you don't understand the current state, it becomes limiting and you don't think about something that ties it all together."

Kaplan discovered that no one had yet developed "a unifying theme or construct—a system, a common language, a common way of thinking about things, conceptualizing work so that you could then train people and all be moving in the same direction using the same methods. We needed a unifying way of thinking, as opposed to what I read in the *Harvard Business Review* last month, and I'm going to try some of that and I'm going to try a little of this."

Kaplan and his leadership team were convinced a piecemeal approach would not work. "We'd always had a history of being innovative, lots of pilot projects, demonstration projects," recalls Sarah Patterson. "That was our culture. But when it came to actual execution across the system, when there was something that really appeared to work, we were not effective in saying, 'This works, it's good for patients, let's roll it out across the system.' So we had well-intended people, good people, but we didn't have a *system*."

And this surprised, concerned, and excited Kaplan: Surprised because with so many really smart men and women in health care in the United States you would think *somebody* would have figured it out. Concerned because if it had not been done that meant it clearly would not be a simple matter. And excited because, well, he and his team were just going to have to go out and do it themselves.

Early in September 2000, soon after Kaplan had taken over as CEO, Virginia Mason's clinical and administrative leaders gathered for a two-day retreat. Kaplan stood before the group and said: "We change or we die." A sense of mourning seemed to pervade the retreat. It was clear that doctors were losing the tried-and-true old way of doing business, a cultural approach so many physicians had worn like a comfortable old coat for decades. The changes precipitating that loss had already begun during the early 1990s managed care phase if not earlier. But now it was clear that change would accelerate, and it would do so in an environment where the very life of the institution was at risk.

Dr. Joyce Lammert, who organized the retreat, says some doctors actually grew tearful at the changes they saw coming. "People were feeling the loss," she says. "You go through college and medical school and training and all those years and all that hard work and you think you're going to get one thing and you get something else. There was an expectation of autonomy—that's a really big thing with doctors, calling the shots on how you practice and what you do. It's gone from doctor-knows-best to twenty-first century medicine where it's patient-centered, collaborative, team medicine—all about working together."

And that was a shift in the tectonic plates, a change that was difficult for many physicians but particularly those who had been practicing for any length of time. And although Kaplan recognized that—and very much empathized with it—he also knew it was essential to move beyond this difficult moment and turn to the future. Toward that end, he invited John Nance to speak to the group about the kinds of changes that might be required moving forward. A Seattle resident, Nance was an intriguing choice for a speaker to a medical group. He was a decorated Air Force and commercial pilot, a veteran of the Vietnam and Gulf wars, and an aviation analyst for the ABC television network. What made him an interesting speaker for the Virginia Mason meeting was his expertise in human factors in flight safety and how aviation's Crew Resource Management (CRM) might apply in other industries. Nance's topic—"teamwork for our future"—focused on safety in the cockpit. He talked about the precision of aviation safety procedures that were designed to get as close to eliminating human error as possible. It was not that flying airplanes and taking care of patients were the same thing, but that both required comprehensive *systems* to prevent mistakes. He maintained that aviation had such a system but medicine did not.

Nance had preached the CRM gospel to executives in countless industries, but he was new to health care. (That would change in the years to come as Nance waded hip deep into health care work. Eight years after he appeared at the Virginia Mason retreat, in fact, Nance published an acclaimed book entitled *Why Hospitals Should Fly.*) Nance argued that significant change would be required if the institution was to succeed in transforming itself into a high-reliability organization distinguished by superior quality.

A critically important change would involve the arrangement between the medical center and the doctors. Gary Kaplan viewed an explicit new deal with the doctors as an essential building block for the future. Without a clear understanding of what was expected from the physicians—and what they should expect from the institution—he believed no real progress was possible. Kaplan knew this would be neither easy nor pleasant, but he also knew it was a prerequisite to any sort of meaningful innovation. He made it clear that the old deal with the doctors would no longer work; the deal that said, as he put it, "'As a doctor I am entitled to patients because I work with a group. I'm protected from worry about business decisions because there are administrators and physicians who also have some business training, and I'm autonomous because I'm a professional.' That didn't sync up with where we needed to go. In some ways, that's what the mourning was about."

Physician-Centric

Part of the problem, Kaplan knew, was that the Virginia Mason culture was very much physician-centric—even as the new strategic plan explicitly stated that the patient always came first. As Dr. Lammert put it, "People would say to physician job applicants 'you really want to work here—*doctors call the shots here.*'"

The reality and aspiration were in direct conflict and something had to give. Clearly, a new deal was needed, yet Kaplan knew that it would be unwise to dictate what that deal would be. That would have to come from the doctors themselves or it would have zero chance of working. Kaplan knew that process mattered to the doctors; the right process would have a chance of yielding a positive outcome, and the wrong process would generate resentment. Thus, Kaplan turned to a consultant who specialized in helping organizations build new compacts, particularly involving doctors. Dr. Jack Silversin—a dentist by training—had worked for twenty years with doctors, board members, and other stakeholders attempting to reach consensus on difficult issues. Silversin was the founder of Amicus, a consulting firm based in Cambridge, Massachusetts, and he had successfully worked with physicians in a variety of states as well as the United Kingdom. Over more than twenty-five years, Silversin had gained a deep understanding of physician cultures and how to help guide them in a positive, evolutionary process. In various organizations he had proven to be an effective catalyst and leader of organizational change.

At the Virginia Mason retreat in September 2000, Silversin spoke about how dramatically the medical landscape had changed and how a new deal was essential to future success. In fact, the aligned vision that a compact would bring about would prove foundational to virtually all of the progress VM would be able to achieve. He pointedly entitled his presentation "Changing Expectations." He had traveled to Seattle a month prior to the retreat to spend a day gathering information—talking to doctors and trying to understand their thinking. He quickly saw that many physicians clung to the traditions of the past, angry about the shifting medical tides.

On the first day of the retreat, after listening to Kaplan's "Preparing for the Future" presentation, doctors broke up into smaller groups to discuss "the GETS—things that providers felt they should get from the organization," says Dr. Lammert. Individual groups were assigned one of five topics from the GETS list: "Participation in decision making, participation in the organization's improvements, compensation, communication, and work expectations." On the second day of the retreat the small groups focused on the "GIVES—what the group owed to the organization, each other, and patients," says Lammert.

Those five areas included "citizenship in VM medical group, relationships with patients and patients' families, administrative staff relationships, support staff relationships, and other VM physician relationships."

When the retreat was over, Kaplan asked Dr. Lammert to chair a compact committee which began its work in January 2001, building on the foundation established at the retreat. The committee worked for six months discussing a variety of ideas, gradually putting pen to paper. With a draft document in place during the summer of 2001, Lammert and her team went around the medical center and sat down with physicians in every department to explain, discuss, and revise—requiring an additional three months of work. Not everybody was happy with the result, of course, but it was difficult to argue with a process so deliberate and inclusive. Everyone had a voice, including some experienced doctors who were deeply angry and resentful about how the world around them was changing.

The process resulted in a compact that embodied a shared vision between doctors and the medical center administration and clarified expectations in the new world as never before. The compact explicitly detailed the responsibilities of Virginia Mason to its physicians and the responsibilities of the doctors to Virginia Mason.

VIRGINIA MASON MEDICAL CENTER PHYSICIAN COMPACT

Organization's Responsibilities

Foster Excellence
- Recruit and retain superior physicians and staff
- Support career development and professional satisfaction
- Acknowledge contributions to patient care and the organization
- Create opportunities to participate in or support research

Listen and Communicate
- Share information regarding strategic intent, organizational priorities and business decisions
- Offer opportunities for constructive dialogue
- Provide regular, written evaluation and feedback

Educate
- Support and facilitate teaching, GME and CME
- Provide information and tools necessary to improve practice

Reward
- Provide clear compensation with internal and market consistency, aligned with organizational goals
- Create an environment that supports teams and individuals

Lead
- Manage and lead organization with integrity and accountability

Physician's Responsibilities

Focus on Patients
- Practice state of the art, quality medicine
- Encourage patient involvement in care and treatment decisions
- Achieve and maintain optimal patient access
- Insist on seamless service

Collaborate on Care Delivery
- Include staff, physicians, and management on team
- Treat all members with respect
- Demonstrate the highest levels of ethical and professional conduct
- Behave in a manner consistent with group goals
- Participate in or support teaching

Listen and Communicate
- Communicate clinical information in clear, timely manner
- Request information, resources needed to provide care consistent with VM goals
- Provide and accept feedback

Take Ownership
- Implement VM-accepted clinical standards of care
- Participate in and support group decisions
- Focus on the economic aspects of our practice

Change
- Embrace innovation and continuous improvement
- Participate in necessary organizational change

© Virginia Mason Medical Center, 2001

Germ of a New Idea

Eight months before the completion of the compact, a serendipitous event occurred that, in retrospect, can be seen as the first step on the Virginia Mason road to emulate the Toyota path. On November 9, 2000, during a flight from Seattle to Atlanta, then Virginia Mason president Mike Rona found himself seated next to John Black, formerly a leader at Boeing. Black had been an Army officer who had served two tours in Vietnam and gone on to work at Boeing for twenty-one years, retiring from the aerospace company in 1999 and setting up his own consulting practice. Black recounted some of his work and showed Rona a PowerPoint presentation about the Toyota Production System (TPS). Rona was fascinated by the conversation and on his return to Seattle, he read Black's book, *A World Class Production System,* in which Black explained the Toyota approach to management and quality improvement.

Rona told Gary Kaplan about Black and Kaplan was intrigued. The fact that Boeing used the TPS gave it instant credibility with Kaplan. He was even more impressed after reading Black's book, and he was instinctively drawn to the notion that other industries operating in competitive global marketplaces might very well have lessons to benefit health care. "The premise of the book is you can do twice what you're doing today with the same resources and create a higher quality, defect-free product," says Kaplan. "Anybody that tells me that—I'd at least like to hear more."

In the ensuing months, Kaplan and many members of his senior leadership team delved into the Toyota methods, reading and studying the system's application at various companies, including Seattle-based Genie Industries, a global company manufacturing industrial lifting equipment. Rona and Kaplan met with Black in 2001 and talked at some length. To be convinced of the applicability of the Toyota system to health care, Kaplan and his team had to understand the concept of waste, which was at the heart of the TPS thinking. (The elimination of waste in the manufacturing process was so central to the Toyota approach that it was also sometimes referred to as *lean manufacturing,* or, simply, *lean.*) Black wrote in his book *The Toyota Way to Health Care Excellence* that "waste is not the fault of the individuals in [a] system, but the system itself, which is overly complex, rife with outdated procedures, and redundant." He observed that "lean operations give us a new understanding of waste. With this new understanding, we find waste in all the ways work is done. With the principles and processes of Lean, we know how to reduce and eliminate waste, including the reduction and elimination of errors (defects)."

There were other approaches out there, of course, including Six Sigma, and the Baldrige performance criteria. Kaplan and his colleagues looked at those and considered Toyota a better fit for them. "We thought Toyota had all the right components, and their emphasis on speed was really important," says Sarah Patterson. "We needed one system, one common language that we could all use, and one set of tools that we could all learn."

Toyota Mantra: Eliminate Waste

The Toyota system was based on identifying and eliminating seven types of waste—waste of time, motion, inventory, processing, defects, transportation, and overproduction. If the task at hand did not help meet a customer's (patient's) needs, it was waste. If the customer was unwilling to pay for it, it was waste. An example of "processing waste" might involve compiling a report that someone used to rely on but that was no longer needed or used. "Waste of motion" might be nurses going off in search of supplies that should be readily at hand. "Defect waste" might involve a doctor's illegible handwriting on an order or prescription. "Inventory waste" meant stockpiling more supplies or materials than necessary.

The idea of waste as a drag on health care was not new. The IOM had suggested that as much as one third of the money spent on health care in the United States was wasted. The IOM recognized that health care was plagued by redundancies and an avalanche of non-value-added services.

"By eliminating waste, you improve quality, safety and reduce cost," Kaplan observes. "When you eliminate waste, you create repetitive processes that can easily be standardized." Early in the process of discovery it was clear to Kaplan that waste—non-value-added variation—was not only of no benefit to patients, but actually served, as the IOM found, as a drag on the system. Sarah Patterson observes that "most people think of waste in very simple terms, and we've learned it's more sophisticated; there are different forms of waste. Part of what we've learned is to identify all the different types of waste and measure them."

The elimination of waste means the patient is receiving only value-added care. It means whoever is paying for the care—the patient, an insurance company, the government, the patient's employer—is receiving excellent value for their dollar. It means the payer does not waste valuable dollars subsidizing an inefficient, wasteful, system. An important benefit to eliminating waste in the health care delivery process, says Patterson, is that it would save enormous amounts of time. "That's where we say there's capacity in our hospital," she says. "If we were to eliminate all the time patients spend waiting in our hospital for things to happen to them or having tests done that didn't need to be done, if we were to eliminate that, they may leave the hospital one or two days earlier than they do now."

Like waste, standardization is also at the core of the Toyota system. Standard work, in theory, means a drastic reduction in defects. Yet Kaplan could see a formidable obstacle looming. He knew that if Virginia Mason were to go down this path and adopt the Toyota approach embracing standard work, he would be confronted by physicians decrying the notion as antithetical to everything they'd been taught throughout their careers—that they were in charge; that they should decide what is best for their patients; that they were independent to act as they pleased and should not be dictated to. Critics would come to derisively refer to standard work as "cookbook medicine."

Was it true that the elimination of waste and standardization could mean greater quality care? More stable finances? The father of the TPS, Taiichi Ohno wrote in his book *Toyota Production System: Beyond Large-Scale Production* that the Toyota approach "is not just a production system," but is "a management system adapted to today's era of global markets and high-level computerized information systems."

The theory—or perhaps the promise—of the TPS was that managers who learned to understand and eliminate waste could help identify process improvement opportunities, improve customer and staff satisfaction, increase productivity, and decrease costs. In theory, the Toyota approach could enable an organization such as Virginia Mason to improve quality while cutting costs. The notion that this might be remotely possible captured Dr. Kaplan's imagination.

Chapter Two

Journey to Japan

A Daring New Path

Gary Kaplan, Mike Rona, and a few senior leaders had studied the Toyota Production System carefully enough so that by March 2001, several months after first meeting with John Black, they were ready to introduce the concept to physician chiefs and vice presidents at Virginia Mason. Presenting the Toyota approach would take some time. Thus, Kaplan scheduled a two-day meeting, and participants were asked to prepare by reading Black's book (an economical ninety-six pages). Speakers for the session included Black, Boeing executive Carolyn Corvi, and leaders from Genie in Seattle and Wiremold in Hartford, two other companies employing the Toyota method. Kaplan knew there would be a certain amount of skepticism within the group, and he wanted to make a strong enough initial case for the Toyota approach to prevent minds from reflexively snapping shut.

At the meeting John Black explained that Boeing used the system to increase efficiency, improve quality, and control costs. This got the group's attention. Boeing, after all, was their neighbor and one of the more respected companies in the world. Boeing Vice President Carolyn Corvi, who would later join the Virginia Mason board of directors, told the Virginia Mason team that she had taken groups of Boeing workers to Japan to study the Toyota method and had applied it to the Boeing 737 line, which she managed. She said that the method enabled Boeing to reduce waste while increasing quality, speed, and profitability.

Assembly time for the 737 was reduced from twenty-two days in 1999 to eleven days in 2005. John Black wrote in his book *The Toyota Way to Health Care Excellence* that from 1994 to 1996, with the application of Toyota methods at Boeing, "defects in production were reduced 35 percent and customer complaints dropped accordingly. Where applied, lean reduced the typical floor space required for operations by 50 percent and cut the amount of inventory kept on hand by 30 to 70 percent." By the end of the 1990s, he wrote "the entire Boeing Company was embracing Lean."

The Virginia Mason group had not previously heard of Wiremold, a manufacturer of wire management products for the electrical industry, but the company's CEO, communicating by speaker phone, made an articulate case for the method. "It's about improving all your processes to eliminate waste and make the value stream flow through your organization," said CEO Art Byrne. "Whether it's a hospital or an insurance company or a manufacturing company, every business is built on a series of different processes. Hospitals are no different." A Genie executive echoed Byrne's remarks.

The essential message of the meeting was that whether it was the manufacture of airplanes, electrical molds, or industrial lifting equipment, the Toyota system helped reduce waste, increase efficiency, and build in quality. On March 27, at the end of the two-day session, during which all members of the executive team were engaged in hands-on learning exercises and discussion, Kaplan addressed the group. "It has never been more apparent," he said, "that now the time is ripe for change. ... These last two days we have experienced an incredible amount of tension—good tension—about our organization." The new path was not about working faster, spending more money, adding more space, or personnel. It was instead "a new way to set targets and to achieve results."

Not surprisingly, there were a number of Virginia Mason leaders who were light years from being convinced that this was the correct approach. John Black, whose company would serve not only as a critically important catalyst for the work at Virginia Mason, but also as the initial consulting guide along this new pathway, observed all of this carefully, and it was clear to him that Kaplan's remarks meant that for some in the group "the air had just been sucked out of the room."

Yet just a couple of weeks later, two different Virginia Mason groups engaged in successful Rapid Process Improvement Workshops, an essential TPS tool. One of the teams was so successful it reduced the number of surgical instruments on the laparoscopic setup from seventy-four to fifty-eight and cut waiting time for patients by 69 percent, all of which resulted in an annual savings of $26,880.

With each step in the process of exploration, Kaplan became increasingly convinced that this was the right approach for Virginia Mason, and he encouraged other members of his team to read and study to increase their knowledge of the TPS. An important part of their education would be seeing the Toyota method firsthand. Kaplan had been impressed with the presentation that Wiremold CEO Art Byrne had given over the speaker phone to the team. Byrne had two decades of Toyota-style management to his credit at both GE and Wiremold, where he increased the company's value from $30 million to $770 million. Byrne was smart and articulate, and he made the connection from manufacturing to health care with ease. Kaplan discussed the next step with John Black and was persuaded by Black's strong recommendation for the Virginia Mason team to visit Wiremold.

During the visit, Byrne expressed the view that the problems in health care were not about resources, competence, or commitment. Rather, they were process problems—precisely what the Toyota system was designed for. The team from Virginia Mason could see that the Wiremold workers were motivated and productive. As the Virginia Mason visitors walked freely through the plant watching operations and speaking to employees, it was clear the Wiremold workers loved the order and reliability of the system. Kaplan was captivated by the efficiency—no wasted energy, time, motion, or resources. Using Toyota measurements, Wiremold had reached a point where the defect rate was nearly zero. Byrne told the Virginia Mason team, in fact, that he believed there were many more similarities than differences between moving a piece of steel and a human being through a process.

For Kaplan and many of his colleagues, the Wiremold trip was inspirational. Afterward, as Kaplan and Rona discussed the trip and the Toyota method with Black and Corvi, it became clear that the next logical step in the process of exploration was a visit to Japan. Seeing the TPS in the United States was certainly instructive, but to see it practiced in its purest form in the place where it was developed and refined, it was necessary to travel to Japan. Both Black and Corvi had led numerous trips to Japan, and they said there was nothing like it; if the Virginia Mason team was serious about pursuing the Toyota method, they had to see it in its natural environment. Kaplan pulled his team together and broke the news. "We've got to go," he told them, "because unless we go, we'll never know—and we run the risk of passing up the greatest potential opportunity in the history of the organization."

Kaplan and his team had laid a solid foundation in preparation for the trip. It had been more than a year since he had first met with John Black and during that time he and his colleagues had engaged in intensive study, met with experienced practitioners in Byrne and Corvi, and were tutored along the way by Black. Nonetheless, a decision to take three dozen top people to Japan to study and work in an automobile factory at a time when Virginia Mason was in financial trouble would surely be seen by some people—some very reasonable people—as lunacy. Kaplan understood that. "It was a gamble," he says, "but it was an educated gamble."

Skepticism

Dr. Donna Smith, then chief of pediatrics at Virginia Mason, plunged into preparation for the trip—intensive reading, study, and discussion with her colleagues. At one point in the preparation process there was a particular area of study she found to be rather hollow and she told Kaplan. "Tell me what you're thinking," he replied. It was not a challenge but a desire to understand, to learn from her. She explained her thinking, and he asked whether she felt that way about the whole TPS approach. Not at all, she said; just that one narrow aspect. "Gary was still very much in the discovery process, too," she says. "We were all discovering this together."

Within the medical center, however, there were many people more focused on criticism than discovery. A substantial number of physicians, nurses, and administrators—especially in middle management—found the whole direction alarming, and the detractors were hardly mindless in their opposition. These were intelligent people—many of them clinicians—who cared deeply not only for the well-being of their patients, but for the future of Virginia Mason. The doctors among them were, of course, scientists very much partial to evidence—to *proof.* What was the proof that an automobile manufacturing system in Japan could help them provide better care to human beings in Seattle? Some of the doctors wondered whether this new direction might actually precipitate the downfall of Virginia Mason.

There were also many people in administration whose experience was in a heroic or cowboy culture where caped heroes would swoop in to save the day on any given problem. When systems break down—or are essentially nonsystems to begin with—this sort of save-the-day culture flourishes. Now, however, the leadership of the medical center was asking all of these people to set aside that approach and work to create reliable systems and standard work that would prevent crises from occurring. This felt like a kind of automation to many managers who resisted the change.

Steve Schaefer, vice president of finance, referred to the pushback as a "resistance movement" that was both covert and overt. "A lot of the resistance movement," he says, "was, 'This is just CQI/TQM/Deming. It's just dressed up in a different dress. This is just a management phase and you know, they go through their phases and then they'll come up with something new. Just smile and wave and it will eventually go away.'"

When word got out of the pending Japan trip, a local newspaper cartoon depicted patients on an assembly line with a caption wondering whether this was the future of health care. A *Seattle Times* front-page story stated that "for the past year, Virginia Mason Medical Center has been nipping and tucking to cut costs, so employees wonder why the hospital is paying for executives to go to Japan to learn to think lean." It continued:

> To better implement a cost-cutting program, the medical center ... is paying for its top 30 executives to go to Japan for a two-week training session ... Hospital officials didn't say how much the trip will cost.
>
> Some employees are furious, calling the expense egregious from a company dedicated to a low operating budget. They say jobs have been cut and morale is poor because of low staffing levels.
>
> "'Outraged' is *not* an understatement," said one employee who wished to remain anonymous. Said a former employee: "This is what makes you think there's no decency left in the administration there."
>
> As part of a four-year strategic plan, Virginia Mason has dedicated itself to "Lean Thinking," a program to help businesses cut waste and become more efficient. ...
>
> Groups of nine to twelve doctors and staff members attend mandatory workshops to examine everything from how long a patient waits for an appointment to the amount of paper used in offices and waiting rooms.

Many senior people within the medical center found the whole approach "very hard to get your hands around" says Ruth Anderson, who was senior vice president of the Office of Process Improvement. "There was huge pushback from the start. People saying, 'Let's put up with this and it will go away.' I was as skeptical as everyone else."

In the face of such criticism, Dr. Kaplan held a powerful trump card: the support of the Virginia Mason board of directors. The directors staunchly supported the notion of exploring this method. It was not that the board members were sold on the Toyota approach from the outset, but they were open-minded about exploring this pathway, and they remained open-minded even as criticism within the medical center mounted. It is difficult to overstate the significance of the Virginia Mason board's support for Kaplan's exploration of the Toyota approach. It was this support, in fact, that made it possible for Kaplan to forge ahead. Absent the board support, the Virginia Mason pursuit of the TPS almost certainly would have succumbed to an early death.

The First Trip

The trip was not undertaken lightly. By the time the team was airborne over the Pacific on June 19, 2002, Gary Kaplan and his team had been immersed in the study of the Toyota method for well over a year. In the months leading up to the trip, the group had undergone a rigorous process including formal classes, extensive reading, and in-depth discussions. This preparation had required a significant time commitment from every one of the thirty-five-person team going to Japan, including the entire senior leadership team of the medical center—physician heads of medical departments, the chief of surgery, and administrators. Significantly, the chairman of the board of directors also participated in the trip. For Virginia Mason clinical and administrative leaders it was not an optional trip. Kaplan told the executive team, including department chairs and vice presidents: "'If you want to be a leader at VM you have to come on this trip.' Not only did we expect executives to take that first trip with us, we also expected them to go on learning and to become certified at a very high level of knowledge about Lean and its application at VM."

The team started in Nagoya, Japan, home to the Toyota Museum, which traces the history of the company from 1902 when Sakichi Toyoda invented an automatic loom that embodied the soul of the TPS: It stopped working when a thread broke. This enabled the weaver to repair mistakes *before* they became embedded in the fabric, thus preventing defects. This was followed by an even greater breakthrough in quality improvement: Sakichi Toyoda developed a way for the machine, on detecting a defect, to repair it without human intervention. In a sense, the first breakthrough was what the TPS would call "mistake-proofing." The second was "setup reduction"—changing the shuttles on the machine without stopping the machine. These two advances combined improved production and reduced defects. Men and women were then freed up to monitor the progress of multiple machines, thus increasing quality and productivity. The Virginia Mason team went through the museum with a hushed respect for the exhibits. Their studies had made them well aware of the process and history. They understood the significance of what they were seeing; this approach had done nothing less than revolutionize the science of quality control. In the first half of the twentieth century, the Toyoda Automatic Loom Works, with its rapid production and defect-free products, was immensely successful and eventually paved the way for the car company.

"When you start in the museum and you think about the evolution of Toyota starting with looms and you see the progression of improvement and the application of these principles you've been reading about, it's inspiring," says Diane Miller, Virginia Mason vice president. The team sought to convey that inspiration to colleagues back in Seattle with a series of letters to the medical center staff. The first communiqué came on June 24, after just four days in the country, and was written by Kaplan and Rona:

Greetings from Japan!

We knew that traveling to another country, to study the principles of Lean manufacturing at their source would be meaningful, but we weren't quite prepared for the amazing experience we've had thus far.

We've found that Japan, one of the most densely populated countries in the world, is a highly customer-oriented culture. People are gracious, service levels are extraordinarily high, trains run on time, and there is not a speck of litter in sight.

A full day at the Toyota Museum of Industry and Technology has confirmed our thinking that Lean principles hold incredible promise for our organization. It is one thing to study Lean principles in the U.S., it is quite another to see the principles in action at their roots.

If the essential question was what a car company management system had to do with health care, Kaplan had an answer in that first letter home. "Toyota has perfected a set of tools and techniques," he and Rona wrote, "that are applicable to any industry." They wrote that there was *not a single principle utilized to produce the highest quality automobiles that could not be applied to health care and to our processes at Virginia Mason"* (Emphasis added).

From Nagoya, the group travelled to Shizuoka, where they worked on the floor of a Hitachi air conditioning plant seeking to identify possible improvements on the factory floor. There they participated in a multiple-day event similar to a Rapid Process Improvement Workshop. "Everybody was nervous on the Hitachi shop floor," says Dr. Donna Smith. "We went in with fear or anxiety because it was so unfamiliar. Then we started using the tools we'd learned—to see with our eyes, to observe the flow, mapping, timing them, and we got to know the work very quickly and could identify the waste and improve the product. We knew nothing about air conditioners, but we could use the tools well enough to actually make productive improvements."

"Whether we were looking at people or at machines," Kaplan and Rona wrote, "we learned very quickly to see waste of movement, time, travel … inventory and waiting.

> We were able to take people out of the process and redistribute the work, leveling operator cycle times and product flow. We were able to identify defects in products from an upstream or earlier process, and suggest changes to eliminate the defects. We were able to suggest improvements that would increase operator safety and operator

flow. We were able to move equipment to make work easier. We were able to suggest changes that would make the ergonomics for the operators much better … .

What impressed us was the ease with which we could understand a totally "foreign" process, implement changes right away and see them work. We were stunned at the willingness of management to apply changes within minutes. Our teams would show the workers how we thought the work should change; they would retrain on the spot if possible and try it … . In one situation, the suggestion of placing parts on a higher platform eliminated bending over and picking up heavy parts hundreds of times a day for just one operator! …

Through rigorous application of the Toyota system, Hitachi improved both production speed and quality. Over a seven-year period Hitachi cut production time for a single air conditioning unit from twenty-eight to eight days. During this time there had been no miraculous intervention, no silver bullet, just relentless, disciplined application of the Toyota method. Thousands of incremental changes had revolutionized the process, but a reduction in manufacturing time from twenty-eight to eight days was just a start for Hitachi. Their interim goal was three days. Their ultimate goal, which they fully expected to reach, was manufacturing an air conditioning unit to the precise customer specifications in a single day—in fact, on the very same day the order was submitted.

An Industrial Symphony

Gary Kaplan had never seen anything like it. He gazed out over the vast Toyota Motomachi production facility in Toyota City, Japan, and felt as though he was experiencing a profound awakening: so many different parts, so disparate, so complex, yet a purity and harmony that was quite beautiful. The assembly line moved along at a rate of less than one mile an hour, as a variety of vehicles were smoothly and precisely constructed. When a Camry appeared the system knew to provide the worker with exactly the right door, mirror, or other part, and the same thing happened with every Camry, every Corolla, and every other vehicle throughout the Toyota line. "It was like watching a symphony," Kaplan recalls. "Everything totally synchronous and you wonder what health care would be like if it actually looked like that."

And then Kaplan saw something that instantly captured his imagination: A worker, apparently having difficulty with a door, reached up and tugged on a cord and the production line slowed noticeably, giving him additional time for the fix. When he still could not get it right, the worker tugged on the cord a second time, halting the entire production line. In seconds, a three-person team of technicians swooped down to the factory floor and huddled with the worker. Within minutes, they had solved the problem and restarted the production line; in so doing they had succeeded in eliminating a defect—preventing a defect from reaching the customer. This was the modern incarnation of what Sakichi Toyoda had built into his automatic loom one hundred years before Kaplan and his team witnessed this unforgettable moment on the Toyota factory floor. Witnessing this stop-the-line event, Kaplan realized that every one of the thousand workers in that factory possessed the immense power to shut down the entire production line in pursuit of defect-free work. As they watched this marvelous performance, Kaplan and his colleagues could see that the stop-the-line technique could have a powerful application in a large medical center such as Virginia Mason. As the team debriefed following their experience at the Toyota plant, it became clear that they were determined to bring this technique home to Seattle.

The members of the Virginia Mason team were amazed not only by the empowerment of line workers, but also by the frontline engagement of supervisors—also in pursuit of quality. Sarah Patterson saw that when there was a problem on the line supervisors did not have to be called from offices in another part of the facility. Supervisors did not respond to workers by e-mail or telephone—they were right there on the *genba*—the shop floor. Patterson learned that tables and chairs in various locations on the factory floor were used by teams meeting to solve problems right there on the floor with the people who actually performed the work.

"It was profoundly different from how we had done our work," says Patterson. "In the past we had not involved the people doing the work in a meaningful way in making improvements. Often it was done by committees who 'represented' the workers, and they would meet in rooms far removed from the shop floor."

Says Kaplan: "Every one of us were blown away. Every one of us said there are huge applications here for health care."

Sarah Patterson was standing next to her colleague, Charleen Tachibana, and both of them marveled at the precision of the system—"watching how they've designed their system to deliver the right door to the right car every single time and the way the door was being handled by the equipment that handled it and the workers. It was done with such precision and care and I remember Charleen saying, 'You know, it is very sad to see that here's a car company that handles its car doors with more care and thoughtfulness than we handle our patients every day at Virginia Mason.' And I'm thinking, 'She's right, that's absolutely true.'"

Part of the Virginia Mason team's mission was to see the process and try and determine what aspects of the Toyota process were applicable in health care. Diane Miller came away from the factories convinced that there wasn't anything she saw "that *wasn't* applicable to health care." She calls the experience of witnessing the work on the floor of the Toyota factory "the most transformational" aspect of the trip. "It's very hard to describe the power of the beauty of those processes," she says. "To see the potential for us was magical. If we could get our systems operating even a fraction that well, it would be a really good thing for health care."

As the group discussed what they were seeing and learning, many were struck by how clearly the Toyota Production System applied to the Virginia Mason strategic plan and the vision Virginia Mason leaders had for putting patients first. In another letter home, Kaplan and Rona called to mind the use of the Toyota system at Boeing, Genie, and Toyota itself—manufacturers of airplanes, forklifts, and cars. "What do any of these products have to do with health care?" they wrote. "Each of the products they produce has thousands of processes involved and many are very complex. Many of these products, if they fail, can cause fatality. They are in many ways, just like us."

And then a new twist—the idea that "the principles and tools of the Toyota Production System may well become those of the Virginia Mason Production System"—an adaptation of the Toyota methods to health care. It was the first time the term Virginia Mason Production System was used, and it was a crucial point, for Kaplan's intent was not to adopt the Toyota method wholesale. Rather, his intent was to learn the history and methods and to adapt the framework to health care. The new method would be a translation and adaptation of the Toyota approach into health care—a process Kaplan expected would take years.

"Aren't You Ashamed?"

While the Toyota facility was an inspirational stop on their trip, it was humbling, as well. The team's work was difficult and the days long. Team members would grow somewhat tense under pressure from *senseis* who were unrelenting. One evening, near the end of a long and arduous day, a team led by Dr. Bob Mecklenburg, Chief of Medicine, and Charleen Tachibana, Chief of Nursing, was huddled with a *sensei* who had been pushing them for hours. The team was studying a schematic of a section of Virginia Mason when the *sensei* pointed to an area on the graphic and asked what it was. Dr. Mecklenburg told him it was a waiting room.

"Who waits there?" the *sensei* asked.

"Patients," Mecklenburg said.

"What are they waiting for?"

"The doctor."

The *sensei* asked more questions, learning that there were dozens and dozens of waiting rooms spread throughout the medical center—waiting rooms in every division of every department and most crowded much of the time.

The *sensei* reacted as though an invisible line had been crossed; as though he was deeply offended by this news. "You have one hundred waiting areas where patients wait an average of forty-five minutes for a doctor?"

He paused and let the question hang in the air, and then asked, *"Aren't you ashamed?"*

It stunned the team, and yet they all knew the answer was yes, of course —they were ashamed. They were ashamed that they had a system riddled with waste where people waited so long for so many doctors. They were ashamed they treated their customers with such disrespect. They were ashamed that this network of waiting areas—well-used every day—was the antithesis of being patient focused.

Dr. Donna Smith thought of the Japan experience as something akin to a ropes course where people are taken out of their element and end up learning more about one another than they do back at work. Nothing about the trip was easy, she says. The whole team was about as far out of their comfort zones as it was possible to get—in a nation few had ever visited with a language none of them knew. They were on factory floors for just about the first time in their lives watching air conditioners and cars being made. Perhaps because there was a genuine spirit of discovery and open-mindedness there was no artifice, no pulling rank. Any sort of veneer that existed back in the United States was stripped away and the team members were direct and honest with one another. The intensity of the experience—of trying to find the application to health care—bonded them together. During debriefing sessions there would be a question on the table and the team members, one-by-one, would speak their minds.

"And if you didn't agree, that was okay," says Dr. Smith. "But you had to speak. We needed to talk about this. It wasn't a given that we would have consensus. It was definitely encouraged that you say what's on your mind. The idea was that we've got to figure this out together. We were pushing each other's thinking, challenging each other to make sure we were making the right decision."

The Missing Piece

The team's third and final dispatch home to the staff came right after their experience at Toyota. They had witnessed a production facility that manufactured 360 cars per day, each car consisting of approximately 20,000 parts. This meant that within this one Toyota plant there were more than 7 million opportunities to make a mistake every day. But the system allowed almost none. The magic of the system was not that it had been devised by some of the finest quality improvement engineers in the world, but rather that *kaizen*—continuous incremental improvement—was a reality. *Kaizen* was the lifeblood of the process. Each year at Toyota, employees offer tens of thousands of suggestions to improve quality and efficiency, many coming from frontline workers. So profoundly attuned are employees to the notion of improvement that many of the suggestions are adopted. Toyota had succeeded in fostering a corporate culture that enhances individual creativity and teamwork while honoring mutual trust and respect between staff and management. The TPS is also characterized by deeply collaborative relationships with vendors, thus enabling Toyota to receive the exact part or tool needed at precisely the correct time in the right place and in the correct amount. Anything more than what is needed at the exact moment is waste. "In every way, they have as their guiding principles and their focus what we want for our organization," wrote Kaplan and Rona. "The piece we are missing that they have in place is the integrated management system called the Toyota Production System."

If there was any doubt back in Seattle about the leadership commitment to implement what would become the Virginia Mason Production System at the medical center it was erased in this dispatch. There was a sense of discovery—even a feeling of euphoria—that emerged in the latest communication back home. Kaplan and Rona wrote that "there was no question that this system of management would work for Virginia Mason." In fact, of course, there *was* a question about whether it would work, but the exuberance inherent in this letter revealed the supreme confidence Kaplan and others had that, in fact, they had come upon the Holy Grail of management. Any doubt about Kaplan's commitment to the method was obliterated in this missive: "There was only reaffirmation that this management method would revolutionize Virginia Mason and, hopefully, our industry." The letter declared unequivocally, "This will be our management method."

After two weeks in Japan the team gathered in Tokyo the night before their flight home. Much had been accomplished. Kaplan communicated back to Seattle that he was committed to a no-layoff policy "related to Lean efforts" to make sure that employees would feel free playing an active role in quality improvement and the redesign and streamlining of work; they had to have the comfort that they would not be innovating themselves into the unemployment line. Kaplan also communicated back to Seattle that Rapid Process Improvement Workshops would be an essential and well-used tool going forward and that value stream maps—charts detailing each step in a process—would be "developed for inpatient, outpatient, procedure areas, and all major divisions of the organization" within ninety days. This value stream mapping process would reveal the systems most urgently in need of improvement. They also noted that all executive leaders at Virginia Mason would be required to become certified workshop leaders by the end of that year (2002). Kaplan and Rona announced that Virginia Mason would implement a "stop the line" system modeled on the Hitachi and Toyota systems that empowered every worker to stop the line to prevent any kind of defect.

It had been an astonishing trip in so many ways. The team had spent hours together in both formal and informal sessions. These discussions—during plane and bus rides, over meals, or at late-night get-togethers—were a critically important part of the trip. Every person on the team processed the experience a bit differently. Some exhibited a sense of robust enthusiasm from the moment they touched down in Japan, whereas others were restrained, questioning, or even skeptical. Conversations were heartfelt and brutally honest. Some of the team members worried that the whole idea was too extreme, too foreign both culturally and practically: *We take care of people, not cars.*

Viewed in retrospect the trip had a linear nature—they went, saw an amazing process, and returned to implement it. In reality, though, it was much more complex and nuanced. There were heated discussions and many doubts. Much of the sense of enthusiasm and discovery was matched by an honest sense of fear and anxiety for how this would affect the future of an institution about which they cared so deeply. It was no exaggeration to say that their collective professional futures were on the line. In his book, John Black characterized the Virginia Mason team's response to the new direction as a mix of "energy, excitement, shock, and some skepticism. It was clear there was no immediate consensus in the room to move forward as aggressively as Kaplan and Rona planned."

Whatever the individual's point of view, the trip was intense in almost every way—physical, emotional, and intellectual. Ultimately what bound the group together was not wholehearted agreement on a point of view—that did not yet exist. What bound them together was the intensity of a unique shared experience. They had gone out to a frontier, pioneers with that western spirit, and they had searched for something new, something no one else in health care had attempted on a systemwide scale, never mind accomplished.

"What occurred in Japan was transformational," says Kaplan. "It was the product of an intense shared experience and intense shared processing."

From the start, Kaplan knew that alignment among the executive leaders was essential. Fractured leadership would surely doom the new effort, yet alignment could not be forced and it could not—and did not—happen overnight. Important progress toward alignment was achieved in the months leading up to the Japan trip as leaders engaged in rigorous study. The team was further solidified when it became clear that participation in the trip was required for Virginia Mason leaders.

As much as anything else it was the experience of the trip itself that most powerfully bonded the leadership in pursuit of the new path. Diane Miller says the group's constant togetherness and ongoing discussions over the three weeks promoted a growing sense of alignment. The fact that the men and women on the trip were thrown together with—as they said at the time—"nowhere to hide"—resulted in a nonstop discussion of the new methods and their applicability in health care. "During the first half of the trip we could not say wholeheartedly that we knew where we were headed with this," says Miller. "But there were dinners and discussions and all of that time we spent talking about the implication this had for health care enabled us to reach a point at the end of the trip where we agreed that this would be our management method."

Although there was a powerful sense of the possibilities that lay ahead—of a future with a dramatically better approach to quality—there was an inescapable sense of loss, even grief, for some. After all, these people had been working a certain way for years, many of them for decades, and the message now was that the old way was not good enough, didn't work well enough, and failed to care for patients in the best possible way. This was a very tough message for people who had devoted their careers to doing the very best that they could. Now, to discover that there might be a much better way was, on one hand exhilarating, of course, but it also meant they would have to relearn so much of what they had been doing for years, even decades.

On the eve of their return home a surge of emotion swept through the group. People were overwhelmed by it all. Whereas some faced the prospect of going home to implement the system with a sense of trepidation—a fear it was simply too much change, too big a gamble—others believed that applying the new approach could transform Virginia Mason, could improve the quality of care for patients, and could save lives! "We were so moved by the power of this that on that last day there was a lot of crying," recalls Diane Miller. "People that I would have never pictured—and to this day have never seen again—cry, but were quite moved by it. On the last evening when we committed to embrace and support VMPS as our management system each of us stated what we would commit to personally do in our individual roles. We were each presented with a Daruma doll, small, round doll heads, red in color. The dolls are a symbol of perseverance and good luck—often a gift of encouragement—to remind us of our commitment. We then signed one another's dolls as a show of support."

Miller and others on the team were carrying home a vision of a journey forward—guided by the Virginia Mason Production System (VMPS)—with the goal of zero defects. "Zero defects, zero infection rates, zero any defect," she says. "Or 100 percent satisfaction. This is a game of zero and 100 percent, and if we have a vision less than that, it's the wrong vision."

While the letters home to the staff were clear enough, but the message Kaplan and colleagues conveyed when they were back on the ground in Seattle would be crucial. It was one thing for the Virginia Mason staff to receive three letters from Japan, but the in-person message back home would be more powerful. Prior to the return, team members discussed communication home about what they were learning. Gathered at the hotel the day before leaving Tokyo, and at the urging of John Black, Kaplan was convinced that returning with one voice was important. It was not that the travelers forfeited their freedom of speech on return, but Kaplan wanted to convey several points quite clearly, and this would be accomplished more effectively if the whole team joined in the communications effort. The central message was as obvious as it was clear: Henceforth, the Virginia Mason Production System (VMPS) would be *the* management system for the medical center.

"We agreed," says Kaplan, "that we were going to say, 'We've been there. We've seen something quite remarkable. We believe it has huge potential for Virginia Mason, and we are committed to pursuing this as our management system.'"

"This Is Ludicrous"

Back home there were staffers eagerly awaiting the chance to implement the new method. Many others remained neutral, adopting a wait-and-see attitude. And then, of course, there were the skeptics, many doctors among them, who considered the trip a colossal waste. "People were saying, 'We're struggling financially and all of a sudden we've got thirty people in Japan for a ten-day boondoggle while the rest of us are working,'" says Dr. Fred Govier, a surgeon specializing in urology who would go on to become Chief of Surgery at Virginia Mason.

Part of the reaction was impatience with what was perceived as yet another flavor-of-the-month management method. "We'd been through CQI in the late 1980s and at least two or three other management techniques," says Govier, "where they'd gotten everybody together for half-day seminars and none of those had really gone anywhere."

There was also a growing sense of concern among doctors at the increasing talk of standardization in the practice of medicine, a concept that was antithetical to the thinking of many physicians. Word had filtered back that the notion of standard work was an essential element of the method and this deeply troubled many physicians. "It first came out that this was the new direction of the organization," Govier says. "And it was all going to be about processes and standard work and people were not the same as cars but there were a tremendous amount of similarities. As a surgeon the last thing I wanted to hear about was standard work. I was taking care of patients with complex problems and the thought that we were going to learn something from an assembly line that made automobiles was just way out there for me."

Another essential element of the new method was creating a Kaizen Promotion Office (KPO) within Virginia Mason staffed by men and women who would achieve enough expertise in the system to be able to work throughout the medical center promoting and managing continuous improvement. John Black had pointed out that at Toyota as much as 5 percent of the workforce was assigned full-time to *kaizen*, and he told Kaplan that creating a robust KPO was essential. He said the same held true for hiring an experienced *sensei* to help guide the work. These moves were hardly greeted with universal enthusiasm, however. Early on the staff from the KPO would show up in various places throughout the medical center armed with stopwatches and clipboards, and they would create flow diagrams. Their measurement and analysis led to suggestions on how doctors might practice in a more efficient, patient-centered manner.

This violation of autonomy rubbed many doctors the wrong way, and when there were mistakes by the KPO team the critics pounced. An early Rapid Process Improvement Workshop, for example, concluded that the pre-op clinic was unnecessary and it was thus abolished. Soon thereafter, however, it became clear that the pre-op clinic was actually very useful and it was restored. Other early missteps fortified the critics. The practice of 5S (sort, simplify, sweep, standardize, self-discipline) is one of the cornerstones of Toyota's success and VMPS implementation. The plan was to apply 5S to all areas throughout the medical center and although staff were informed, trained, encouraged, cajoled, measured, and held accountable, the new 5S efforts sometimes produced poor results. An effort to simplify by labeling became a circus as employees went on a spree labeling everything in sight, including co-workers and where their bottoms should rest on chair seats. This sarcastic rebellion greatly amused the critics.

The "standardize" in 5S was problematic as well. Few employees were comfortable when told how they had habitually performed a task was no longer going to be okay. Each step or two forward usually included one backward. The 5S audit process contributed to this two-step. Trained observers performed 5S audits by visiting departments and asking to see their "5S book," which documented their 5S work. Although the need for data mandated audits, there was initially less focus on the actual 5S process and more on its documentation, with the result that complex busy work was created to document the simplification effort!

These sorts of things "fueled the fire," says Govier. "Physicians were saying 'What are the crazy people in the Kaizen Promotion Office going to decide next? Physicians don't have any say anymore.'" Govier was eating lunch in the doctors' dining room soon after the group returned from Japan and deep resentment about the expense of the trip pervaded the room. Part of it, of course, was the notion that Toyota makes cars and cars are not people—but it was much deeper than that. Most of these doctors had been at Virginia Mason for a while, and this new direction seemed to many of them the latest in a series of ominous signs. There had been consecutive years of financial losses. Plans for a new hospital building had been scrapped. A major policy change from the board deprived doctors of the power to elect medical center leaders as had traditionally been the case. Henceforth, the board decreed, leaders would be appointed rather than elected. And then the ultimate insult—modeling a medical practice on a car manufacturing company. "Physicians have always been a very conservative group," says Govier, "and change came very, very slowly and the Virginia Mason Production System was tremendous change."

A few months after the team returned from Japan, Kaplan announced there would be a second trip. For many skeptics, this was gasoline on the fire. During a professional staff meeting doctors angrily criticized Kaplan. "There were several very, very angry individuals who stood up," says Govier, "and said, 'This is ludicrous.'" The resistance movement was difficult for Kaplan. Many of the dissenters were longtime friends and colleagues—men and women he greatly respected and admired. But he was on a path he felt confident was right for the medical center. If it was clear before the trip that this path would require the most resolute possible leadership, it was doubly so afterward.

Inevitably, there were casualties. A handful of physicians were so put off by the changes that they left Virginia Mason. It was not one change, but rather a series of changes that pushed them to do so. First had come the physician compact and with it a difficult cultural shift from autonomy to team medicine; from doctors being at the top of the heap to patients being there. The governance change—appointing rather than electing department heads and the CEO—was a break with longstanding tradition and an affront to some doctors. On top of it all, came the application of VMPS and with some physicians—*"People aren't cars!"*—that did not sit well.

No Going Back

The challenge from the resistance group at Virginia Mason was formidable but an order of magnitude more challenging was the difficulty and nature of the work itself. Since day one, John Black had emphasized to Kaplan that the journey would be arduous. In his book *The Toyota Way to Health Care Excellence,* Black wrote that "the journey to becoming a world-class health care organization isn't quick or easy, or for the impatient or faint of heart ... Toyota has been engaged in its change effort for decades and hasn't run short of improvement ideas yet." Black wrote that "without an understanding that real change is hard and takes time and commitment, your improvement effort will not survive the first year."

At Virginia Mason it was important to start fast building momentum to combat what Black called "the inertia of organizations, the behavior that goes with it, and the resistance to change that is typical in all organizations." Black told Kaplan that during the first year he might feel as though he was taking two steps forward and one step back and that there would be triumphant moments, but maddeningly frustrating ones as well. Black told him he would just have to keep trusting the process.

Kaplan knew there were people on staff whose strategy would be to lay low and wait out what they considered nothing more than the latest management fad, but he made it clear that he would demand active engagement. "If you want to be a senior leader here," Kaplan told colleagues, "you have to be certified, which means you have to go through the certification training, take the exams, and continue to be certified to hold your job as an executive." This applied to *every* leader, Kaplan included, and it required real work—a deep dive into the theory and application of the process. Kaplan was trying to make it impossible for any leader in the medical center to sit on the sidelines, unengaged in the improvement work. There would be no hiding under the desks.

Certification of leaders in the VMPS was crucial. Diane Miller and other leaders saw it as essential to embed this new thinking among all Virginia Mason leaders. "We had proposed taking people just below the vice president level—director, executive director level, or senior director—offline to have them learn the methodology," she says. "The thinking was that this will just be another CQI if we don't embed it at the front line. So I suggested that we take these folks offline, have them certified with really in-depth learning, and they could then lead in significant areas—radiology, perioperative services, cancer services, GI, internal medicine."

But there was pushback, says Miller. There was real angst about certification because it required seven days of classroom work and much other study as well—all in addition to one's normal job. "That first group all went in saying, 'This is ridiculous. I don't have time to be offline. What are you talking about I have to do that? Who's going to do my work when I'm not there?'"

It was not long before the reaction was completely different, however. The managers taking the classes could see the application to their work. "Within a month, they were changing how they were working, how they viewed the world," says Miller. "The whole certification process, spending a lot of time really understanding these principles, is what changes people's ability to manage and think differently. That's the only way we can really change the culture of the organization and that does start at the top. I do believe being certified helps us continue to understand this as a management method, not a set of tools that you pull out occasionally to solve a problem."

Chief of Medicine Bob Mecklenburg knew the cultural and process changes that lay ahead would require personnel changes. "I had to find leaders to lead the change in creating a much different approach to delivering health care," Mecklenburg says. "Each of the eighteen Section Heads in the Department of Medicine had been elected to their positions because they were superb physicians, yet few were interested in insisting their friends and colleagues abandon their personal preferences in delivering medical care to practice medicine according to the standardized pathways that were the path to reducing costly variation in health care." The result, over the next three years, was that leadership changed. Mecklenburg did not view any of those who moved on to other positions as failures. With VMPS, leaders were required to take on a very difficult new task—leading transformational change at the speed of light. Very few left Virginia Mason. Instead, says Mecklenburg, "They just decided that they'd rather practice and do their usual great job at teaching and research rather than lead change. We made these choices together, and the result was a good resolution for all concerned. From my perspective this period of change management, conflict resolution, and alignment was satisfying, produced strengthened relationships, and provided an outstanding leadership team."

The long-term nature of the work was daunting in the early days. "Everyone was telling us that this takes twenty years," says Kaplan, which was not at all what he or anyone else wanted to hear. As CEO, Kaplan wanted results and he wanted them *now*. It was not long, however, "before you realized that this is incremental and really a long-term strategy. So early on you're hopeful that you're going to see some really significant wins, but people said you're going to be in it for the long haul. Given the unacceptability of the status quo in terms of quality, safety, cost, workforce satisfaction … there was no better option."

Kaplan had spent some time with Edgar Schein, the former MIT faculty member and organizational culture guru, and Schein says that leaders of organizations—*by their behaviors*—shape the culture. To Gary Kaplan, that meant he and the other Virginia Mason leaders would have to engage with the method, learn it, practice it, and teach it. Only then would they have a chance at changing the culture. Kaplan was convinced this was the right road, but he also was clear-eyed in understanding that it would be a long and difficult journey; there would be bumps in the road, detours, collisions, and worse. But, he was committed, his key senior leadership team was committed, and, crucially, the board was committed as well. "The board signals to the entire organization that going in this direction is absolutely essential," says COO Sarah Patterson. "There's no going back. We've burned the bridge."

Chapter Three

The Blue Yarn

The first major initiative at Virginia Mason using Toyota methods and tools actually started six months prior to the first Japan trip. When Dr. Kaplan and his leadership team were deeply engaged in the study of the Toyota methods. In late 2001, the need to improve the Virginia Mason outpatient cancer service presented itself as an ideal opportunity to test the new methods on a difficult, real-life problem within the medical center.

It was, perhaps, the first time since Hippocrates that a ball of blue yarn made an impact—and a considerable impact, at that—in modern medicine. A ball of blue yarn told cancer doctors and their team a story with a kind of clarity the physicians, nurses, and other staff members had rarely seen. The team gathered to envision and design a new Virginia Mason cancer center, and their first step was to understand the reality of the current state. What exactly did the process of delivering cancer care look like step-by-step? What was the patient experience, step-by-step? This required measuring, observing, and detailing every segment of a cancer patient's journey through the medical center.

Thus, the blue yarn. Team members huddled over a large piece of cardboard with blue yarn tracing the path of an ambulatory cancer patient's meandering journey throughout the medical center—to the lab on six, radiology on five, up to fourteen for the clinic, down to the infusion center on twelve, then across twelve to radiation. The yarn looked like some sort of abstract art as it went up and down one building then into another and up and down and around and then into yet another building and then doubled back and wrapped around itself in horizontal and vertical lines from one end of the cardboard to the other.

On one level, it was just a piece of yarn on a cardboard diagram, but at a deeper level it revealed a system riddled with flaws and centered on the provider, not the patient. Dr. Henry Otero, a physician in the Hematology/Oncology Section, and Michaelle Wetteland, RN, were amazed when they saw the blue yarn reveal the truth about the patient experience.

"We saw that blue yarn and said, 'Oh, no,'" recalls Dr. Otero. The fact that the sickest ambulatory patients were forced to walk all over the medical center for treatment made no sense whatsoever, and it had to change. Something else occurred to Otero as his eyes followed the circuitous path of the blue yarn—as he scanned the whole diagram: He was looking at a tool that might very well help him understand how to improve the treatment of cancer patients.

A Revealing Value Stream

Michaelle Wetteland, a nurse in charge of the infusion center, could clearly see that a new cancer center was needed. "The infusion center and the clinic were on inpatient floors within the hospital and that was just not ideal for our patients," she says. It was confusing for patients to show up on a hospital floor and have to walk past a series of inpatient rooms to the end of the hallway to the outpatient infusion center. "There was a lot of noise and activity," says Wetteland. The fact that the patient experience was less than ideal was obvious to Wetteland and her nurse colleagues who experienced firsthand patients' frustration with delays and long waits. In addition, says Wetteland, the facility itself "was not the kind of healing, comforting environment our patients needed."

In the old days, constructing a new cancer center would have meant an architect huddling with facilities staff, creating a design, and running it by administration. That approach, however, was antithetical to creating a design to eliminate waste and provide defect-free care to the patient. Although they were still a half-year shy of making the first Japan pilgrimage, Kaplan and his team had learned enough about the Toyota methods to know that they could help guide them through the process of designing and building the new space.

The cancer center staff was certainly a clean slate when it came to VMPS. Nurse Wetteland and administrators Denise Dubuque, Julie Sylvester, and Richelle Bagdasarian were deeply devoted to the patients but had no experience or familiarity with the VMPS approach. The same held true for the two physicians who would be most involved in the work—Otero and department chief Andrew Jacobs. Both were experienced, respected clinicians who had focused their professional lives on treating patients with a wide variety of cancers. Jacobs had previously been on the faculty at the UCLA Medical School, as well as in private practice in Los Angeles, and Otero had previously been at the Fred Hutchinson Cancer Research Center in Seattle.

Before encountering the new methods, Otero characterized himself as having been "fairly unaware of the patient experience. I was physician-focused. If I was delayed I was upset, but if I was delaying someone else I either didn't know it or had that sense of entitlement that we're providing good care so it's okay if the patients wait."

A number of months before the work started on creating a new cancer center, one of Dr. Jacobs's patients expressed a level of frustration that captured his attention. After colon cancer surgery, the patient was undergoing six months of chemotherapy treatment. It was bad enough that she had cancer, bad enough that she was afraid, bad enough that she was missing so much work, bad enough that the chemo made her sick and exhausted. What she did not understand, she told Dr. Jacobs, was why the whole process was so difficult at Virginia Mason. "I'm here all day for chemo," she told him. "I'm walking from here to there. I have to walk to three or four different locations, and I spend a huge part of the day not doing anything except waiting for the lab, waiting for the doctor, waiting to get my chemotherapy. Waiting and more waiting. It's a whole day I've lost to work."

Jacobs was struck by this. The notion that the sickest ambulatory patients in the medical center had to trek all over the campus pursuing treatment was indefensible. He was struck particularly with the waste of patients' time. "For someone with cancer, time is the most precious commodity they have, particularly for people whose cancer has spread," he says. "Their life span is limited so time is precious, and we were wasting a considerable amount of it." When Jacobs looked down at the cardboard and the meandering blue yarn he wasn't seeing the yarn any more—he was seeing his patient's experience.

"Our cancer patients are taken care of by pretty much every part of the medical center," observes Virginia Mason COO Sarah Patterson. "They come into the emergency room often, they're in the hospital on and off—sometimes for chemo treatments, sometimes for palliative care, sometimes for surgeries. They're in radiation therapy, our outpatient infusion center, in our lab, in our radiology department, and we thought we could be doing a much better job. It was an opportunity to demonstrate by going deep within a particular service line what the possibilities were and how it impacts our patients." The idea was to break down the silos that get in the way of patient-focused, coordinated care.

A fundamental principle of the new approach is that when work is to be redesigned it is done by teams that include all of the stakeholders in that work: Those who create the product or service as well as those who buy or use the product or service. It is a notably egalitarian process that routinely sees the creation of teams that might include the chief of medicine alongside a member of the housekeeping or maintenance staffs. The theory is that on such teams all voices are equal. The idea was to take the old vertical way of top-down decision making and flatten it into a horizontal model where every voice is heard; where every participant is respected and valued. The cancer center redesign team included Drs. Jacobs, Otero, and Michael Glenn, chief of surgery; Nurse Michaelle Wetteland; the cancer services administrator; nurses from the clinic and infusion center; a facilities staff person; schedulers; and two patients. Dr. Otero is candid in recalling that at the time he was puzzled by the inclusion of scheduling staff, wondering what they could contribute to "this high-level design process." Otero knew most of these men and women, but he had had no real interaction with many of them.

The decision had been made to move the cancer center out of hospital floors to the Lindeman Pavilion ninth floor, among the most appealing spaces in the medical center. For one thing, it was a shell, enabling the cancer service to design whatever it wanted from scratch. In addition, it offered stunning vistas of downtown Seattle and Puget Sound.

The team started work with a tool called 3P—production preparation process—that was typically employed to redesign a process when breakthrough rather than incremental change was required. It had been used countless times in industry, particularly manufacturing, but this was apparently the first time it was ever used in health care. John Black and Associates played a pivotal role in the specifics of how to go about redesigning the cancer center and two Black colleagues, Jon Sutter and Mark Barnett, facilitated the cancer center 3P.

Typically, a 3P process lasts for five days. Every team member's calendar was cleared, and they were ready to take the process on. On the first day, there was a sense of curiosity and some restrained excitement, but there was also a healthy dose of skepticism—subdued for the most part, but clearly there. Perhaps the most vocal team member at the outset was the cancer center administrator, who made no secret of his belief that this would all be a waste of time and that the end results surely would not justify the cost of taking so many valued employees offline for a week.

On the second day of the 3P the team began using the "fishbone" tool. This involved creating a drawing that looked like a fishbone with the spine being the patient flow and the lateral bones being a wide variety of procedures and events needed to get the patient successfully through the process. Lateral bones from the fish spine might represent, for example, the patient having blood drawn, checking in for chemotherapy, visiting the doctor, and so on. This required the team to detail who was doing what and when, and it very quickly laid the process bare—revealing that the work of nurses and doctors was overlapping at nearly every step in the process. It also revealed that communications among nurses, doctors, schedulers, and others was so poor that it required constant rechecking, interruption, and rework. No one on the team had ever seen the process revealed so completely. It was during this process that Otero began to gain a sense of enthusiasm. He discovered that he and his nurse were often repeating the same work, and he had never realized that before. And he could see that many mistakes happened during sloppy handoffs. "It was very eye-opening," he says. "It was sort of 'Wow, this is our current process, and it seems to be cobbled together over the years without any thought to the *entire* process.'"

An essential part of the 3P process was analyzing the flows of medicine to the existing process to identify opportunities for improvement. In this case, the team looked at the flows of patients, providers, family and relationships, medications, supplies, equipment, and information. This is where the blue yarn made its appearance. As the team called out the patient steps in the process the blue yarn kept getting longer and longer and more complicated and twisting and turning in its journey.

Next came the yellow yarn representing the chemotherapy distribution process. The chemo order would be written by a physician on the fourteenth floor and brought by the patient to the twelfth floor treatment area, where a pharmacist would process it. The order was then faxed to the inpatient pharmacy in the basement to be prepared. The chemotherapy was prepared then brought by transporter back to the twelfth floor, but, because the courier had a hospital routing schedule of many deliveries, it took up to two hours for the return to the twelfth floor. This meant that a patient arriving soon after the courier left the floor would wait as much as 150 minutes before the chemotherapy might be ready to infuse.

"They sit and wait, patients with cancer, delayed by the system we created to deliver the chemotherapy," says Otero. "That was not patient first. I had never really thought about the patient experience until that moment and I thought, 'I *know* we can do better.'"

The Patient's Voice

A crucial part of the process was listening to the patient members of the team. They told of long waits and unpleasant surroundings in the infusion center; of a lack of privacy and comfort: "If we have to be there for chemo infusion for two hours or four or even in some cases six hours, shouldn't the space be more comforting? More of a healing environment?"

During the 3P Otero noticed as the team members worked together the first couple of days that silos began to break down and that for the first time team members began to understand the work of others on the team—doctor, nurse, scheduler, and so on—and they began to think about their work in flow and as a team rather than in separate silos the way it had traditionally been.

After only a couple of days Jacobs and Otero were both enthralled with the 3P process. It enabled them to see with new eyes; to see processes right under their noses they had never before thought much about. They and the other team members discovered various defects within the process that were easily fixed, and many of those discoveries were at a granular level. "It was very, very exciting because we were going to create something *around the patient*," says Otero.

During one of their discussions, Wetteland asked a simple question: "How would it be," she asked, "if we brought everything to the patient? If the patient didn't have to walk *anywhere?* They're tired, they're beat up, they don't feel good. How about if they didn't have to walk anywhere, and we brought all the services to the patient?" The team members sat around considering this notion, and it struck them all the same way: Of course! That's exactly what we must do. This notion of bringing everything to the patient became the team's rallying cry. "We really wanted a healing environment where we could put the patient in a calming room and bring everything to the patient," says Wetteland.

In a matter of a couple of days the team designed twenty-one different layouts and discussed each one, eventually narrowing their choices to five and finally down to three. The various teams named their designs: Red Carpet, Rays of Light, and the Waterfalls. Wetteland says there was a healthy competitive spirit among the three teams and that after each team presented its ideas the moderator asked the 3P members to select the best ideas from each proposal. Although all were different in terms of layout, they shared a desire to gather services—lab, pharmacy, social work, physicians, infusion, and so on—around the patient. As part of the process, the team shared its models with others from oncology who had not participated in the 3P process—an important step designed to elicit new ideas, refinements, and feedback.

Then the team hit a brick wall. Or, more accurately, they came to a harsh realization: The coveted Lindeman 9 space with its beautiful views would not work. More specifically, it would not work for the patient-centered facility they wanted to create, for it would still mean that patients would have to trek around the medical center for too many services. "When we studied the space, it was quite a distance from the other services," says Wetteland. "We thought, 'Wow this is really far away from radiation oncology and that's not best for the patient.'" "The beautiful view," observed Dr. Otero, "was at the expense of the patient."

This was one of those crucial moments: Would the vision become reality or would it end up being forgotten, altered, set aside for the sake of the comfort of providers? Viewed through a traditional lens it was a difficult decision. Viewed through the new lens of the patient-first mentality, however, it was an obvious decision: They had to find a new location. Says Dr. Otero, "It was the only principled decision that could be made. "

There was considerable angst over what would happen, however. Otero was concerned that the administration's response would be "That's the space you're going to get. Deal with it—make it work." The team, now with a clear understanding of what space would work, identified a particular area they considered ideal—Buck 2, the second floor in the Buck Pavilion, just two floors above the radiation center and steps from radiology and radiation oncology. However, the Buck Pavilion second floor was already occupied by the Dermatology Department. If they were to be moved in favor of a new cancer center it would cost a good deal of money and delay the new cancer facility by more than a year. Undeterred, Dr. Jacobs wrote a letter to Gary Kaplan and others in senior management in an effort to make the case for Buck 2. Jacobs noted that the original selection of Lindeman 9 for the cancer center was made the old way—because the space was empty and available. Jacobs argued that the work of the 3P team revealed that Lindeman 9 met neither the most fundamental Virginia Mason commitment—patient first—nor the basic principles of the Toyota Production System—eliminate waste. It was true that the Buck 2 space would require a greater expense to convert into a cancer center, but the location would enable patients to remain close to radiation, radiology, and surgical and medical specialists.

Gary Kaplan did not blink—he was entirely persuaded by Jacobs' argument. There was no doubt in his mind that Jacobs and the 3P team were right: Buck 2 was the place.

New Space, New Process

In October 2003, a second 3P team convened to plan the space—and, more important, the *process*—for treatment on Buck 2. The new team included Jacobs and Otero; Michaelle Wetteland, along with other nurses; facilities workers; scheduling staff; pharmacists; two patients; and, this time, the architect who would be designing the facility. The second 3P was quite different from the first in that team members had accumulated some experience with various tools, particularly with Rapid Process Improvement Workshops (RPIWs). There was a greater understanding of waste, standard work, value streams, and flow—of how to analyze a process in some depth. Dr. Jacobs says that having two patients on the team rather than one, as had been the case with the original 3P, "was really powerful. And we also had the architect for the unit on the team, and he was a cancer survivor who had had chemotherapy so he knew *exactly* what we were talking about."

During the second 3P, the team conducted a deeper dive into the data by using a Product Quality (PQ) analysis, which allows demand to be categorized into specific types of products or services. Through this analysis the team learned that nearly half of all patients coming through the cancer center were there for relatively brief visits of less than an hour—some for fifteen- to twenty-minute injections of medications. Others were there simply to have blood drawn or for a growth factor injection, both of which could be done in a matter of a few minutes. The PQ analysis revealed that these patients usually got stuck in the system's heavy traffic when really all they needed was to get in and get out. As a result of this discovery, the team designed a high-volume area for patients whose visits would last less than an hour (and who did not need to see a doctor). Although the new short stay unit occupies a small space with few employees, it nonetheless efficiently serves a very large number of patients.

The 3P on Buck 2 revealed two other broad categories of patients: those coming in only for a discussion with their doctor and patients scheduled for chemotherapy or other infusions lasting anywhere from two to six hours. The patients on the team were clear about what would improve this experience. They said it was important to have private space—to be able to reflect, to meditate, to think, to zone out—and to be alone. "On the second 3P team the patients were a man and a woman," says Michaelle Wetteland, "and we would say to them, 'Tell us what's important to you,' and they had the freedom to voice their opinion. And the man said he wanted a private room every time and under the old system that was hard to get. I did a survey among patients and a majority did want a private room."

As the team progressed through its work it became clear that there were not enough rooms with windows to accommodate both patients and doctors. Ideally, of course, both would have windowed spaces, but now a choice had to be made. Traditionally, in almost any outpatient setting, the space on the perimeter of a building—windowed offices with views and natural light—is occupied by doctors. The assumption here among some members of the design team was that this tradition would hold true—that the doctors would occupy that same prime space in Buck 2 with patient treatment rooms on the window-less interior. But Drs. Jacobs and Otero wondered aloud whether that was put-ting the patient at the top of the pyramid as Virginia Mason had pledged per their strategic plan.

"What does it mean to be a patient-first organization?" Jacobs asked. Chemotherapy infusion treatments can take six hours. Should the patients spend that time in the interior of the building or in rooms with windows and natural light? Jacobs told the group he thought patients should get the outside rooms. Though the views weren't great—they were only on the second floor, after all—they nonetheless afforded a connection with the outside world with a few trees and natural light. The group discussed it, and it was clear that the doctors were not often sedentary during the course of a day—they were on the move the great majority of the time. Did it *really* matter where their space was located? In fact, some in the group observed that if you put the doctors, nurses, schedulers, and other personnel in the core of the space together, it would make communication more efficient.

To many on the team it made perfect sense, but some doctors strongly objected. Says Otero, "Some said, 'I'm a doctor and I work hard and I deserve an office with a window where I can close the door and have my private space away from everyone. That's what I deserve.'" This sense of entitlement was bred deeply into the culture of American medicine, and it was not easily challenged. In a sense, it was not at all unreasonable for doctors to want the outside offices. They had gone through many years of extremely rigorous training and had chosen to become healers; as such they were special members of society and, in a sense, they did "deserve" special treatment. However, Virginia Mason had made a fundamental promise to put the patient first and that meant ahead of the doctor. This was more than rhetoric, more than a vision. It was, in fact, embedded in the compact that every doctor at Virginia Mason had signed and agreed to live by. It helped make the patient-first vision a reality. In this instance, putting patients first meant they would get the windows. And that was the decision—one that Jacobs said "sent a message" throughout the medical center.

Continuous Improvement

The Floyd & Delores Jones Cancer Center at Virginia Mason Medical Center opened in January 2005. From a patient perspective, it was magnificent. There was a meditation room for quiet reflection and a café area with coffee or tea where patients and families could relax. The design placed these areas in the "patient corridor"—a space where patients, families, and friends are undisturbed by staff. The design separates the staff and keeps congestion away from the patients so their area is friendly and comfortable. "We have a very quiet, calming environment," says Wetteland. "We have little refrigerators in each room in case a patient wants to bring a bag lunch or wants a cold drink. Patients had suggested that. A couple of our patients, from the old facility called our new facility the 'cancer spa' when they saw it the first time."

In the new facility when patients arrive, they are immediately directed into the area most appropriate for their needs. Patients requiring only brief visits for injections, medications, to have blood drawn, and so forth, go directly to the short-stay clinic where they can move rapidly through the process. The team implemented self-rooming for those patients who were frequent visitors. When they arrive they simply find a room card and walk to the short-stay section. They know the nurses and the nurses know them. They receive their injections and sometimes they are out the door in less than five minutes. Patients requiring longer infusions are escorted on arrival to private rooms, where they are seated in a comfortable recliner. There is space for a family member or other companion as well. While patients are there they can enjoy a flat-screen TV or wireless Internet.

"The nurse comes in and assesses them and draws the blood, which gets sent up to the lab," says Jacobs. "The doctor will come into the room. The social worker can come into the room. Pain management can come to the room. Whoever is needed will come into the room. If the doctor gives the okay, the chemotherapy is made up very close by so there isn't the wait for it to be delivered from the pharmacy in the hospital. There is a little satellite pharmacy right there, and the nurses pick up the chemo and take it to the patient, who is sitting in the same room—from start to the finish of their treatment. It cut down by almost 50 percent the amount of time the patient is here, and nothing that affects safety or quality was done faster."

Dr. Jacobs emphasizes that the focus is on identifying and providing only value-added services—services the patient values most highly. Anything in the patient experience that does not add value—sitting around a waiting room, for example—would be minimized or eliminated. "The doctor's visit isn't shorter, it's the same," he says. "That's value-added time—that's precious time. You don't touch that. The time spent with the nurse is value-added. You don't touch that. The speed at which you give the chemotherapy treatment or the blood or whatever it is you're doing, you don't touch that either. It's all the waste in between. It's all the waiting, the preparation time, and so on—*that* you can speed up."

The soul of the Toyota Production System is continuous improvement and one of the most common tools for improving any process using TPS is an Rapid Process Improvement Workshop. These workshops involve a representative team convening for five days to break a process down into its component parts, identify and eliminate waste (any non-value-added part of the process), and ultimately reengineer the process to reduce time and cost. It is a rigorous process that must be "commissioned" by a sponsor, nearly always a senior executive within the medical center. Two certified workshop leaders convene and lead the group, which includes staff members directly involved in the work and many times personnel from the KPO. Prior to the start of the five-day workshop, a series of meetings take place to refine the goal of the RPIW, establish the metrics that will be measured, set specific targets for improvement, and select the team. Between May 2002 and August 2005, Jacobs, Otero, Wetteland, and their colleagues held thirteen RPIWs to improve various aspects of the cancer center. Workshops were conducted to improve a wide variety of processes including patient flow in the oncology infusion center, lab and pharmacy services for medical oncology patients, flow for breast cancer patients, treatment day lead time for radiation oncology patients, and more.

During a separate RPIW focused on the delivery of chemotherapy and biological agents, the team discovered that medications for patients were prepared by the pharmacy and sent to the infusion floor for patients but would sit there—often for quite a while—before being administered. There was no system for nurses to know the medications had actually arrived on the floor. The team reported that it had created "a visual control system using magnets. … A red magnet placed on the patient white board indicated that a medication had arrived on the floor. This notified the RNs that the medication was ready to be administered to the patient." The impact of this simple fix reduced the time it had previously taken for meds to be administered by 88 percent. The new pathway created by the RPIW team eliminated trips to both the Lindeman and hospital buildings for many patients. A representative time and distance under the new plan was seven hours, forty-five minutes and 181 feet—a reduction of three hours, forty minutes and 564 feet.

Patients immediately recognized that the new facility was built around *their* needs, and the level of patient satisfaction with the cancer center climbed from about 70 percent up over 90 percent. The more efficient systems enabled the cancer center to improve productivity and capacity. With patients spending less time in the cancer center, there was space and time for more patients.

There was an important *but* to the cancer center story. Although the cancer center work was a great success both for patients and in demonstrating the power of the new tools, an unfortunate result was a certain level of staff frustration. Some doctors remained irritated with the office arrangements, but a more nettlesome issue was dissatisfaction among nurses, including those who worked with patients in the infusion center. Previously, the center had been off by itself—an island where nurses operated with a significant degree of independence. In the new facility, nurses worked side-by-side with physicians, and the nurses did not always react positively to guidance from the doctors. "We were redefining some of the nursing work, clarifying some jobs," and seeking to establish standard work, says Otero. "It was a new process, and the nurse staff really struggled with standard work." Some nurses objected to the constraints of standard work. "I've been doing it one way for twenty years and it's the best way," was the objection of some nurses.

In the early days of the new center there was enough complaining from the staff that Dr. Otero felt compelled to write a plea for a more positive attitude. He asked that the staff direct "negative comments" to him or other specified managers. Otero sought to place the issue in a broader context. He wrote to colleagues that being pioneers—"the first to apply a new methodology to the improvement of medical process, the first to design a medical facility under the 'patient first' mandate, and the first to work in a design driven by the way we work and flow"—would generate a certain amount of stress. He wrote bluntly that adopting the Toyota approach would require change "which most of us will find difficult." The letter was sent to all staff but was really aimed at providers.

> We will do everything possible to make corrections and listen to concerns. Many "fixes" are already in the works ... Blanket statements of disgruntlement to the staff only lower morale and cannot help us. Our informal interview of staff finds they are enthusiastic about the place mainly because the patients love it! Satisfying the patient makes the staff happy, and it should make us happy too. The staff's biggest complaints are the negative remarks by the providers ... please, whip me ... not them. ... They deserve better from us.

Otero was most surprised by what he saw as fundamental resistance to change. "I'm not referring to anchor draggers or bad people," he says. "There is some innate aspect of human nature that resists change even when shown all the technical reasons why it's appropriate. It was the feeling of loss, uncertainty, skepticism that occur when we replace the familiar way of doing things with a new uncertain process, and we hold on until the new process 'proves itself' to be better and worthy of emotional investment." Toyota had experienced countless difficulties during its long journey, Otero knew. And he had heard a Japanese proverb that served him well during the difficult times: "Fall down seven times, get up eight."

Jacobs and Otero later realized the enormous value of change management, particularly in an environment where drastic changes were happening much faster than normal. An important lesson centered on the significance of simulation as a technique to prepare staff. Otero says it would have been beneficial to do more simulation of the new processes "before the go-live date. We found ourselves making changes early and often for issues we could have foreseen had we done more simulation. This was frustrating for the staff."

In the midst of the turbulence that change so often brings, important and visible leadership was provided not just by the doctors, but also by Michaelle Wetteland, center administrator Denise Dubuque, Julie Sylvester and Richelle Bagdasarian. They were there in the cancer center—out on the floor—visible, moving around watching, listening, and responding to concerns. Since that experience, change management has become a top priority for managers at Virginia Mason.

Standard Work

For many doctors and nurses the most difficult part of the change involved the focus on standard work. "A lot of poor quality comes about through variation and a lack of standardization," says Dr. Jacobs. "If you go to most places, if there are six oncologists they can be treating breast cancer six different ways. Or if you go to a surgery department, there are people that are operating on gallbladders, and if you've got six surgeons, they're using six different sets of equipment and they're doing it six different ways, because they're all trained in different places, and, 'This is the way I did it at Stanford,' and, 'This is the way I did it at Harvard, and it's the best way.' But they're all doing it different ways. They're all doing it the 'best' way. So you get variation and the variation leads to errors and when you have variation, you don't really have a quality standard. You've got six different standards. In a lot of medicine, there are established best practices, so if you get everybody to conform to a single best practice where that exists, you end up with a higher quality, reliable, and measurable product."

Doctors reflexively resist standardization, says Jacobs, because doctors "don't like to be told what to do. You'll hear them call it cookie-cutter medicine, because they say, 'Patients aren't all the same.' Well, we know that, but there's a lot about them that *is* similar. If you get past the emotional part of it, a lot of what doctors do is very repetitive. It's the same thing again and again. Maybe 20 percent of the time people have different anatomy or different pharmacology or they're allergic to a medication or they have personal religious preferences. However, much of the time, we do the same thing again and again. It is repetitive, and it lends itself to standardization at least 80 percent of the time. When you standardize, you reduce variation and you end up improving the quality by conforming—norming people's behavior to a best practice."

The issue of standard work is at the center of a fierce collision between medical tradition and the VMPS approach. Jacobs argues forcefully in favor of standardization because he has no doubt it results in higher quality, safer, more consistent care. He points to the gold standard of medicine—clinical research trials—built on a platform of rigorous standardization. "If you have somebody on a clinical research trial, their care is standardized," he says. "The care is standardized because if you don't do it the same way, then you cannot compare the effectiveness of the new experimental treatment to the old treatment. The meaningful comparisons of process outcomes cannot be made."

Because the measurement of clinical performance is one of the most powerful and sustained trends in health care, the trend toward standardization is growing as well. "Without standardization," says Jacobs, "you have no ability to measure what you're doing."

A well-known quote from Taiichi Ohno is that "without standards, there can be no improvement." Rather than looking at standardization as constricting clinicians, this notion from Ohno suggests standards are actually the building blocks of excellence. When rigorous standards are set and then met by providers, further improvement requires identifying ever higher standards, thus raising the quality bar ever higher. This is truly patient-centered care, for it is all about improving on the standard of care. To improve on a better standard requires rigor, creativity, and innovation—all of which result in anything but cookbook medicine and all are part of the strategic plan.

Virginia Mason has achieved significant progress in standardizing treatment of certain cancers. With breast cancer, for example, there are established standards for preoperative evaluation of the patient, testing, and surgeries. Jacobs says they have "standardized and narrowed the variation" on postoperative chemotherapy and hormone treatments, and they have sought to achieve as much standardization as possible in other areas, as well, including treatment of colon cancer. In cancer, as in many other specialties, national, evidence-based practice guidelines have been established by various professional societies. At Virginia Mason, the idea is to select one professional society's approach—*one* set of standard work—and apply it.

To illustrate the intense resistance to standard work, Jacobs tells the story of a conversation he had with one of the directors of the Fred Hutchinson Cancer Research Center in Seattle, a world-renowned center where bone marrow transplantation was developed. The director said he did not think Jacobs and Virginia Mason would be able to get doctors to abide by standard work. "Doctors don't want to be standardized," the man told him. "They value their autonomy." The irony was that the Fred Hutchinson Cancer Research Center was a model of standardization. Every patient there, in fact, is part of a research trial. "I said to him, 'Everything you do is standardized on those trials,'" recalls Jacobs. "'You don't give any of your doctors wiggle room to treat people off trial.' And he stopped me and thought about it and he said, 'You know what? You're right.'"

Jacobs readily concedes that many doctors do, in fact, resist standardization because autonomy is so precious to them. Yet the scientific method, in which all clinicians are trained, depends on a certain level of standardization and establishing a baseline from which to measure and compare. Otero agrees that doctors feel "threatened by standard work. The biggest threat to doctors is losing their autonomy. 'Somebody is going to tell me how to do something, and they're going to tell me it's better when I know it's not.' They're worried that standard work would be *average* work."

A Singular Success

The cancer center was perceived throughout Virginia Mason as a wonderful success. It demonstrated what could be accomplished using VMPS tools and systems techniques that remained distinctly foreign to many. It certainly helped accelerate the pace of change within the medical center. "As soon as one group lets go of something, lets go of a myth, it becomes more permissible for other people to do it," says Otero. "You get peer pressure. You know, if they can do it, why can't you do that, and so on. I think it helps to accelerate change and improvement. It helped set an example."

Jacobs says it helped set a precedent by exploding the myth that the TPS methods did not apply in health care. "It's not about what industry you are working in, it's more about all of the complexity and the process around what it is that you're doing. It's a management method to improve processes, and health care has some of the most complex, high-risk processes imaginable. It's about delivering higher quality care by making those processes safer, more predictable and reliable and less expensive."

At the start of the work on the cancer center, Dr. Jacobs knew almost nothing about the Toyota method, but now he is one of its staunchest champions. "It gets to really increasing the value of the encounter and what you're delivering," he says. "So what does value mean? It means delivering the highest quality care or outcome that you can at the best price. It's not just about price and competition on price. It's about the quality of what you're delivering, too. And that resonates for every health care system whether it's Canada or the U.K. or the U.S. That's really what people want. This method lets you get at quality and safety, and it also helps reduce the cost of the delivery of care."

In the first full year in their new space, the cancer center was so much more efficient that it increased visits by 1,100 (to 14,927) with no increase in the number of employees. Although there have been clear benefits in terms of efficiency, productivity, and finances, the major benefits are patient-centered. After the second year in the new facility, Michaelle Wetteland asked her nursing staff how they thought things were going. In general, the staff thought that things were much better than in the old facility; that the new center was much better organized, was more patient-focused, provided dramatically reduced wait times, and that the flow was working very well. Overall, the nurses thought things were much better all around. "I looked at our numbers, and we had seen 1,100 more patients in the second year with the same number of nurses, and they thought things were *much better*," says Wetteland. "You would expect comments about more work with the same number of staff, but they did not know we saw that many more patients."

On top of that, patient and staff satisfaction levels reached the 93rd and 95th percentile, respectively. "It isn't just about efficiency," says Jacobs. "It improves quality, it reduces error, so it improves safety. It gives you better quality time with the patient, so it improves the quality of the encounter. It touches the things that they can see and feel during that visit …. It changes the experience for the patient …. The system enables us to change the patient experience by removing all of that waste and error and lack of transparency and lack of clarity."

"I'm a cancer doctor," says Jacobs. "The Virginia Mason Production System doesn't tell me how to talk to a family who are going to be losing a loved one. It doesn't get to that, but it gets to a lot of the aspects of the care of that loved one and whether they're getting the right safe dose of treatment and whether they're getting it on time and whether the nurses have been trained to do what they need to do and are following the best practices. And it makes the delivery of care a better experience when there's less chaos, more safety, and more predictability. Palliative care, which is a lot of what we do, is about maximizing the quality of life. When I have what I need where I need it when I need it, I'm able to do a better job, and I'm better able to give the patients the attention that they need."

Chapter Four

Safety Crusade

Mrs. Mary McClinton, age sixty-nine, arrived at Virginia Mason Medical Center on November 4, 2004, having been diagnosed with a brain aneurysm, she was scheduled for a complex, but not particularly dangerous invasive radiology procedure. The plan was for doctors to insert a miniscule stent to keep blood flowing freely through an artery and then inject dye enabling doctors to see her bloodstream flow on an imaging test.

The procedure seemed to go beautifully. Mrs. McClinton, a beloved member of her church and community, was wheeled to recovery. But she awakened from anesthesia in horrific pain, her legs swelling visibly. The interventional radiologist immediately called a Patient Safety Alert and a clinical team worked feverishly to try and save her life. Doctors and nurses struggled mightily throughout the night and in the ensuing days, but Mrs. McClinton steadily worsened. As the hours ticked past her vital organs began an inexorable process of shutting down.

This chapter tells the story of what happened to Mary McClinton and why. More broadly, it tells the story of Virginia Mason's safety journey—a journey where the loss of Mrs. McClinton would mark its low point, at the same time inspiring the entire medical center to new and much safer heights. It is the story of a safety journey that was transformed into a safety crusade.

Patient Safety Alerts™

Five years before Mrs. McClinton arrived at Virginia Mason, the historic 1999 IOM report *To Err Is Human,* was published. It detailed the epidemic of medical errors in the United States and made clear that the American medical culture—Virginia Mason included—reflexively resisted disclosing and discussing medical errors. Dr. Gary Kaplan and his Virginia Mason colleagues wanted to change that. To do so, they sought to probe the level of comfort providers within the medical center had for reporting and discussing safety issues. Thus, in 2002, they started measuring the "culture of safety" using a proven measurement tool developed by a provider insurance conglomerate (Physician Insurers Association of America (PIAA); Virginia Mason switched to an Agency for Health Care Research and Quality (AHRQ) tool in 2005 and has used it ever since).

"We wanted a baseline measure and, not surprisingly, it showed there was low trust in terms of being able to report," says Cathie Furman, RN, senior vice president for Quality and Compliance. The research found that most Virginia Mason employees believed that if they self-reported medical mistakes they would be punished or would lose their jobs. There was very little trust that the administration would adopt a blame-free approach and use information about errors to improve the safety of care. At the time, like every other hospital, Virginia Mason used what were known as quality incident reports (QIRs) each time an error was discovered. Typically, however, the QIRs would sit on a shelf collecting dust for months, only to be filed away and forgotten.

The Virginia Mason Production System (VMPS) presented an entirely different way to deal with error prevention. Cathie Furman joined Kaplan and the team for the first Japan trip and was amazed that every worker in the Toyota plant was empowered to stop the line to prevent a defect. When she saw a worker stop the line she thought, "That's interesting. In the health care environment that would mean that someone's going to yell and scream at you. I mean, how could an assembly line worker stop a multimillion-dollar line? And all these people came, but they weren't coming to yell and scream, which is exactly what would have happened if it was a nurse. They felt that it was more important for that worker to get the resources that he or she needed to fix the problem before it went to the next worker. They weren't going to pass that defect on. That was *huge* in our eyes."

As they embarked on a process to establish a stop-the-line system at Virginia Mason, one concern raised was that mistakes in health care were so numerous that a stop-the-line approach might potentially stall or even paralyze the system. "The fear," says Furman, "was that we would never get the line started again."

Kaplan insisted, however, that such a process be developed and put into place at Virginia Mason. To demonstrate a seriousness of purpose, the responder to a stop-the-line call would not be a supervisor or manager but an executive—someone senior enough to send a message that Virginia Mason Medical Center was serious about protecting patients. During an executive committee meeting, Kaplan asked for a commitment from everyone present to drop what they were doing and respond to stop-the-line calls—or, as they were to be called at Virginia Mason—Patient Safety Alerts (PSAs).

Implementing the program was not a simple matter. Defining a defect in a medical setting presented a challenge. During the committee meeting there was agreement that a PSA would be called when an event constituted a near miss or inflicted actual harm. During preliminary conversations, though, doctors pushed back. They argued that many instances of harm—ventilator-acquired pneumonia, for example—should not be considered an error because these things happen in medicine. Complications, they argued, were inevitable. "If I have to do surgery on a dirty wound, there's going to be an infection," one doctor said. "Am I supposed to call a PSA on that?" The definitions were not so neat and tidy—not at the start anyway. During the next year or so there was a good deal of discussion seeking to define more precisely terms such as "error" and "near miss."

There were other complex questions. What would happen, for example, in the event that a clinician and administrator disagreed on whether an event met the standard of a PSA? What if a clinician called a PSA and the executive in charge did not agree it met the standard? These were difficult discussions where the correct path was often not at all obvious. The Virginia Mason leadership was passionately committed to improving safety, however. An indication of this commitment came early on with a clear rule: If there was a disagreement over whether a problem rose to the level of a PSA, it would go directly to Cathie Furman for her judgment. Then, if she was uncertain for any reason, she would go to Gary Kaplan. Thus, if a PSA was to be overruled it would have to be done with the agreement of the executive in charge, along with Furman and, in certain cases, Kaplan as well. This sent a signal throughout the medical center: With the CEO directly in the PSA loop, the message was clear—*this matters*.

Nonetheless, the team struggled from the start working through definitions and designing policies. Only significant events could be categorized as PSAs; all other mistakes fell into the old category of QIR. "It was not smooth from the get-go," says Furman. Yet they persevered, learning with each step along the way, fixing, amending, and revising as they went.

"The other thing we learned in the first couple of years was deciding that PSAs had to be *significant* created all sorts of complexity because what was significant to the eye of the reporter versus the executive who owned it could be quite different. We would spend so much time trying to figure out whether it was a PSA or not that we really increased the lead time, and we weren't actually focused on the necessary corrective action."

An important step forward came in February 2005, when the QIR category was eliminated at Virginia Mason, and it was decided that all events involving the safety or well-being of a patient would be deemed a PSA. Three color-coded categories were established based on potential severity. Red PSAs involve anything life-threatening, any never-event, and anything that poses or could pose serious harm to a patient. Also included within the red category are actual or near misses, wrong-site surgery, accusations of sexual misconduct, security issues, and disruptive behavior by staff or patients. In addition, the red category included all issues considered to be reportable events by the National Quality Forum, including falls with injury and Grade 3 or 4 pressure ulcers. Orange PSAs are somewhat less severe in intensity, but they often involve interactions between or among different specialties or departments. Thus, getting to the bottom of the matter will likely involve more resources and a more intense, cross-departmental effort. In all, about 1 percent of PSAs are red, 8 percent orange, and the rest yellow. A yellow PSAs is a slip or a latent error, something that employees recognize as carrying the potential for error but not immediately life threatening. Furman says yellow can be "anything from an outdated tuna fish sandwich"—which could sicken a patient—"to nurses being frustrated that the elevators aren't functioning properly," thus delaying patient treatment.

Because the PSA program was somewhat complex, at least at the outset, and because it was new, it required extensive staff education. Furman and her team developed case studies—real stories from Virginia Mason—to make the PSA concept clear. At monthly meetings throughout the medical center, including gatherings of managers, department heads, professional staff, and so on, she and her team would tell a new story. This was important because she was finding a reluctance on the part of many staff members to call a PSA. Staff members were deeply committed to protecting patients, but they worried about repercussions. "Staff have told me that they don't report because they have reported before and nothing ever happened," says Sarah Patterson. "They say that if they reported they would be shunned by their co-workers for telling and that it takes too much time to report. These reasons sync up with what we have learned from other high-risk industries about why people don't report errors." Nurses feared the wrath of doctors who, in turn, feared committing a breach of camaraderie, perhaps professional deference. No one, it seemed, wanted to be seen as stepping on anyone else's toes. And with the program still in its infancy, there was no proof yet that it could have a real impact on protecting patients.

A Nurse's Courage

Then came a dramatic episode that served as a powerful catalyst supporting the PSA program. A nurse was ready to provide chemotherapy to a cancer patient when she noticed that the patient had not yet received an echocardiogram (to ensure a strong heart) and given a urine sample (to determine alkaline level). This was a simple oversight, she thought. She pointed this out to the doctor, who she assumed would order the testing. He did not. Instead, the physician grew annoyed with her and ordered the chemo to commence. Trying to be positive, the nurse noted that the protocol required both tests before treatment. The doctor brushed her aside and told her to begin treatment.

The nurse had a decision to make: do as instructed by the doctor or make a stand that she believed to be in the best interest of the patient. She chose the latter and placed a call to Dr. Jacobs, Chief of Cancer Services. After she explained the situation, Jacobs thanked her and contacted the doctor, making a point to say the nurse was correct—that the echocardiogram and urine test were necessary prerequisites to the chemo infusion. After the call from Jacobs, the physician, now livid, called the nurse and let loose, verbally abusing her on the telephone, dressing her down for challenging him and then for reporting him.

Her response? She phoned Dr. Jacobs again and explained what had just happened. Jacobs did not hesitate. He promptly called a PSA saying the doctor had been abusive and unprofessional. The doctor was called, told he had acted unprofessionally by ignoring protocols and verbally abusing a nurse, and taken offline while the matter was investigated.

Word of this story raced through the medical center. Senior executives in the hospital personally thanked the nurse and encouraged all staff members to report anything they deemed a threat to any patient. The message from executives was emphatic: You call in a PSA, we've got your back.

A Doctor's Courage

For generations the cultural norm in medicine has been that mistakes were discussed in private circles within the hospital or physician practice—if at all. It is this very culture, says Sarah Patterson, that must be challenged and broken down to create a genuine culture of safety within the medical center. "It's really changing the mindset in health care about defects and errors," she says, "that we shouldn't talk about them, we've got to hide them. The system puts it all on the backs of individual doctors and nurses, saying, 'You've got to do the best you can to protect your patients. There's no system out there. It's just all you.' We've got to change that mindset, and we've got to change the culture."

Given the nonstop, high-risk nature of the work, Patterson says doctors and nurses, just to make it through the day, "have to minimize in their minds the risk their patients are exposed to. It creates an environment where people tolerate things that shouldn't be tolerated: Lapses, not following standard work, not building in enough checks. The PSA system is really our signal to the organization that we need to change this culture. We're making good progress, but it's a big change. People come to us trained at other institutions, then we have to start from scratch again every time we get a new nurse, a new doctor and say, 'It needs to be different here, and you need to be a part of this.'"

This message was delivered with tremendous force in an incident during 2003, when Dr. Daniel Hanson, a talented young hospitalist who had served for five years as Chair of the Quality Assessment Committee, made a mistake. Dr. Hanson was filling out a paper prescription one day (this was about nine months before Virginia Mason had computerized physician order entry). He wrote an order for atenolol, a beta-blocker, for a fragile, elderly patient. In doing so, Dr. Hanson wrote: "25 mgms QD"—calling for 25 milligrams daily. There were two immediate problems: First, the Joint Commission had made it quite clear that QD was a potentially dangerous abbreviation and had recommended that clinicians discontinue its use. Their fear was that in the world of physician scribble the abbreviation could be too easily confused with QOD (every other day), and QID (four times a day). The second problem was that the 25 was scribbled so that it was not entirely clear.

"It was late in the evening, and we were all busy trying to wrap things up for the day," recalls Dr. Hanson. "The patient was very sick and fragile with heart disease. The atenolol would help slow his heart rate and lower his blood pressure." Dr. Hanson wanted to start the patient on a low dose of the medication and then increase it if needed. When the order reached the pharmacy, however, the pharmacist read the 25 as 75. Some patients tolerate such a dose well, but this patient was much too sick for that. When the medicine was administered, the patient's heart rate slowed dangerously and his blood pressure dropped to an unsafe level. That night, he was transferred to the intensive care unit (ICU), where the staff sought to reverse the effects of the drug, but it was too late. It was clear the patient was in very bad shape and, in fact, he died soon thereafter.

The reality was that the patient was so sick that his life expectancy would have been months, at best. Nonetheless, an error had contributed to his death. Dr. Kaplan asked Dr. Hanson to address his colleagues at a physician meeting about the incident. Doctors had talked about errors in the past, of course, but almost always in small groups. Hanson brought a couple of slides, including one showing his handwritten order. About half those present thought it read 25 mgms and the rest thought it read 75. It was an order, in fact, that any one of the doctors present could have written. Hanson's handwriting was hardly perfect, but neither was it as illegible as that of many of his colleagues in the room. Doctors sat in silence, watching as Hanson became openly emotional about the incident.

Dr. Hanson took the blame, yet a PSA investigation found that there had been a series of breakdowns along the way. The ward clerk who received the prescription from him should have stopped the line on seeing that QD was written on the script. The same was true of the pharmacist and the patient care nurse. The problem was not Dr. Hanson—the problem was that the system had failed. There was not a culture of safety yet at Virginia Mason. "We can't just write orders and walk away—we have to be good team members," Hanson told his colleagues. The message to all physicians was, as Hanson put it, "we can't just step in, fire off an order and not be accountable for how it's interpreted." Hanson's colleagues listened carefully to his remarks. They knew how difficult it must have been for him and many expressed admiration for the courage it required for him to stand up in such a large forum and talk about the mistake.

Seven years after the mistake, in 2010, Dr. Hanson viewed the safety culture at Virginia Mason as dramatically transformed. He says when he goes to conferences around the country it is quite clear that Virginia Mason is far ahead of most other medical centers in its safety journey. "I go to these national meetings and see people struggling with things we are way beyond," he says.

Cathie Furman sees this a defining moment on the Virginia Mason safety journey. "For a well-respected hospitalist who is chair of the quality committee to stand up in a room full of his peers and describe what he had done—it was a profound moment. Everyone talked about it for months afterward. It was such a powerful example, and I have no doubt that countless times after that doctors stopped and thought about that before writing a prescription. I suspect some real mistakes were avoided because Dan Hanson had the courage to stand up there and tell his story."

Why Shouldn't *Everybody* Get a Flu Shot?

Every year in the United States an average of 35,000 people die from influenza, and it was clear to Virginia Mason clinicians and administrators that they needed to provide immunization for as many patients and staff as possible. It was especially important to protect the large number of geriatric patients cared for within the medical center, for these patients were especially vulnerable to the flu. To streamline the immunization process, an RPIW was convened with a diverse team of staff members, including doctors, nurses, administrators, and a medical assistant. The goal of the RPIW was to design the most efficient way possible to deliver flu shots to patients and employees. In the process, a drive-thru flu shot plan was established that would enable patients to get their shots far more quickly and conveniently—no parking, walking to the clinic, sitting in a waiting room, and so on. Under the plan, patients would drive through a circular drive, where teams of clinicians would deliver the shots in seconds. The major effort by patients would be to roll down their windows and roll up their sleeves.

During the course of their work designing a plan for patients, the team came across some alarming statistics about the failure of most health care workers to get immunized. They discovered that on average, only about 40 percent of health care workers in the United States received the flu vaccine each year. Nurses tended to run below that level—somewhere around 36 percent. At Virginia Mason overall it was slightly better, with about half the employees receiving immunizations annually. In the past, few had paid attention to this fact, but now that the patient was at the top of the Virginia Mason strategic plan, it seemed somewhat embarrassing that so many doctors, nurses, and other staff members—people in daily physical contact with sick patients—were not immunized.

Dr. Joyce Lammert was a member of the workshop team, and she says after the team had conducted its basic review of the literature, Suzanne Tyler, a Virginia Mason supervisor, cut to the heart of the matter. "What's with the 30 or 40 percent" immunization rate among health care workers, she asked. "I don't understand why we don't require *everyone* who works here to get the vaccine. Do you know that 50 percent of the people with flu have no symptoms? So half the people in this room could have the flu during flu season and not even know it and not even feel bad and when we cough or breathe or touch we could be spreading the flu. If we're putting the patient first, we're not protecting them when they come in here."

It was an amazing moment—not unlike the breakthrough moment on the cancer center design when a nurse had said "Let's design it so we bring everything to the patient rather than having the patient chase around the medical center for services." Suzanne Tyler was not a physician or a nurse and did not hold a particularly senior position at the medical center. Nonetheless, it was the quality of her idea that mattered. It was a moment that revealed the power of welcoming all voices on an RPIW. When Tyler made her point, the workshop team members looked at one another and knew immediately that she was right—that immunization against the flu should be required of every employee in the medical center. Dr. Bob Mecklenburg, Chief of Medicine, was sitting across the table from Tyler when she asked why they didn't require everyone to get the vaccine, and he was struck by it. "You know," he said, "that's a very good question. That's a *very good question*." Says Dr. Lammert, "It was so obvious that this was putting the patient first."

The workshop recommendation requiring all employees to receive a vaccine every year was readily approved by medical center leadership including the board. Gary Kaplan was excited by the new policy, seeing it as the embodiment of patient-focused care. "We're going to be the first in the world to say if you want to be a Virginia Mason employee, you must have a flu shot as a fitness for duty requirement, just like the TB test, just like a background check," he says.

Lammert then led an extensive effort, beginning in the winter of 2005 in preparation for the 2006 flu season, to educate the Virginia Mason workforce about the new policy. Predictably, there was pushback. "I remember a professional staff meeting where we had more than a hundred physicians in the room," says Kaplan, "and I was explaining why this was important, and one of our physicians who is from another country raised his hand and said, 'I came to America for freedom. You can't tell me what to put in my body.' And I was about to say, 'You're right, you have choices, and you can choose not to work here.' But I didn't have to, because one of our pulmonary and critical care doctors stood up, turned to him and said, 'Let me tell you something. I take care of those people in the ICU who get respiratory failure from the flu and never again are we going to give our patients the flu in my hospital.' So that's when I knew—and I got chills just standing there and thinking about it—when I knew that we were getting serious traction on putting the patient first."

The most intense pushback came from the nurses' union, which filed a grievance against the medical center, arguing that the policy should be part of the collective bargaining process. An arbitrator and federal court agreed with the union, resulting in union nurses having the option to be immunized or not. The union also opposed Virginia Mason's policy requiring nonimmunized staff to wear a mask during the flu season, but an administrative law judge rejected the nurses' assertion and ruled that Virginia Mason had the right to require masking as part of its infection control policy. The result: 98 percent of Virginia Mason employees received flu vaccine and 2 percent wore masks.

Mecklenburg considered this a key moment in the Virginia Mason journey: "This story is important because what might well become national policy some day comes from an administrator who steps back and takes a look and says, 'What's wrong with this picture? Why doesn't *everybody* at VM have a flu shot to protect our patients?' The breakthrough concept did not come from any of us executives who were hoping for an incremental change. She changed the rules for 5,000 employees—and possibly many more health care workers in our community and in our nation."

An interesting footnote to the issue was that the following year, as flu season approached, whether to be vaccinated was, for the great majority of Virginia Mason employees, a nonissue.

Mrs. Mary McClinton

In November 2004, Mary McClinton was dying and nobody at Virginia Mason knew why. Throughout that night and into the following days the team worked feverishly to try and solve the mystery.

After intensive study of every step during the procedure, there came a breakthrough: The radiologist said the only explanation he could think of was that the medical team had inadvertently injected something caustic into her system. It was the only explanation that made any sense. Everyone involved had gathered together to try and figure it out—interventional radiologist, anesthesiologist, endocrinologist, radiologist, nurses, and prep table technician. This thinking led the team to the prep table in the room where the procedure had taken place. On the table were a variety of instruments and supplies used in the procedure, including three stainless steel bowls containing contrast dye, saline solution, and chlorhexidine, an antiseptic used to cleanse bacteria from the skin before an incision is made to reduce the chances of infection. All three liquids were clear—identical in appearance.

During the course of such a procedure the interventional radiologist stands over the patient and is handed whatever he needs from the prep table. The experienced technician in charge of the prep table might have wanted to make sure he not only kept up with the demands of the procedure, but that he was a step ahead—anticipating the radiologist's need. Thus, in advance, he placed a label on an empty syringe marking it as "contrast dye." But then, a calamitous mistake: Instead of filling the syringe with contrast dye, he mistakenly filled it with chlorhexidine. During the procedure, the interventional radiologist was handed this syringe and unknowingly injected chlorhexidine into Mrs. McClinton. Nineteen days later she died.

Mrs. McClinton had been a patient of Dr. Robert Mecklenburg for many years. As it happened, Mecklenburg was not only Chief of Medicine, he was also Mrs. McClinton's primary care physician, and the night of the mistake he happened to be on call when he received a request for a consultation to see a very sick patient in the ICU. Mecklenburg was stunned to see that the patient was Mary McClinton. Mecklenburg not only knew Mrs. McClinton, but he knew members of her family as well, and he sat with them at the hospital during their vigil even as her condition steadily worsened. In the days after the procedure, Mecklenburg, along with so many other Virginia Mason clinicians, tried to understand what had gone wrong and then tried everything they could possibly think of to save Mrs. McClinton's life. As chief of the Department of Medicine, Mecklenburg felt strongly that the entire Virginia Mason community needed to know what had happened to one of their patients, reflect on it, and learn from it.

Mecklenburg and Dr. Mindy Cooper, chair of the medical center's Quality Assurance Committee, authored a memorandum to Virginia Mason staff explaining what had gone wrong. Mecklenburg and Cooper knew that sending the memo throughout the medical center would result in the press getting a hold of the story, but this deterred neither them nor Gary Kaplan nor the board of directors. The Virginia Mason community—and the greater Seattle community they served—deserved the truth. One week after the incident, the memo was sent electronically to all Virginia Mason employees. It explained that "the solution used to clean skin before and after procedures was recently changed from a brown iodine-based solution to a colorless antiseptic," and thus was identical in appearance to the dye. "At some time during the procedure, the clear antiseptic solution was placed in an unlabeled cup identical to that used to hold the marker dye ... that is injected into blood vessels to make them visible on x-rays ... The antiseptic solution is highly toxic when injected into a blood vessel. Acute and severe chemical injury to the blood vessels of the leg blocked blood flow to muscles, causing profound injury and swelling of the leg. Kidney failure, a sudden drop in blood pressure, and a stroke followed." The essential truth of the matter, the doctors wrote, was that no individual should be blamed—no individual *would* be blamed—because it was a system failure. Responsibility for the error, they wrote, rests with "all of us."

Mrs. McClinton's death was a grievous loss, not only for her family, including two brothers, a sister, and four adult sons, but it was also a loss for many others in her community of Everett, Washington, where she worked at the Greater Trinity Missionary Baptist Church helping needy people find work. She had done so much fine work for disadvantaged people—including during the years she worked as a vocational coordinator in Alaska prior to moving to Washington in 1996—that she was made an honorary member of the Tinglit tribe, a great honor for anyone not born into the tribe.

After thirty years of practicing medicine, Mecklenburg had seen many medical mistakes, and he had witnessed patients dying, but, as he put it, "I had never seen the full effect of a death like that on the larger community and the family." Perhaps this was owed to having been Mrs. McClinton's physician, or perhaps his familiarity with the family. Perhaps it was even in part due to his heightened focus on the patient as a result of the new approach at Virginia Mason.

"What I really hadn't seen before through thirty years of being a doc was the collateral damage of a medical mistake," he says. "This family was torn apart by this, as was the community, and the ICU nurses and the providers at Virginia Mason and the sense of self of the entire medical center. So this was two orders of magnitude more devastating than I had ever seen before. What you may not fully realize is that you may have affected hundreds of other people in a profound way that will never be redeemable."

In a newspaper article about the matter, reporters cited Virginia Mason's forthright admission. In a front-page story, the *Seattle Times* noted that Virginia Mason "took the unusual step of publicly explaining, and apologizing for, the error." In the article, Mrs. McClinton's son Gerald said he was pleased the hospital did not try to conceal the mistake. He said physicians at Virginia Mason had treated his family well and that the hospital had approached his family about a settlement. Given the preventable nature of the mistake he was deeply upset. Then he added a crucial point—a point that speaks as painfully as it does eloquently to the nature of this as a system failure. Gerald McClinton said that although he was "getting angrier by the minute," he added, "I don't know really who I should be getting angry at."

Publicly, Virginia Mason officials expressed deep sorrow and regret along with a determination to learn from this event. Dr. Bob Caplan was quoted in the newspaper saying that "we just can't say how appalled we are at ourselves and the suffering of this patient and her family and friends. ... In many ways, this open and honest communication is our way of trying to honor her." Learning from such mistakes, he said, was essential, adding that "you can't understand something you hide."

Privately, however, the men and women of Virginia Mason wept. They pounded the table in anger. They felt a sense of despair. How could they have done this? After all their hard work to protect patients, how could they not have seen the massive flaw inherent in the three clear liquid bowls on that prep table? It was a shattering moment for Kaplan, his leadership team, and the board of directors—for every staff member at Virginia Mason. They were two years into an arduous yet intoxicating journey on the VMPS path—far enough into it, they believed, that this sort of catastrophic event was not supposed to happen. Very quickly, however, they realized that their journey had barely begun; they had a great deal of work to do to make Virginia Mason a safe environment every day for every patient. No sooner had that realization settled on the medical center than the clinical and administrative leaders vowed that they would do whatever was necessary to make Virginia Mason the safest hospital anywhere.

As would be expected, the death of Mary McClinton prompted the Seattle press to compare Virginia Mason with other medical centers in terms of safety. The *Seattle Times,* citing data from the state's Department of Public Health, wrote that "Virginia Mason had reported more 'adverse events' over the past three years" than the three other major Seattle hospitals. Within the article there was a critically important caveat added by the Department of Public Health official, however. She told the newspaper that, in fact, Virginia Mason was generally more conscientious about reporting such incidents.

Mistake Proofing

The PSA system failed to save Mary McClinton's life, but the team wanted to make sure that never again would a patient receive an injection of chlorhexidine. The PSA deep dive made it terribly obvious that there should never have been three unlabeled stainless steel bowls of clear liquid on the prep table. That was a fundamentally flawed system where human error was not only possible, but seemed inevitable. Was mistake-proofing achievable in this case? In fact, the team found, it certainly was. Why did chlorhexidine have to be in a bowl at all? Why not place it on a stick that could be used to swab the skin? That would make it impossible to place the solution in a syringe. It would ensure that what happened to Mary McClinton never again happened to another Virginia Mason patient.

That particular fix—chlorhexidine on a swab stick—was a wonderful example of process improvement and mistake-proofing. Another example involved altering the arrangement of instruments on an anesthesia cart. Traditionally, a couple of dozen items were placed on a cart in no particular order. Often the carts appeared messy and unprofessional. However, no one ever thought of the cart in quality or safety terms. No one had ever thought about the cart and its design as a way to increase safety for patients. But knowing the tools and concepts of VMPS, Dr. Bob Caplan had exactly that thought. Working with his team, Dr. Caplan redesigned the cart in a much more orderly fashion. He did so by creating a shadow board showing the exact location for each tool or piece of equipment. A photograph of the proper arrangement was placed atop each anesthesia cart under a clear piece of Plexiglas (wiped down between cases). Each piece of equipment would be placed on a picture of itself, leaving no doubt where anything should go. The cart also instantly showed gaps—which pieces were missing. As Dr. Caplan puts it, "At 3:00 a.m. you don't need to worry about your memory. All the essential information is there. At 7:00 a.m. a faculty instructor can tell at a glance if the resident—new or experienced—has set up the anesthesia workspace according to specification. At any time of day, an assistant can enter the room and determine at a glance if there is something missing that needs to be replaced or provided. The very first time that I had a novice resident use the shadow board, she looked up at me and said, 'Dr. Caplan, I've been training for three months, and this is the very first time that I've been confident that I've set up correctly!' What a marvelous experience for her … and what a telling lesson for those of us who are educators."

A Culture of Safety

The question now for Virginia Mason was this: What's next? How do we go about changing—in the most fundamental way possible—the culture of safety within the medical center? In the answer to these questions, the death of Mrs. McClinton became the essential catalyst for change, for it coincided with the Virginia Mason goal-setting process for the following year. When Mary McClinton died, each major department had set goals and the list of major goals for 2005 was up to thirteen. After her death, Gary Kaplan and his senior leadership team made a decision to set all that aside and establish a single goal for the entire medical center: Safety. "It was the catalyst that bumped us into really being passionate about safety," says Dr. Bob Caplan. "I think after that we really began to appreciate the meaning of stop-the-line. We knew that some people had come into the radiology suite before that event and had looked at the setup and had wondered in their head, 'I wonder if that's safe?' But the wondering hadn't gone any further. This is the event that taught us that stop-the-line is a real concept. You really have to call out the safety hazard when you see it. After that our Patient Safety Alert system really took on meaning in our organization. It became evident to people that you need to inspect to be safe, and you not only need to inspect your own work, you need to—no matter how difficult it might be—inspect the work of others, and you have to be ready to call out the defects and take action."

There were many changes in the aftermath of Mrs. McClinton's death, including the alignment of executive compensation with measurable safety improvements. More than anything else, though, it was the commitment by the organization—the leadership in particular—to continue along the VMPS path that spurred work toward greater safety. Elizabeth Dunphy, RN, believes that the death of Mrs. McClinton helped to solidify the notion that "I have a duty and responsibility to report a problem, and I trust nothing bad will happen to me in doing that." Mrs. McClinton's death, she says, "developed a level of trust and accountability that 'I need to stand up, and I need to do the right thing no matter what.' … It also gave this organization clarity around what the PSA process is and that the intent behind it is true discovery and prevention and the rigor it will take for us to mistake-proof it, to make it perfect. And we can't make health care perfect until we make every single process perfect. So it's to the level of detail of every syringe, every bowl, every basin, anything you touch needs to be done correctly. It really pulled us back into the reality of what we were trying to do. We were a few years into our journey, and we thought we were pretty good, and we learned humility, and I don't think we have forgotten it, nor will we ever forget it."

After Mrs. McClinton's death, Virginia Mason leaders heard that other hospitals had precisely the same conditions—unlabeled clear solutions in stainless steel bowls on procedure tables. The public disclosure of Mrs. McClinton's death served as a catalyst for these hospitals to change their process and adopt a new medication/solution labeling policy several months prior to the Joint Commission issuing a sentinel event alert based on the type of error in the McClinton case. The reality is that transparency on the part of Virginia Mason led to many other organizations significantly improving their safety procedures—and perhaps saving lives.

Evolution of the PSA System

The PSA system had not saved Mrs. McClinton, but it had done a great deal of good, and it was evolving into a powerful method for protecting patients. The system had been inaugurated in the fall of 2002 and by the start of 2004 informal surveys revealed that 100 percent of the medical center staff knew what a PSA was and an estimated one third of employees had reported a PSA. Why so much progress so quickly? The key was that when a PSA was called revealing a system flaw, the administration responded immediately by fixing that problem. Thus, when employees saw that they were getting rapid action in response to PSAs, it generated confidence and trust in the system. People believed in it because they had seen it work on problems they cared about—problems in *their* department, on *their* floor, affecting *their* patients. It was no longer an abstraction—a shiny new program from Japan. Thus, the more PSAs were met with prompt corrective action, the deeper and broader the belief throughout the medical center in the system.

Cathie Furman heard increasing levels of positive feedback from the staff about the PSA system. "They'd say, 'Oh, wow, that's been bugging me forever. You guys finally fixed it. Maybe you're really serious about this,' she says. "That's when the floodgates really opened."

Still, there were questions, discussions, and disagreements about what warranted a PSA call and what constituted a red PSA versus an orange. With the most serious PSAs revealing a process or structural problem, there were sometimes disagreements about when the underlying system problem was truly solved—solved enough to make sure that whatever had gone wrong would never go wrong again. "We were still learning how to mistake-proof," says Furman. "When is it closed? When have we fixed it? Sometimes the executive, quite frankly, would just want to get rid of it and would be wanting to close it and the Patient Safety Specialist wasn't sure, or maybe the Patient Safety Specialist thinks it's ready to close and I don't think it is ready."

A significant change to the PSA process came in January 2007 when Virginia Mason established a requirement that all red PSAs would have to be presented to the Quality Oversight Committee of the medical center board of directors by the executive responsible for that PSA. Furman considers this a breakthrough. These executives are quite senior within the medical center, accomplished men and women accustomed to giving many presentations, but Furman notices that when they have to go before the board committee on a red PSA they tend to get anxious. "They make sure they've got their ducks in a row, but the board doesn't always accept their corrective action plan," she says. "Sometimes they say, 'You know, I am not convinced this isn't going to happen to another patient. You've got to go back, and we want you to do A, B, and C.' That's been really good. I think it's really increased the robustness of the process, and the public board members are very much engaged in this work."

The deep involvement of board members in PSAs is another powerful signal to the medical center staff that the process is taken seriously. Whenever a red PSA occurs board members are immediately notified and receive a monthly update on the case until it is resolved. No red PSA can be closed until the board says it is closed. "We're saying the board members are the ones that are going to decide if we've adequately mistake-proofed our processes," says Kaplan. "They're smart people, and they want to make sure it is mistake-proofed and sometimes they send it back: 'You need to look even closer at this. We're not sure this is yet fully mistake-proof.'"

In addition to overseeing red PSAs, board members also come face-to-face with patients at board meetings. Patients—or patient family members—are invited to tell their stories and engage in discussion with board members. Some stories are positive, but many—even most—are not. The board pushes to hear cases where the hospital has not performed as well as it should. "It's extremely powerful," says Lynne Chafetz, Virginia Mason general counsel. "It really connects the dots to 'what are we here for.' It is one thing to have a manager talk about a patient, but it's much more powerful to have a patient in the room."

Initially, there was a fear within the medical center that PSAs might increase the exposure of clinicians at Virginia Mason—as well as the hospital itself—to medical malpractice claims. Had this been the case, of course, the program would have been doomed. But not only do PSAs not increase the likelihood of malpractice, Kaplan argues the program actually decreases such risks. Importantly, the state of Washington has in place a regulation allowing health care organizations to file a Coordinated Quality Improvement Plan with the state Department of Health. If a plan is filed, information and documents specifically created for, collected, and maintained by an approved plan are provided a higher level of protection from discovery in legal proceedings. This encourages organizations to improve quality through careful and thorough review of its processes without an increased fear of medical malpractice claims.

The folks at Virginia Mason had found that for every eight patients who encountered an adverse event, only one sued. "And that's generally because of two things," says Furman. "They want an apology, and they want to make sure that nobody else is affected in the same way. With the Patient Safety Alert system, because we know sooner rather than later that something has gone wrong, the first thing we do is apologize. We disclose, we apologize, and we take care of whatever their additional costs are for the harm." One particular case, for example, involved surgery gone awry. The surgeon operating in a difficult area made an error, immediately announced that there had been a mistake, and summoned help. When the patient woke up the doctors informed the patient and spouse precisely what had happened. Although there was a financial settlement, there was a belief on the part of Virginia Mason executives that the amount of that settlement might have been dramatically different if they had not been apologetic, honest, and transparent.

The dollars-and-cents result of this openness policy has been significant. Malpractice actions against the medical center have decreased significantly since implementation of the PSA system and transparency. From 2007 to 2008 Virginia Mason professional liability insurance expenses declined 26 percent. They declined an additional 12 percent the following year. (Symbolic of the sweeping change has been changing the name of the risk management department to the Patient Safety Department.) Says Cathie Furman, "We have risk insurance carriers who are clamoring to get us on their program," carriers who want Virginia Mason to teach other medical centers a similar approach to risk mitigation. Insurers, she says, see the Virginia Mason approach "as huge risk mitigation." Thus, while other providers in their area are experiencing increases in the costs of their malpractice premiums, Virginia Mason is achieving double-digit decreases.

As the PSA system develops and matures, clinicians are able to tackle more complex issues. There are many errors throughout the country, for example, with antithrombotic medications. Too much of the medication and patients bleed; too little and they clot. At Virginia Mason clinicians found that these medicines were among the top drugs that triggered PSAs. Thus, they instituted a program in 2009 specifically targeting the safe use of these drugs. Data over time also showed that oversedation was another PSA trigger, and the medical center convened a medication collaborative to tackle that issue.

Falls were another significant trigger for PSAs. "Hospitals around the world are actually quiet factories for falling," says Furman. "About three patients fall for every 1,000 patient days around the world. We didn't really pay much attention—it was just business as usual—until we began to look at our Patient Safety Alerts, and we realized this is something we really need to focus our attention and focus our abilities on." They have done so in a variety of ways, including probing the link between medications and falls. Pharmacists now investigate every fall resulting in injury to determine whether there might have been a pharmacological explanation. They've made significant headway in reducing the number of falls with injuries by establishing Falls University, a multidisciplinary team that reviews all falls, completes root cause analyses, spreads the lessons, and implements best practices throughout the medical center. This process has revealed that a majority of falls occur while toileting. The solution: standard work including hourly nurse rounds where nurses help guide the patient to the bathroom, reducing the need for patients to venture out on their own. Nurses also make sure the bed is in the safest position to prevent falls and that the bed alarm—for patients who are not supposed to get up on their own—is switched on. "But here's the conundrum," Furman says. "Next year we're going to be focused on reduction of urinary tract infections, which are caused by indwelling urinary catheters. We've got some improvement work going on there, which is great, but when we take out the catheters on patients, guess what? They're going to get up and go to the bathroom. The number one reason for people falling is going to the bathroom. So how do you measure when we're doing better?"

Such vexing issues notwithstanding, PSAs have made an enormous difference in the quality and safety of care at Virginia Mason. The more than 15,000 individual cases where a PSA has been called since 2002 are obvious places where quality and safety were improved—and in some cases lives saved. But much more broadly the PSA data help identify systemic problems that need to be solved with new policies and processes; by implementing standard care or by going back and conducting an RPIW to try and find a solution. In the moment, PSAs help clinicians provide higher quality, safer care to an individual patient and if they accomplished no more than that, they would be enormously valuable. More fundamentally, though, PSAs are learning opportunities where benefits go far beyond an individual patient. They result in changes to processes that lead to standard work and mistake-free procedures. This benefits many patients now and in years to come.

Bob Caplan uses the example of a patient with a deep venous thrombosis, a clot in his leg, which was treated in a very conventional way with a devastating outcome. "By going back and studying that event in our Patient Safety Alert process," says Caplan, "we realized that we weren't content with conventional approaches to the management of deep venous thrombosis. We could discern by looking at the current medical literature that there's about to be a shift and there's about to be a better way to do it. That Patient Safety Alert drove us to those realizations, allowing us to take care of our patients with leg clots in a much better way than if we had just continued on with the conventional and standard approaches.

"This is a great example of how Patient Safety Alerts make a difference. If you're a practitioner and you get back a report that says your patient has a clot in the lower leg, it's not really clear in the current literature what is the best way to treat that. And this case that I'm talking about, this Patient Safety Alert, involved a clot in the lower leg that was treated in a conventional manner. We didn't like the way it evolved. As we investigated this PSA our radiologist said,

'You know, every time we give a reading that a patient has got a clot in the lower leg the practitioner asks us almost invariably what to do about that.' It's because the state of knowledge was so indistinct about that. Now what we're doing is at the bottom of the radiology report we're providing the practitioner with what we consider to be better guidance and guidance that's going to give us better outcomes. That's an example of how a Patient Safety Alert makes a big difference and pushes us forward in care."

The PSA system was significant enough that five years after its inauguration, Cathie Furman and Bob Caplan published an article about it in *The Joint Commission Journal on Quality and Patient Safety* (July 2007, Vol. 33, No. 7), in which they concluded:

> The PSA system has proven to be the single most important tool to make our care safer. It provides a quick, timely process for improvement and feedback to our staff that their concerns will be listened to. Lessons learned are …
>
> 1. Executive leadership is a prerequisite.
> 2. Reporting should be easy, with multiple methods available.
> 3. "Significant" is in the eye of the beholder: Open the floodgates for all concerns.
> 4. Claims management staffing will go down as Patient Safety Alerts go up. Right before the start of the PSA system, we had six claims managers and three RN reviewers; we now have three claims managers and five patient safety specialists.
> 5. Be prepared to change the processes of care as the organization learns from the PSAs.

In the culture of safety consciousness at Virginia Mason one of the most important events each year is the awarding of the Mary McClinton Patient Safety Award. There is an air of reverence around this award that is perhaps unlike anything else within the medical center (a staff focus group rated this award as the number one form of recognition given to staff). It is awarded annually to one of the teams within Virginia Mason that has made outstanding progress toward a safer patient environment. At the second annual presentation of the award, in 2007, Gary Kaplan stood up to speak.

"The auditorium was packed," he says. "Mary's sister was there, all four of her sons and her pastor was there, our staff, managers, physicians—standing room only. I was making a presentation of our progress on our safety journey; it was really a chronicle of our progress. I had not planned on doing this but on the spur of the moment I said, 'How many people here have actually called in a PSA?' Well over two thirds of the audience of 300 or more people raised their hands. And I got chills. I said, 'Wow, could you raise your hands again, please and just look around. Think about what this says about our community and how we are now behaving in terms of patient safety, and how we are thinking.' … To me, that was awesome."

Chapter Five

Ambulatory Care Breakthrough

On the front lines of primary care, change and innovation are as difficult as they are rewarding. Despite the immense challenges presented by primary care, some of the most innovative work at Virginia Mason has been focused in this area. It is important work with broad application for primary care practices throughout the country—and for specialty care practices as well.

By applying basic VMPS tools and eliminating waste, the medical center has realized enormous quality improvement gains in primary care. This chapter focuses on work done at a suburban clinic staffed by a dozen primary care physicians. Although the chapter focuses on Virginia Mason Kirkland Clinic, the innovations initiated there have been spread across the Virginia Mason system.

Stress on Primary Care

Kirkland, Washington, is an attractive city set across a broad expanse of Lake Washington, with a dramatic waterfront panorama and striking views of the Seattle skyline and the Olympic Mountains to the west. The Virginia Mason clinic in Kirkland, just ten miles east of Seattle, is home to ten primary care physicians (including Gary Kaplan, who practices here a few hours each week), as well as numerous specialists in areas ranging from cardiology to dermatology.

It is in this pleasant setting that Virginia Mason physicians and administrators have been waging a determined effort at quality improvement in ambulatory care for nearly two decades. At the heart of the Kirkland facility is its primary care practice, where internists and family practitioners provide more than 45,000 patient visits per year. The practice has its own unique elements, of course, but in many ways it can be seen as something of a microcosm for the realities plaguing primary care practices throughout the United States, many of which are under severe pressure. Patients are not entirely satisfied, providers perhaps less so. Far too many primary care doctors are feeling more strain than satisfaction from their practice. They feel both underappreciated and underpaid, and they are too often inundated with paper, phone, and e-mail messages. In a way, primary care doctors these days are somewhat like the daring performer on horseback, standing upright on a racing steed while spinning a stack of plates in the air—all while Blackberry, pager, and computer screen incessantly beckon.

Moving the Mountain of Waits

At the beginning of the VMPS journey, Virginia Mason did not have a robust patient satisfaction measurement system, but informal feedback was not always positive. Dr. Brian McDonald, Chief of Satellites at Virginia Mason, recalls an encounter with a patient during those days: "I'm booked out 8 to 12 weeks, using our walk-in clinic at Virginia Mason Federal Way all the time for overflow of almost all 'urgent' care needs, doing service recovery all the time at the outset of office visits. A long-term patient of mine comes in and goes through her story of a recent acute problem for which I was 'not available' and just before I could give my usual standing response, she posed the final question that stopped me in my tracks and really made think about the care I was (or was not) providing. She looked me right in the eyes and asked, 'Are you really my doctor?'"

The scheduling mayhem preventing that patient from seeing Dr. McDonald in a timely fashion had many causes. At Kirkland, a study of work flow found that during more than half of patient visits physicians were forced to leave exam rooms to search for supplies or seek help from staff they often could not find. Struggling to stay on time, physicians were compelled to postpone documenting visits and responding to messages until the end of the day. This delay resulted in staff overtime and repeated phone calls as angry patients reacted to untimely communication. Physicians spent hours completing the postponed visit documentation, ultimately incomplete as physicians lost important details throughout the course of the day. Staff turnover and job dissatisfaction mounted. On top of it all, the clinic was losing money. Elsewhere in the primary care universe beyond the Virginia Mason boundaries, burned-out physicians left standard fee-for-service practices and sought refuge in concierge practices.

In the 1990s and early 2000s, Dr. Kim Pittenger was as frustrated as anyone. He had been in the forefront of the improvement effort at Kirkland since 1990 and had pushed for a series of innovations years before VMPS was the new pathway. There were numerous problems plaguing primary care and one of the more obvious was the scheduling problem his friend Dr. McDonald noted. A day never passed in Pittenger's experience without at least one and usually several patients complaining about being made to wait—for the phone to be answered, for an answer to a simple question, for an appointment, to get into the exam room. In the late 1990s, Kirkland primary care patients faced appointment delays of up to forty-seven days. Because appointments were so precious, patients crammed as much into them as they could, not knowing when they would get another opportunity. The waits were infuriating, but worst of all, Pittenger knew that when patients were not seen in a timely fashion it hurt the quality of care.

Pittenger and the other doctors and administrators at Kirkland decided they had to tackle the access issue head on. As they studied it, they realized that solving the problem would require a very difficult first step—paring down and eventually eliminating the appointment backlog. This was not greeted warmly by doctors already feeling overworked. Some had to get past the cultural notion that a sure sign of a thriving practice was a three-week wait for an appointment. The idea that it was often due to poor systems, inefficiency, and a lack of patient-centeredness rarely occurred to them.

Partnering with two consultants Dr. Kaplan first heard at an Institute for Health Care Improvement national forum—Mark Murray, MD, and Catherine Tantau, RN—doctors at Kirkland developed their own access wonk, Rich Furlong, MD, an internist. He led the Kirkland primary care physicians while McDonald and former vice president Marnee Iseman pressed every group to gradually pare down the appointment backlogs by working extra hours. Over an arduous nine-month period, Kirkland did something rarely accomplished in the primary care universe: They eliminated the backlog altogether. A detailed analysis informed them that a predictable number of patients would call in each morning seeking an appointment, and the physicians built schedules matching the predicted demand. Once they worked down their backlog, they arrived on that magic day when they started work with a half-open schedule. The unfilled schedule was initially unsettling to doctors who depend on production for their revenue.

However, the new system worked just as promised: The available slots were quickly filled and patient satisfaction rose. The Kirkland team had accomplished a rare feat then in American medicine—advanced access in scheduling: no backlog and same-day appointments available to any patient. This meant more timely treatment and much less anxiety on the part of patients dealing with symptoms for weeks before being seen. Suddenly patients routinely thanked the doctors for being seen so easily and promptly. It seemed the patients' anxieties about a precious visit simmered down, and their lists of concerns for each visit shrank a bit.

The Kirkland team next tackled one of the more nettlesome problems primary care sites face: Phone access. Every day hundreds of calls poured into the Kirkland office in an unrelenting drumbeat. Part of the problem was that the people answering the phone were rarely able to help the patient. Over time, Kirkland's management team continued to ask one another the same question: Why do we have operators? "Operators would answer the phone," says Pittenger, "and they can't do a thing other than basically say, 'Hi, I can't help you. I'm not medically trained. Can I find somebody for you? I probably *won't* be able to find them, but can I at least put you in a queue to wait for somebody who's medically trained?'" In 2002, they reached a breaking point. "We'd had a terrible week of phone service, just nothing but complaints."

"I've been trying to call all day. I cannot get a call back."
"I cannot get anybody to answer the phone!"
"I have a simple question."
"All I want is a refill."
"I haven't heard about my lab results. Can I have them, please?"
"I need some help!"

The following Monday, Kirkland Clinic administrator Shirl Diaz, nursing supervisor Sandi Nagel, and reception supervisor Sharon Peep made a decision to shift operators over to receptionist duty and put trained medical assistants (MAs) on the phones. They had done some preparation. They knew, for example, the various buckets of phone calls that came in—pharmacy refill, billing questions, medical questions, results reporting, requests for appointments, and so on. "Why should a phone call that's destined for a pharmacist come to a primary care doctor first?" Pittenger asks. "If we hadn't succeeded in reporting test results to somebody the medical assistant could at least say, 'Here's what the results are and I'll tell you the abnormal and I'll have Dr. Pittenger call you back and tell you what they mean and I'm so sorry he hasn't gotten back to you yet.'"

On a Tuesday morning, with the MAs answering the phones, the improvement was immediate. Calls were answered more quickly and the MAs had the training and knowledge to satisfy many callers with answers. It wasn't exactly the discovery of ether, but it was an important accomplishment, for it showed the team that certain steps could have an immediate beneficial impact for patients and improve the efficiency of the clinic's operations—and that meant less hassle, pressure, and stress. It also provided renewed energy to work on all of the other items clogging the clinic arteries. Pittenger, in fact, was after bigger fish in the quality improvement effort—*much* bigger fish.

Mistake-Proofing Care: Early Steps

In 2003, a landmark study by Elizabeth McGlynn and her colleagues at RAND found that on average Americans get about half the recommended care even for patients with chronic diseases. This statistic played out in reality within the Kirkland Clinic. Routinely, patients would come in for a complaint and the doctor would focus on that complaint and often do an excellent job in diagnosing and treating it. But other things—quite often much more important things—would be missed.

"If I'm seeing you about your back pain," says Pittenger, "and whether you have a cold or sinusitis and you need two refills, and if it so happens that you haven't had a mammogram in three years and I don't know it, you're basically walking around in an unsafe state, and so it would be good if I knew in the setup of the visit that you were late for a mammogram." This notion of a physician being responsible for things far beyond the visit had been an interest of Pittenger's—perhaps an obsession—for years. He had long believed that it was his job as a doctor to take care of the whole patient and not just what they happened to come into the office complaining about. As an intern at the University of Cincinnati in 1980, he vividly recalls reading a groundbreaking work by Frame and Carlson in *The Journal of Family Practice* that showed "a grid of what was thought at that point to be important to do for preventive care and disease management. It was a simple paper tool on a medical chart listing what was needed and at what intervals: mammogram, sigmoidoscopy, stool hemoccult test, tetanus shot at ten-year intervals, pneumonia vaccine at age sixty-five, and a screening lipid test.

The idea of the grid came from the last of a four-part series of critical reviews of Periodic Health Screening by P.S. Frame in 1975," says Pittenger. "I adapted my own to add a screening lipid test since that was just coming into vogue, recommended by the experts at our medical center."

It drove Pittenger crazy that the medical profession in general—doctors in particular—"accepted no responsibility for getting these things done unless somebody came in for a physical. So I was busy making charts for my patients at the family practice center at the University of Cincinnati, and I would check them every time somebody came in." In 1990, when Pittenger was at Virginia Mason, he was invited to join the Patterns of Practice Task Force convened within the medical center by Dr. Fritz Fenster, a gastroenterologist specializing in liver disease. "Fritz was always interested in how patterns of medical practice were or were not based on evidence, were or were not appropriate," says Pittenger. Dr. Fenster also thought it was preposterous that his water heater company could alert him about preventive maintenance to avoid flooding his condo, and we couldn't alert patients that they needed a mammogram without plowing through a paper chart. The Patterns of Practice Committee evolved into the Clinical Guidelines Committee and made an effort to extract the best and latest evidence from the literature and apply it in a variety of clinical areas.

In 2003, when Pittenger was chair of the Virginia Mason Clinical Guidelines Committee, a major study of Type 2 diabetes was published. The U.K. Prospective Diabetes Study spanned two decades and included 5,000 patients across the United Kingdom. Its breakthrough was demonstrating that life-threatening complications of Type 2 diabetes could be significantly mitigated by comprehensive disease management using known and accepted treatments. The findings presented Pittenger and his colleague, Dr. Kenneth Gross, an endocrinologist, with precisely the opportunity they needed. They extracted elements from the U.K. study to apply in the daily operations of outpatient diabetes care at Virginia Mason.

"The question is whether you're going to organize care and try to deliver a reliable, uniform pattern of care," says Pittenger, "along the lines the literature spelled out—good control of glucose, LDL less than 100, blood pressure less than 130/80, smoking cessation, physical activity, and weight reduction—or whether you're just going to tell docs about the results of the study and organize nothing in the infrastructure. We wanted to organize the infrastructure to make better care."

The idea was to create a registry of diabetic patients in the Virginia Mason system and determine whether those patients were in control or not and make that knowledge available to providers at the point of care. This was very different from what doctors were accustomed to doing during a visit—diagnose whatever symptoms confronted them at a given moment. Doctors often tended to deal with diabetes on the fly during an episodic, complaint-related visit. They did not preplan visits devoted entirely to diabetes. Additionally, there was little in the way of longer term thinking, making sure that all of the screenings and preventive measures called for were applied to each diabetic patient.

Yet times were changing. Increasingly, payers were pushing for more disease management and as pay-for-performance contracts were rolled out, performance metrics increased in significance. It was not that providers did not want to treat the whole patient—it was that they had neither the method nor the tools to do so. Under constant time pressure, doctors did not have the "luxury" of thumbing through a thick paper chart to see whether prevention and disease management tests were up to date; whether targets were met for blood pressure, A1C, LDL, and more.

Pittenger and Gross wanted to develop something that would scan the patient's record and pull out salient markers of care needs that had not been met. However, they realized that they would not be able to get doctors to take the long view in diabetes care unless they created a specific tool to make it easy to do so. If this was seen as just piling on more work, it would be doomed from the start. Then they made their work more comprehensive. "We thought, well, there are populations that need it besides patients with diabetes," says Pittenger. Shouldn't they create something that could be applied to hypertension, asthma, coronary disease, mammograms, colonoscopies, LDL levels, and much more? Says Pittenger, "We thought, 'Shouldn't we build a tool that tries to mistake-proof care for *everybody,* not just diabetics?'"

Creating a New Tool

At the time they initiated this work in 2002, Virginia Mason ran on paper medical records (although billing records were computerized), making any sort of population health management extremely challenging. Pittenger and Gross created a list of important tests and interventions they wanted their patients up-to-date on. To figure this out, they worked with creative programmers who devised a way to derive this information from computerized payment data. Then they built a crosswalk to the lab results database. The idea was to try and create a list of patients scheduled for appointments tomorrow and have the computer kick out the tests or interventions each of those patients hadn't had and needed, or had had and what the result was.

"If we could do that we would have a list first thing in the morning," says Pittenger. "Here is this patient who has or hasn't had a mammogram and needs one and she has or hasn't had an A1C in the last six months with result numbers for you to see."

They engaged an adventurous programmer from their Clinical Decision Support team, Vicki Berman, and a thoughtful IT architect, Steve Poole. Both were eager to build something that had practical daily use at the point of care, not some data mining project that just led to a report to an accreditation agency or the finance department. They built a system that scanned both the billing database and the lab result database and fused whether a test had been done with the result. This had never been done. Because it was so good at "spying"—legally of course—into the patient's clinical situation, they dubbed it the 007 Program. After about six months of work the team had built a new point of care tool that operated off of 007, which they called the Primary Care and Prevention (PCP) Report. The paper report would be generated each morning, and the clinic staff would be able to anticipate the needs of every patient for screenings and other preventive measures.

With this new approach, Virginia Mason "transitioned from being an institution that really only tracked administrative data into becoming an institution that invested in a clinical data repository," says Pittenger. "We built a process that put the tool at the point of care."

Doctors differed in how they used the information. Some would start out the visit going right to the overdue tests or screenings, and others would casually raise the issue later in the visit. Pittenger loved the tool and was aggressive about it in part because it was the year that his wife developed breast cancer. "If somebody was three years out from her last mammogram and her life was crazy, I'd say 'Let's just solve it right now.' Press 5, 'Hi, this is Dr. Pittenger. Mary really wants a mammogram and she can't find time. Let's make one right now,' and hand the phone to her. 'Okay, next Friday at 4:00? I'll be here. Thank you very much.'"

Change in health care is rarely easy or smooth. Doctors, in particular, tend to be skeptics. They are, after all, scientists trained to probe and question. When they do so, it frequently makes change contentious. During the course of this work there were some physicians who asked what Pittenger refers to as "a core question—one of those separating questions at Virginia Mason: 'Do you mean when I'm seeing somebody about his back pain and a possible sinus infection and by the way I need two refills you expect me to manage his preventive care and disease management, too?' And we would say, 'Well, what do you think the patient expects? Do you think the patient expects you to see him about his back pain and a possible sinus infection and by the way I need two refills and specifically neglect whether I've had a mammogram, specifically overlook that my last A1C was 9.2—and that was nine months ago and we haven't worked on it? So flip that card the other way. Is that the kind of doctor you want to be or the kind of practice we want to have?'"

The few doctors in Kirkland's group who resisted grew progressively unhappy about standardized work and eventually left Virginia Mason. Many other doctors, however, long frustrated by the hit-or-miss nature of getting important screenings and tests for their patients, embraced the new tool. Eventually, just about all the doctors came around to believing that there was inherent value in the tool as a way to work on prevention while still covering other issues requiring attention. The PCP Report, in fact, was so innovative that Pittenger and his colleagues were runners-up in the 2003 Acclaim Award from the American Medical Group Association for quality improvement for creating and implementing the report. On a more personal level, in 2006, Pittenger was awarded the James Tate Mason Physician of the Year at Virginia Mason for excellence in a variety of areas including his role in creating the PCP Report.

Inventing the Flow Station

For generations in medicine, the consensus was clearly that the doctor's work was all about the patient visit. Conversely, there was little regard for the amount of work involved in indirect care of patients—phone calls, refills, forms, outside records, lab results, and more. Over the years, all that indirect care came to be known as "junk." But as the framework of VMPS was applied to the medical center in 2002 and 2003, it became clear that although indirect care was time-consuming and too often wasteful, much of it was extremely important.

Primary care leaders saw indirect care as an ideal target for *kaizen*. They would use the VMPS principles and tools to take on what they called the medical "junk drawer." "Because we're traditionally trained to do visits, we thought all that other stuff was junk," says Pittenger. "We even called it junk. Everyone was so focused on doing a great job on today's visits that our attitude was 'What I'm really good at is having a great visit with the patient and achieving therapeutic effect and all this other stuff is junk.' We needed to break that cultural construct and convince people that the junk was not junk."

Junk or not, it was annoying. It often caused doctors to run behind and was the major reason physicians would remain at their desks for hours most nights well after their last visit was completed. For this and other reasons the junk bothered physicians—and *really* bothered some of them.

"I remember one doctor. She's very good and patients loved her, but someone asked me to go down and talk to her because they were afraid she would leave Virginia Mason," Pittenger says. "And I said, 'Gee, what's wrong?' and she said, 'I am very efficient. I see twenty, twenty-two patients a day, I am done at 5:30, and I come back to my desk in my office and there's this pile of crap. Now what's with that? I've got to get home.' And I said, 'Well, what's in that pile of crap?' And she said, 'Well, you know, it's refills, it's forms, it's result reporting, it's labs from outside Virginia Mason, consults from outside Virginia Mason, it's drug company junk, it's insurance company junk. *It's junk.*' And I said, 'But this is part of your patients' care. Didn't this happen because of something you did in the recent past with a patient during a visit?' 'Well, of course, that goes without saying.' I said, 'So is it junk?' And she said, 'As far as I'm concerned it's crap, and you'd better solve it or I'm leaving.' Well, we didn't solve it, and she left."

This was an extreme case, of course, but every primary care doctor Pittenger knew had the same complaint. Junk distracted them from patients. Junk made them run late for appointments. Junk forced them to stay late at the office working their way through a stack of paper.

Former Virginia Mason Vice President Marnee Iseman initiated a Rapid Process Improvement Workshop (RPIW) at Kirkland to take the issue on and the RPIW revealed a critically important truth: There were, in fact, two kinds of care—direct care (a patient visit) and indirect care (everything else). They found that indirect care consisted of about sixty pieces of work per day for each physician—an average of three for every patient visit.

A basic truism in manufacturing is that making products in batches reduces quality while increasing lead time and cost. The question then was how to get the junk quantified and broken down into small enough lots so it could be dealt with *throughout the course of the day rather than in a batch at the end of the day.* The RPIW team—including personnel from the Kaizen Promotion Office (KPO)—gathered at Kirkland to study the work of one family physician—Dr. Laurel Morrison. They set her up to try small lot production of junk. The team would observe how she moved about, how she handled a piece of junk, timing her work. When she emerged from a patient visit a KPO staffer would suggest she try something slightly different. Move this way instead of that. Respond to an e-mail, then another. Sign a form, perhaps two more. Everything was measured and timed. Throughout the process, especially after each slight change in routine, the team would ask Dr. Morrison how that particular move felt—Was it logical? Easy? Did it make sense? It was important that the new system should be efficient, of course, but it was essential that it should be comfortable to comply with, not physically or visually awkward.

"In between each patient," says Pittenger, "they would say, 'Okay, we're going to change the layout or the sequence. Now when you come out of the exam room, we've set these pieces up here. We want you to do them in this order and then go into the next exam room.' And she might say, 'But I'm already 20 minutes behind,' and they would say, 'Just please do it. We'll time it. Trust us. We may get behind today. We'll all apologize to the patients, but we have to figure this out.'"

Through three consecutive days of the RPIW, Dr. Morrison did exactly what was asked of her in rearranging her movements and her physical space over and over again. While she did this the RPIW team timed every movement, looking to eliminate as much waste as possible. The process revealed a key lesson: Working closely with an MA, the physician could manage all the nonvisit care in about one to three minutes between visits throughout the day. This was a huge stride, for it meant that by day's end there would be no forbidding stack of work left. "We found out that there was really less than a minute for most of the pieces," says Pittenger. "Some of them are so perfunctory you just sign or pitch it. If your medical assistant could actually manage this flow and have rules by which she could judge what is true junk and can be pitched and what's clinically important, she could arrange them and that way you would do the meaningful work."

The team huddled with MAs to guide their work, which involved defining what was junk and what was not. "So a piece of advertisement from a drug company is junk," says Pittenger. "We don't even want the docs to see it. Pitch it.

A glossy journal from a drug company consortium is junk. A name brand journal is not. An endoscopy report, an outside lab report is not junk."

The essence of the improvement during the RPIW was the seamless interaction between physician and MA. It was clear from the start that most of the MAs had a keen instinctual sense of what was junk and what was not, and the improvement team guided them in how best to feed the nonjunk items to the doctor in what the team called the flow station—a U-shaped area in the hallway with slots for each category of nonvisit care, as well as a computer terminal and a phone. There was a white Formica counter with a series of filing slots above it in the cabinetry. Dr. Morrison picked up the phone to her right—everything in the flow station was within arm's reach—and dictated a note about the visit she just completed. She then filled out a billing sheet and placed that in a designated slot. A staff member would come by hourly and deliver the small lot of billing sheets to the billing clerk for online charge submission. The next slot to the left, labeled "paper flow," contained paper results from inside and outside the Virginia Mason system as well as paper forms to sign. She selected one sheet, signed it, then placed it in the next slot to the left labeled "Done/for MA." To her left was the computer monitor where she could see that a phone call from a patient, taken earlier by the MA, had been translated into an e-mail for her review. She read it, responded to the MA, and the MA would then call the patient back. All of this work had been preselected by the MA who had gone through the nonvisit pile and made rapid decisions. Only work that required the physician's attention made it to the flow station.

It was thrilling in those early days to see Dr. Morrison emerge from a visit into the hallway where the MA would already have her nonvisit work ready—an e-mail to return, a form to sign—and literally two minutes later she would see the next patient. There was almost no down time. While the doctor was in the flow station between visits the MA was rooming the next patient, checking the PCP Report to determine whether the patient was due for tests or screenings. The MA was empowered to schedule a wide variety of appointments for things such as colonoscopies, blood work, mammograms, and so on. She gave needed vaccines, as well. After the RPIW, nobody was more enthusiastic than Dr. Morrison. She told her colleagues, "You guys have got to try this! I'm goin' home!"

Breakthrough

The creation of the flow station was a huge breakthrough. "The impact was very exciting conceptually," says Pittenger, "and everyone said, 'This is great, we're going to be wonderful,' and they then spent eleven months *not* doing it, because it's fine if you rearrange the processes of care. Doctors like that. Get rid of the operator, put an MA there. Doctors love watching somebody else solve these 'hotel' problems of medical practice. But the little things you do as a physician, the way you move, what tools you use, what sequence you move in—doctors really don't like people telling them how to do that. And they're also very nice and they simply smile and say, 'This is going to be really great' and then they don't do it."

The Kirkland leadership tried an experiment: They redeployed the more assertive MAs to work side-by-side with doctors who had tended to avoid using the flow stations, and it seemed each month the number of physicians working in a flow station would increase slightly. Even for those deeply committed to the concept of the flow stations, it was difficult to break old habits.

An important breakthrough came when Shirl Diaz, the clinic's administrative manager, intervened. She approached a few physicians and worked with them on the clinic floor, helping guide them through the course of their day. "When we came out of a room and looked like we were going to bolt for the next room," says Pittenger, "she said, 'No, no. Wait.' And she gently guided us and said, 'Turn here and do this. Just do one. Okay, that was 30 seconds. Now do another. Do one more. Good, it's been two minutes. You can go in.'"

Pittenger wasn't sure what the answer was at that moment, but he was sure of something: This idea of working "in flow"—of doing a couple of pieces of nonvisit work between visits—was simple, easy, and made the day move much more efficiently than the old way of batch production. "After just a few months it was obvious that most of the physician–MA teams were in sync," he says. "The MA knows how to feed that now. She may not know that a potassium of 3.1 is or isn't dangerous, but she knows it's abnormal, so she might say, 'I'm going to go room this first patient, but would you look at these three things? They're abnormal.' That's how we're starting our day. And if it's an abnormal lab that needs action I take action right there—calling the patient, changing the medication, whatever is necessary."

Skill–Task Alignment

At the heart of successful flow production in primary care is the concept of skill–task alignment. Under the old system, MAs were underutilized. They would room patients, measure weight, take blood pressure, and so forth, but little else. Yet their education and training made them capable of doing significantly more clinical work and nearly all the MAs were eager to take on greater challenges. Under the new approach, with significant new responsibilities, the MAs flourished. They were energetic and enthusiastic about their new duties and finally working up to their capacity. They felt more engaged in the care of patients and most were excited by their added responsibilities and the increased sense of satisfaction it gave them. If the MA is engaging patients in value-added work such as 'What are your allergies? Are these medicines correct?' and checking on preventive tests and screenings, it puts the patient at ease. Patients can see it is important work, and they are not anxious about getting the doctor into the exam room right away—giving the doctor a few minutes to work the flow station.

Dr. Ingrid Gerbino, section head and internist at the Virginia Mason Lynnwood Clinic, summarizes it this way: "The MA/flow manager is best for determining and scheduling preventive needs, setting the agenda, and directing the provider's flow throughout the day. The RN care manager is best used for goal setting, education, and creating a shared care plan with each patient. The pharmacist is most skilled at following patients on multiple medications and making dose or medication adjustments as needed, partnering with providers. Providers are best utilized for making new diagnoses, and providing oversight to the team caring for patients with chronic/complex illness. Leveraging the team is paramount to obtaining an 'activated and informed' patient, reaching improved worker and patient satisfaction, while improving clinical and financial outcomes."

Pittenger says skill–task alignment enables the team "to apply the correct brain at the correct time. We didn't invent the use of nurses, pharmacists, and MAs to leverage the skill of the team, we just conceived of it a bit differently than other groups. We were careful to do it in a way that enhances the personalized nature of care and makes 'Team' obvious to the patient. This unfolds best for diabetes patients. At the beginning of the day the team huddles. The RN has scanned the schedule for diabetics and creates her day's schedule to include seeing them whether they are coming for diabetes or not. When the diabetic patient arrives, the MA rooms her, using the standard rooming sequence. The MA will set up a self-scheduled colonoscopy or get agreement for vaccines after the visit. It is standard work. The RN enters and joins with the patient briefly then elicits her goals for the visit. She blends the patient's goals with whatever target needs work—blood pressure, glucose control, LDL, or exercise and weight control. They work it down to two goals for this visit. At about the tenth minute she pages the physician. They then have a joint visit with the MA and doc in the room together. The RN tells the physician what the visit agenda is and assigns the physician work. The doc might give a lecture about insulin resistance using online images, might do a vascular exam, might examine a complaint that is accessory to diabetes. The RN is the closer who ties the whole care plan together after the physician leaves. The patients love it and the results are impressive."

A series of RPIWs focused on the standard work of planned care visits for diabetics has reduced the waste of poor quality. In 2007, when the primary care physicians were not avidly engaged in joint visits with nurse care managers, Virginia Mason diabetes results were mediocre. A1C control less than 7 (a debatable ideal) stood at 43 percent of their patients. Over two years it has improved to 56 percent. A1C < 8, a better target for older diabetics with multiple diseases at once (the majority) rose from 47 percent to 72 percent. Most importantly, LDL control < 100 rose from 40 percent in 2007 to 62 percent in mid-2009 and is the fastest improving metric.

How did the primary care teams manage the change and improve integration? They did it by making the RPIW results standard work, slated for implementation at every site:

- The Best Practices Task Force within the medical center created an accountability grid to mark and identify where each site was in their implementation journey.
- The Planned Care Collaborative recruited a primary care physician and an RN care manager from each site and monthly brainstormed their barriers to change.
- The Best Practices Task Force showed side-by-side comparisons of sites and providers. (The section heads asked their physician friends why they differed so much? Was it their patients' biology or their own?)
- The section managers made sure the teams implemented the setup for the physician, but there still had to be a change "when the door was closed" for the visit.

Paradoxically, by giving up traditional autonomy, physicians gain the freedom to improve, to focus on the work they do best, and reduce the waste that used to rest squarely on their shoulders. The external set-up their team provides preserves their time with the patient. Kirkland has very low turnover in MAs unless they go on to nursing school or college to focus on premed studies.

Standardized skill–task alignment became an essential element in team design across all Virginia Mason sites. Dr. Kim Leatham of Virginia Mason Winslow pushed the skill–task alignment concept furthest. The practice she and her colleagues run on Bainbridge Island, across Puget Sound from Seattle, spreads care of depression, diabetes, and medical frailty across a team of physician, nurse, care manager, pharmacist, and MA. It transformed their practice and results. "We are moving ever closer to that ideal of physicians doing only physician work, RNs doing RN work, MAs, etcetera," says Leatham. "Skill task alignment has made our staff happier with their jobs and has enabled flow."

Coupling skill–task-aligned teaming with flow production of indirect care became the new neural network for Virginia Mason. It felt visceral. Doctors and MAs felt it when they were in flow, and they quickly felt it when they slipped out of flow. Now that the doctors have seen that flow *works,* it is extremely popular throughout Virginia Mason. Doctors like the fact that MAs are there to handle so much nonvisit care. They like the fact that they feel a sense of control over their day and are free to focus on the needs of their patients. They love the fact that the tools enable them to provide higher quality care, especially for important preventive tests and screenings. They certainly do not mind getting home in time for dinner with the family.

Primary Care Transformed

By the end of 2005, the flow production approach had fundamentally altered the nature of primary care at the Kirkland Clinic. With a much more efficient system, patient needs were responded to more quickly and efficiently and patient satisfaction scores reflected the new reality. Under the old system, 40 percent of patients said they were very satisfied with phone access at Kirkland, whereas under the new system it is 85 percent. Answering calls efficiently under the new system also had significant impact on the Kirkland finances.

"If you don't answer them in flow, they call back," says Pittenger. "So when we started answering them in flow, our incoming phone calls for ten doctors went down by 1,000 calls a week and that's been maintained for all the six years we've been doing it"—50,000 fewer calls each year! "Anybody now can see twenty-one or twenty-two patients per day and go home on time and have very little work in process left, no toxic lab results left, no unanswered phone calls hanging to the next day," he says. "If people are in flow production of indirect care and reducing their costs, any group of ten primary care doctors can make a positive margin."

Kirkland's financial turnaround has been dramatic. The year before the flow stations were introduced, the family practice group of five providers lost $301,000. Two years later, they turned a profit of $112,000. With MAs working in flow and leaving on time, MA overtime was essentially eliminated in 2005. Also, family doctors working in flow were significantly more efficient—so much so that they were able to increase their patient load in the same number of work hours. In prior years, the volume of patient visits had been increasing by about 1.5 to 2 percent a year, but in 2005 visits increased by 5.6 percent, despite having "mature, saturated practices."

The margins allow reinvestment in the team. In successive years they have hired more nurses while area practices hired none. They allocate their nursing FTEs to their diabetic population because visits are predictable in that group, based on how many have A1C > 9 and A1C 7 to 9. The nine-member primary care physician team had a 2009 margin of $800,000.

Kirkland is just one example of the turnaround due to VMPS in primary care. The entire Virginia Mason primary care system has turned around using flow production. Primary care margins were a negative $4.6 million in 2003. In 2009 they were a positive $4.3 million. (The financial gains represent contribution margin, meaning the clinic has covered its direct expenses and made a contribution to overhead costs shared by the whole enterprise.)

Is everything perfect at Kirkland? No, says Pittenger. "We have created this production environment that has more capacity and have not yet mastered flow. So, we see twenty-five to twenty-eight patients per day, not twenty to twenty-one. And we're here ten to eleven hours per day if we do. We walk around this place and see batches, rogue uses of the flow station, inconsistent application of new standard work. We have yet to master flow. We're only exceptional compared to other groups that flop along in batch production."

The real gold, however, is the improved quality the VM primary care groups provide. Pittenger and his colleagues have no doubt that the flow they have achieved makes for higher quality, more timely, and more responsive care. With flow stations and nearly real-time attention to nonvisit care, the chances of missing a critically important lab result are far lower than they once were—as are the chances of letting a patient go for an extended period without essential tests or screenings.

Under the old system there was always a concern about what might be hidden in the pile of nonvisit work. The doctors knew instinctively that the new system provided better care, and then they knew it anecdotally when a particular physician was away on vacation. Under the old system, the vacationing doctor would have returned to a massive stack of work that would have likely taken a few days and maybe longer to slog through. Under the new flow system, however, another physician and MA covered for him in his absence and when he returned there was no stack at all. On that first day back, one of the doctor's patients dropped off a letter that, under the old system, would have sat in his inbox for a week. But because he was in flow, the physician opened the letter in his flow station and read that his patient was intending to commit suicide. The doctor immediately got services to the patient—who did not take her life.

In another instance, a different physician was seeing a patient complaining of elbow pain. When the MA was rooming the patient she noticed he was overdue for a colonoscopy and scheduled it while she was in process of rooming the patient. A few weeks later the patient was found to have treatable colon cancer, and it was promptly surgically removed.

"The other part is the engagement," says Pittenger. "If patients are constantly frustrated by waiting for every little thing, direct care or indirect care, then we believe, they're less engaged in the diseases we want to manage." Improved patient engagement improves the quality of care. "If you've got a system that makes you calm down mentally and you feel in control of interactions with your patient then you settle down and focus. It's a paradoxical calming effect of standard sequence—submit to the control of a well-designed sequence and you get to feel better. You talk to doctors privately and they tell you that every time they made a mistake they were distracted. 'I didn't listen that well. There was too much to do at once, too much clutter in the brain.'"

Pittenger has little doubt that it harms the quality of a visit when patients are frustrated or angry because they have had trouble getting through on the clinic phones, or waited to get a return call, or had difficulty making an appointment. "Let's say we're working on weight loss as part of blood pressure management and to prevent diabetes," he says. "You've got a family history of high hypertension, you're overweight, your blood pressure's creeping up, and you've got an elevated fasting blood glucose. If your visit is frustrating and then at the end of it I'm going to tell you, 'But the main problem is you never exercise, you're overweight, and you're headed down the road to ruin,' the entire negativity of the scenario is not going to engage you in change. You'll say, 'Yeah, get in line. Everybody wants me to change, my boss, my wife, whoever.' But if at the beginning of the visit they're fresh and want to know what we're working on and we have a mutual agenda, then they engage in what the visit's really about."

Going to *Jidoka*

A Virginia Mason doctor tells a painful story: "I had been in practice for many years, functioning in a chaotic setting, in which health maintenance and prevention concerns relied primarily on my memory and my attention span at the moment. Nonetheless I had gotten by, always feeling satisfied that I provided the best possible care, while not really appreciating the inherent lack of reliability in our care processes. One day a long-term patient came in for a visit. Typically, our visits together were disorganized, bouncing from one complaint to the next, invariably extending beyond the appointed time, but addressing all her concerns. ... On this day, while checking through her chart, I realized that in fact she was overdue for a screening mammography by one to two years. At the end of her visit, I ordered a screening mammogram, and it returned indicating the finding of breast cancer, advanced beyond early stage. I only saw her back once more after that. She had completed the initial phase of her treatment and came in to see me in follow-up. Her focus was to ask me why I had not ordered a mammogram earlier. It was a very difficult conversation. I acknowledged that she was right, and I felt very bad."

This is a primary care physician's nightmare. Information sitting in a thick medical record that sits open in front of the doctor during visits over the course of time, and the doctor never turns over enough pages to see that the mammogram is due. By 2007, Pittenger had been working on this problem for nearly three decades. "The off-the-shelf electronic medical record buries text and doesn't enable you to do mistake-proofing," says Pittenger. "So we wanted to take what the PCP Report had been doing for us and find a way that the electronic medical record could do that for us. And if you look at the way the PCP Report worked, it made a batch of reports every morning and then you used the paper tool as the day went on. The question was could we put this information into flow production and make it part of the standard work of a visit to check through some kind of on-screen tool that would alert us to what this patient was due for?"

Could they take the PCP Report and create a computer program that would integrate it into the flow of care so that it would sort through each electronic chart identifying disease management and preventive testing that was due or overdue? Just about this time Dr. Keith Dipboye, an internist in the large downtown internal medicine department, joined the Virginia Mason Best Practices Task Force, bringing multiple talents—including a knowledge of IT—to the group. Dr. Dipboye worked closely with the Virginia Mason IT team and doctors at both Kirkland and the downtown primary care facility and essentially invented the fusion of VMPS into the system's electronic medical record system. He worked with Pittenger and Dr. Rich Furlong on crafting an electronic tool that built on and improved the paper PCP Report.

"It took us over a year, but we built a set of rules about important chronic diseases like diabetes and hyperlipidemia in high-risk patients and then the preventive care tests, like mammography, colonoscopy, pneumonia vaccine," Pittenger says. "And we built rules so that any time you had a patient's chart open, you could go to the safety screen, and it would tell you what they're due for or overdue for. That put us into a new era of testing whether or not we can get doctors to do standard work. They had adopted standard work with the PCP Report because it allowed an engagement with the patient, it made them feel they had meaning in their work, and they had great hope that it would improve the rate at which we did mammography and other tests.

"But we were and to some extent still are stuck at a very good rate of mammography, 82 to 84 percent of our patients over fifty have had a mammogram in the last two years. But there are things that we're lousy at, such as Chlamydia screening, for example, which was not in the PCP Report. We wanted to write a rule into the system that would show us Chlamydia screen due or not at the outset of every visit. We wanted to do better, and we thought that putting this into flow production would be the way."

Partnering with RN programmers Sally Roberts and Teri West, they built a tool called the Health Maintenance Module that does exactly what Pittenger hoped. Now, when an MA is rooming a patient, the standard sequence of operations includes looking at the Health Maintenance Module—along with the patient—to see what is due. And the MA is empowered to do what is necessary to get the patient up to date—give a tetanus shot, schedule a mammogram, or set up a lab slip for an LDL and a lipid profile. At the start of the patient visit, in fact, the first thing staring the physician in the face on the computer screen is the Health Maintenance Module or, *as Pittenger calls it, the safety screen.* He will tell the patient that the safety screen is "screaming at me that you still haven't gotten your colonoscopy, so what's up with that?' And patients do *not* say, 'Hey, I'm here about my back pain, a possible sinus infection and by the way I need two refills. Intuitively, they know it's an act of caring, and it's, 'Yeah, I know. I've just got to grow up and do it.' And I say, 'Let's get you the appointment right now' and I flip up my phone and in a minute it's done."

The Health Maintenance Module had an immediate impact. In just the first six months of use it increased the rate of providing on-time, age-appropriate, gender-specific, and evidence-based preventive health interventions to an adult primary care patient. It caused an increase in primary care mammography volume due to the ability of the call center to make appointments for women overdue for mammography no matter what their appointment request was. Women were getting mammograms as a result of calling to make an appointment for any reason. It also caused a jump in the LDL < 100 goal rate of 6 percent for high-risk patients at Kirkland in its first six months of operation. Of these two improvements, the mammography increase inspired primary care supportive staff more than the potent LDL impact—preventing heart attacks years hence. Any increase in mammography has a predictable impact on breast cancer diagnosis. With their PCP Report experience, the 2005 increase in screening mammography allowed the Kirkland leadership to predict that they would diagnose three breast cancers that year that wouldn't have been enabled without the PCP Report and standard rooming by the MA. This gave them great pride. Now, with the Health Maintenance Module feeding information to telephone service reps at the call center they, too, are in the mistake-proofing business, causing real clinical impact.

External Setup

"We're striving for zero-defect production in medical care," says Pittenger. "So could you have a visit in which nothing is neglected, everything is corrected? You maybe can't do the mammogram right then, but you get an appointment scheduled. You maybe can't get the LDL down today, but you've measured it today and you're going to be able to set up a conversation by phone to modify medicine or whatever. And so this had to be done in a way that allowed the MA to do her check with the patient and then a successive check by the doctor. This means that the doctor is becoming like an airline pilot and has a checklist and this is the next big step for us. Can we submit to standard sequences like pilots use to make every visit zero defect and modify what's been our traditional visit interaction?"

The practice of "self-check" on quality by the MA and "successive check" by the MD operating atop a platform of mistake-proofing in the Health Maintenance Module came from the work of Shigeo Shingo, a master of the Toyota Production System. Shingo used such a system and achieved zero defects in electric clothes dryers at Matsushita in Japan in 1974. A full month's production of dryers was flawless. No dryers needed repair before shipping. Production costs fell. This was landmark work in manufacturing and Virginia Mason aspires to achieve the same in medical care.

Before he engineered zero-defect production, Shingo had achieved the "single minute exchange of die." He found a way to change the massive steel unit that casts or stamps a part on an assembly line. Traditionally, these units were bolted in place and were so large that the production line had to shut down for days to change them and install a different die to make a different model. This meant that dies were changed only after a large batch of a single model of product was completed. Days changing a die meant flow production ground to a halt, resulting in increased lead time for other products as they waited for huge runs to be completed. Shingo composed a special team that got a new die ready alongside the line. They calibrated it, lubricated it, and had it on rollers that enabled one or two people to slide it into place and switch the old die out in just a few hours. Then, with practice and *kaizen,* they could do it in a single minute, thus enabling Toyota to change model production on the fly, eliminating huge waste and, realizing the savings inherent in flow. Changing the die away from the running line and thus enabling a quick changeover was dubbed "external set up" (a critical concept in specialty care in Chapter Six).

Primary care is naturally a mixed model line, with unique patients arriving one after another. Pittenger huddled with Virginia Mason Chief Operating Officer Sarah Patterson one day on a bus during a Virginia Mason trip to Japan in 2008 and wondered "What are our die changeovers? How can we be instantly ready for every 'model' of patient?" Patterson thought about it and replied, "I'll bet it's your huddles."

On their return to the United States, Pittenger and his colleagues developed huddles that preplan changeovers. This patient will need a wound cart wheeled into the room. That one will need the PHQ-9 depression scale administered during rooming. That one will need postural vital signs. The diabetic patient at 9:00 a.m. who is visiting for back pain has an A1C of 8.6 according to the Health Maintenance Module. Therefore the RN care manager needs to wheel into that room right after rooming, before the physician enters. "We will externally set him up to get diabetes care and back pain management in one visit. We will manage this mixed model line of patients in flow, saving time by being absolutely ready and having all aspects of care 'on rollers' ready to slide into place."

Few provider organizations have a tool as advanced as the Health Maintenance Module. There are, of course, health maintenance organizations (HMOs) that do population case management using registries, but few academic medical centers have a system as advanced as the one at Virginia Mason. Commonly, places that provide key information do not provide it at the point of care, which the Virginia Mason team believes is essential. The system enables any provider from the medical center—doctors, nurses, MAs, pharmacists—*anyone* who deals with patients—to access the safety screen and work to get patients compliant. A version of the safety screen, in fact, appears on the computer terminals of telephone service reps when a patient calls in for an appointment. The rep can instantly order whatever tests are needed using a physician's electronic signature. Commonly, says Pittenger, pharmacists will notice on the screen when a patient needs a refill that he or she is also due for a preventive screening or test. In such cases, pharmacists send an e-mail to the MA and the tests get scheduled.

Pittenger thinks of this system as a descendant of Sakichi Toyoda's automatic loom developed in 1902. At the Toyota Museum in Nagoya, Japan, Pittenger saw the loom and was amazed by its wizardry. The brilliance of the loom was that it achieved *jidoka,* which builds knowledge into the system.

In the Health Maintenance Module the Virginia Mason team applied the principles of *jidoka* and the loom by embedding rules for each individual patient based on past lab results, family history of coronary disease, as well as lifestyle issues such as smoking and more. These bits of information, taken together, allowed the computer to detect whether a patient was out of range on an LDL level, for example. The program identifies patients at high risk for cardiovascular disease and sets their LDL goal at less than 100. It sets different goals for patients at lower risk. It can then identify patients whose LDL is not at goal—a broken thread in the clinical loom. When the computer makes such a finding it instantly signals the provider in bold orange letters on the screen. Because it is standard work to always leave a patient's chart set on the Health Maintenance Module so the next user sees it first, Pittenger gets information from the program on any patient the minute he opens the chart. Usually, in fact, whatever issue has flashed on the screen in orange is taken care of even before Pittenger enters the exam room. This happens during the rooming process when the MA sees the patient is overdue for an LDL level and schedules it on the spot.

A worthy addition to the repertoire of standard work, flow production, and *jidoka*-laden processes that mistake-proof care in the production system would be a move from standard visit-based production to "pull production." This would involve pulling patients in for care before they realize they need it.

Virginia Mason had already developed pull production of planned diabetes care using the registries and the efforts of RN care managers pulling patients in back in the days of the PCP Report. The result had been steady improvements in A1C and LDL to target, far above national averages.

Pull production became Pittenger's focus when he was awarded a Kaizen Fellowship at Virginia Mason in 2008. He and the other fellows engaged in fifteen months of study of the production system, and he chose to build a pull production system for preventive care. Vicki Berman, the talented programmer in clinical decision support, generated lists of patients who needed mammography, Pap smears, colonoscopy, or blood tests for diabetes and vascular disease in the coming month. The call center worked with Pittenger to use their down times to initiate calls to patients. They refined a production sequence that enabled them to reach a rate of appointments made from these "cold calls" of 24 to 34 percent in 2009.

Spreading the Kirkland innovations to other primary care sites throughout Virginia Mason proved quite successful in most locations although the main Virginia Mason primary care site in downtown Seattle—known as General Internal Medicine—proved particularly challenging. It was a chaotic environment where silos prevailed, skill–task alignment was badly out of kilter, and there was little sense of team medicine.

Cindy Rockfeld took over as administrator of the clinic and saw that it would be necessary to "fix the foundation" before she could attempt to introduce flow stations or other advances. Over several years, Rockfeld and her clinic partner Dr. Joyce Lammert succeeded in breaking down silos and applying a variety of VMPS tools to reduce waste and increase the patient-centered nature of the clinic. (A more detailed accounting of the work at General Internal Medicine can be found in the Appendix.)

Biggest Room in the House

When the Virginia Mason Kirkland Clinic started its journey, Pittenger says, "we had almost no system for managing direct care and indirect care. We had the right to be random, and we had the right to get through the day as best we saw fit and that basically equated to the right to have profoundly negative margins, less than optimal patient outcomes, and care that wasn't mistake-proofed. Now we have the right to all the autonomy we want when the door is closed with the patient—and do what we do best with our own personal techniques and style, but we have a system set up around us that mistake-proofs care so we are less likely to make mistakes. That involves accepting some standard work and some standard sequences. We are accountable to each other for the cost of indirect care, which is really what kills the economics of primary care. We have now adopted a new neurology that I'm in flow or I'm not in flow. And if I'm out of flow, my job in the next hour or two is to get back in flow."

Through a rigorous auditing process run by Rosemary Temple, RN, Virginia Mason knows that the Health Maintenance Module is used 60 to 80 percent of the time and correcting defects 60 to 80 percent of the time it is used. "That's nowhere near good enough," says Pittenger. "It's not 100 percent and that won't lead to zero-defect care, but in this kind of cultural and technical change journey, it's a great start."

In 2009, 92 percent of Virginia Mason Kirkland patients rated their overall satisfaction with care at the top of the survey scale in an externally contracted satisfaction survey. Staff satisfaction was in the same range. Sixty percent of diabetics have conventional ideal control rates (A1C < 7), 80 to 85 percent have an A1C < 8 (ideal for older diabetics with multiple chronic diseases) and fewer than 7 percent have poorly controlled diabetes. LDL is at target for 78 percent of high-risk patients. The primary care team of nine providers, four RN care managers, two pharmacists, and a dozen MAs achieved an $800,000 margin for 2009. No one has been laid off in the recession, unlike the situation for their competitors.

Unexpected good fortune enabled a breakthrough in the Kirkland production environment that matches their production methods. The neighborhood hospital offered to buy the Kirkland Clinic building in 2008, enabling Virginia Mason Kirkland to build a new facility specifically designed for flow production. On arrival, patients skip the waiting room (there isn't one), check in to identify themselves, and receive a self-rooming card. An RFID device is clipped to the card and sensors in the ceiling track its movement. Patients follow hallway images and signs that match their card as the tracking system shows the MA that they have entered the exam room. The MA follows the patient into the room within ten seconds—entering through a sliding door opposite the patient entry. The MA invites the patient to sit on an exam table that lowers to nineteen inches above the floor and configures into a chair position. The system tracks the time spent, with eight minutes being the goal for the standard rooming sequence. The MA weighs the patient privately in the room and measures blood pressure only after five minutes of sitting to make that accurate. Health Maintenance Module, medication list reconciliation, and agenda setting are accomplished.

If the physician does not enter the room in five minutes, the system notifies the MA and the provider is paged. The pressure is on to use all available external set-up and production planning to start on time and preplan the visits to run on time. The visit proceeds with the doctor and the patient sitting side by side, sharing the electronic medical record and its information. By the end of the visit prescriptions have been sent by fax to the pharmacy, future labs have been set up, and a care plan is in hand.

The provider team's flow stations are in the "beehive" offstage where indirect care hums along out of the patient's view. Natural light floods this area for the workers as the beehives follow the circumference of the building. All exam room supplies can be delivered through the backside of the room's cabinets which contain backside doors as well as in-room doors. All supplies are in two-bin systems so the provider can never run out during a visit. Most procedure and sampling materials are "kitted" for quick access. MA–physician communication happens via cell phones to cover special needs without the physician leaving the room.

There is a phone room where three or four MAs answer incoming calls in thirty-six to fifty seconds. They resolve 50 to 60 percent of these calls themselves. They convert the rest into e-mails that the physicians answer in flow. MA students are constantly present, being groomed to replace MAs that move on to nursing school. Visiting physicians and administrators from their programs at the Virginia Mason Institute routinely tour through their clinic seeking inspiration and confirmation that the approach truly works.

All of this came to fruition because of systematic application of the Virginia Mason Production System, a corporate mission to apply that system, and the drive to apply the redesigns at a local level, improving the daily life of patients and medical workers alike. The alignment of standard work, mistake-proofing, flow production, *jidoka,* and pull production into a humming system that constantly improves care is a dream come true for these people. They would never go back to traditional doctor-centered methods. There is no goal line on their improvement field. Like the Japanese say, they live in the biggest room in the house—the room for improvement.

Chapter Six

Transforming
Procedural Care

The Virginia Mason Production System (VMPS) has had a transforma-
tional impact on procedural care within the medical center. There are
countless examples, two of which are detailed here: creation of an inno-
vative new experience for surgical patients and a new space to support it,
and creation of a landmark Center for Hyperbaric Medicine.

Creating a New Ambulatory Surgical Experience

It was clear by early 2007 that Virginia Mason would soon face a shortage of
operating rooms. The medical center was running at full capacity in its main
ORs and there was a need for additional capacity, not only for existing surgeons
with growing practices, but also for a number of new surgeons coming on board.
Facility limitations created a less than ideal experience for patients who were
required to travel long distances and were corralled in ward-style surgery prep
and recovery areas. They waited for surgeries to start, experienced a number
of providers coming to do their "part" of the process, and then recovered in
spaces that were not designed to address the emotional and practical needs of the
patients and their families. Like many health care processes, it was a patchwork
of disconnected pieces quilted together over a number of years and shoehorned

into the existing physical space. Virginia Mason had no intention or desire to replicate this traditional model. It was only through the dedication of the staff and providers that patients experienced such great outcomes.

Patients would check in for surgery, where they would be asked a series of administrative questions and then be handed off to a nurse for a series of clinical questions. The patient would then go to a crowded waiting room until he or she was called by a staff member, who would take the patient to the induction (surgery prep) room. At this point—very early in the process—patients were separated from family members—a separation that distressed many patients and loved ones.

The induction area afforded no privacy. Patients were separated by curtains and were able to clearly hear conversations between clinicians and other patients barely a few feet away. In the induction area a patient care technician would help get the patient changed for surgery, label personal belongings, and assist with other logistics. At that point the patient was handed off to a nurse who would ask the patient another series of questions. Following that, an anesthesia team would interview the patient and discuss the anesthesia care. An OR nurse would then arrive and explain to the patient what to expect in the OR.

At this point, the patient would be wheeled on a gurney along a lengthy corridor leading back to the OR. The surroundings had a distinctly clinical feel with a tangle of machines, gases, and gauges that patients often found unsettling. Already anxious patients would grow more so. After the surgical procedure, patients would wake up in the postanesthesia care unit, which was a ward or bay type setting where, again, there was no real privacy. "You're in your most vulnerable state, coming out of anesthesia, you don't feel well, you're disoriented, your family is nowhere around," says Vice President Katerie Chapman. This had to be fixed.

Early in 2007, Chapman, then administrative director for Perioperative Services, met with a team of colleagues, and it was clear that transformational change was necessary. Chapman and her colleagues had no interest in building a traditional set of ORs. They were well enough along on their VMPS journey to set lofty expectations based on their belief that the principles and tools of VMPS would enable them to address the problems in an innovative fashion that best serves the needs of both patients and staff.

Design Challenge

"Once we knew the location, we had a more challenging task, which was to determine the design," says Chapman. "It had to directly reflect VMPS. It had to lead us in our pursuit of the highest levels of quality, safety, and efficiency.

It could not be more of the incremental process improvement that we had done in the main ORs. It had to be a breakthrough." And, it had to reflect the concepts they had learned from VMPS.

It was a measure of the team's experience with VMPS that they went into the process with a level of confidence that they would be able to achieve truly fundamental change. "We knew that something better was possible for the patients' experience and for our staff within their work environment," she says. "We knew we could transform the flow of patients, staff, and information. We inherently knew something could be built so dramatically better utilizing these tools and focusing on the VMPS principles." The team's confidence stemmed from having adopted VMPS as their management method. "For many of us," says Chapman, "it had become the way we think, the way we do our work."

To ensure that the new design embodied VMPS principles, Chapman put together a team that was well-versed in VMPS. Robbi Bishop had worked closely with Chapman in the Kaizen Promotion Office (KPO) before both moved to Perioperative Services, and Bishop had recently become the Manager of VMPS Strategy and Implementation for the department. Dr. Steve Rupp, the medical director for Perioperative Services as well as Chief of Anesthesia, had been steeped in VMPS methods since the start of the work at Virginia Mason and had, in fact, gone on the first trip to Japan with Dr. Kaplan in 2002.

Chapman, Bishop, and Rupp were aware of the traditional method of planning and constructing hospital facilities, both at Virginia Mason and elsewhere. Typically, a few doctors might be asked what they wanted or needed—perhaps a nurse as well. Someone from the facilities department would likely have an old set of plans from when the original ORs were constructed, which might be used as a guide. An architectural firm accustomed to having built similar ORs in various hospitals would bring their experience to bear.

The worst part about how it was done in the past was that little thought in the design effort would be given to how the *processes*—as well as the physical facility—might also be redesigned. To Chapman and the others this was the golden opportunity—a chance to redesign the facility, yes, but, more important, an opportunity to improve the process, flow, and experience of patients being treated in the OR.

"In the past," says Chapman, "they would have designed the physical space without any consideration of process, functions, flows, and then as we moved in we would have been forced to figure out what those new processes looked like, what those new flows looked like to accommodate the space. Our approach with VMPS was to understand and improve the processes and *then* determine the space required to support the flows and needs of the patients and staff." And most important, says Bishop, "it had to be all about the patient."

Listening to Patients

Rupp noted that "the architects presented the traditional concept of an ambulatory surgery center being built in a circular layout. Patients move in at a point on the circle and then move to preop preparation, the OR, phase one recovery, phase two recovery, and finally returned to the point of entry for discharge. This configuration has traditionally served to consolidate staffing for the surges of patient admits in the morning and the completion of final discharges at the end of the day. We needed to free ourselves of these biases to really entertain how the flows of the patient might best be served. In the end, through the 3P process and subsequent planning, we settled on a linear flow model."

In this model, the total distance traveled by the patient in the final design was roughly equal to the diameter of the circle, a much shorter distance than the circumference. "Reducing the total distance traveled by the patient was critical," Rupp noted. "All the other flows of medicine (providers, equipment, supplies, medications, etc.) follow the flows of the patient. If you reduce the distance traveled by the patient, you reduce the distances traveled by all those other elements of care and hence maximize the improvement in efficiency. This is a critical component of reducing overall cycle times."

The team had no shortage of ideas, but by following the principles of VMPS they knew that creating transformational change would require the thinking, input, and buy-in from a larger group of people ranging from housekeepers to surgeons—each with a critically important role in the process. They selected the 3P method to set the vision. The leadership team guiding the effort—Chapman, Bishop, and Rupp—began planning for an event that would have an unusually large inter-interdisciplinary team, including administrators, surgeons, anesthesiologists, nurses, scrub techs, admission personnel, architects, patients, and more. In addition, they invited leaders from other parts of the medical center to join in thinking about a vision for the new facility. The diverse perspectives of the 3P team members would prove greatly valuable.

"One of the things that events like 3P and RPIWs do is they bring everybody together," says Chapman, "and you begin to see where you overlap or what that next person either up or downstream is doing and how you impact one another. It allows you to get a real sense of interconnectedness."

Before the team could begin, there were two major tasks—to understand the needs of the customer, the patient, and to know the current state of the processes inside and out. When thinking of the customer, team members wanted to go beyond the typical consideration of waiting room carpet and lobby décor. They were interested in designing a process from top to bottom that exceeded the patient's expectations at every step of the journey. Beyond that, they recognized that the patient's family was a vitally important customer and wanted to understand their needs as well.

They began to understand the customer by conducting a series of patient focus group discussions with men and women who had had surgery at Virginia Mason. Over a couple of months, Virginia Mason's patient relations team and the 3P leaders talked with scores of patients—some in the structured setting of a focus group interview and many others more informally, often one-on-one. Chapman and others probed to get the clearest idea possible of what they wanted in a surgical experience. "We would talk with patients about their care experience and what it feels like for them and for family members," says Chapman. Communicating with patients and family members was "extraordinarily valuable," she says. It was "the key element for us in our improvement efforts."

The feedback and ideas from patients and families were collated and summarized to inform the 3P team and the vision. Clear themes emerged and four customer elements were identified that would prove foundational to the new surgery center:

■ Family involvement in the process
■ Privacy
■ Fewer handoffs
■ Reduction of the clinical feel

Patients talked a lot about family involvement and being able to keep family members not only nearby, but actually a part of the process to the greatest extent possible. Patients emphasized that they did not want to be separated until absolutely necessary. "It is so silly if you think about it," says Bishop. "I was present for the birth of my two children, but in our current OR system, a loved one cannot be present in the surgery prep area when we start an IV."

Patients talked a good deal about privacy as well. Usually, in induction areas or surgery prep areas, there is nothing more than a curtain separating patients from one another. Patients could overhear detailed—and sometimes quite intimate—conversations happening just a few feet away. "They deserve privacy," says Chapman. "We need to give that to them. Considering how we could build that into our new facility was very important for us."

In the course of the focus group discussions, patients also expressed concerns that they were seemingly passed from one provider to another. In medical terms, patients wanted to reduce the number of handoffs from one caregiver to another.

Finally, the team heard something surprising from the patients—something they would never have considered had they not included patients in the process. A number of patients said that there was a mystery to the surgical process that was unsettling; that exacerbated their anxiety. Chapman and her colleagues knew that patients would often get anxious in a forest of high-tech medical gadgetry, but this was different. "We knew that just the nature of a clinical area promotes some angst," says Chapman. "But the thing that came out in the focus groups was a sense that the ORs are very deep into the building. They're so far away that it's sort of a mystery, if you will. It causes a lot of anxiety and even fear in some patients that they're being taken back to this mysterious, secret place. It was interesting how they articulated that. So one of our aims was to reduce that mystery."

Setup Reduction

The next important step in preparing for the 3P was to have a detailed understanding of the processes and functions of the entire perioperative OR realm. As was the case with all 3Ps and RPIWs, preparation, supervised in this case by Bishop, included observations with stopwatches, "spaghetti charts" and other VMPS tools to fully grasp the process and identify waste. "I was not trained to work in the OR," says Bishop, "so I was able to separate myself from the clinical details of the ways ORs are 'supposed' to look. This allowed me to focus on understanding the process of each provider, the patient flow and experience, and the waste that surrounds the work." It became clear to Bishop and the project team that the principle of *setup reduction* would become critical in how the team approached making improvements in flow, capacity, utilization, and productivity.

Typically, when employing setup reduction, the target is a bottleneck in the process that needs to be released. The constraint in this case was the operating room itself. The goal was to reduce the thirty-minute turn time so that the OR team could maximize the use of the room itself—by definition a limited resource. The 3P planning team set a challenging target of turning over the operating room in under ten minutes. The team intentionally stayed away from the time the surgeon was operating and instead focused on all of the time surrounding the procedure, which was generally non-value-added from the perspective of the customer. After all, patients did not come to Virginia Mason to be wheeled up and down a hall or repositioned on yet another bed—they came *for the surgical procedure itself.*

Despite the substantial reduction goal, Liz Dunphy, RN, one of the leaders for the 3P event, took the goal in stride. "We modeled the times and, we'd had a lot of really good data to help us understand how long it really takes to turn a room and what are the key steps. We were far enough along in our journey that we could pull from our data and our knowledge to trust the process."

With data in hand and the experience of several 3P design events in her back pocket, Dunphy urged team members to let go of old ways of thinking. The team set a roadmap for the improvements that would seek to transform peri-operative services and the patient experience. The work of the 3P was to address the customer and process elements that had been identified. The team leaders started off by employing the setup reduction techniques that the planning team identified would be so crucial.

The first step for the 3P team was to separate internal from external setup. Internal setup includes processes that must be done in the operating room itself—cleanup from the previous case, arrangement of the equipment, and final operative site preparation, for example. For all practical purposes, the team had been treating all of the work that occurred in the thirty minutes of turnover as internal, thereby holding up the use of the room for the value-added activity of surgery itself. The key to reducing the bottleneck of the room was to identify what could only be done in the room versus what could be done outside the room in the prep area.

Part of the 3P process is recognizing and confronting *mental valleys*—typical or traditional ways of thinking. An obstacle, says team leader Dunphy, was the mental valley that certain aspects of surgical preparation could *only* take place within the OR, such as positioning of the patient or setting up instruments. The 3P team recognized in its search for waste that doing these types of setup activi-ties in the OR was, by definition, a waste of the resource of the room.

After elements of setup were categorized, the next step was to convert what is now internal to external setup. The team wondered, "What if we could do some of the preparation of the patients *outside* the OR?" That would mean more OR time for surgery rather than prep—and the team devised a new method that accomplished just that.

One of the tasks that occurred inside the room and took a good deal of time was transferring and positioning the patient on the OR table. In the traditional model, when patients arrived in surgery prep, they were placed on a gurney and then transferred to the OR table when they arrived in the OR. After surgery, they were transferred back to the gurney and moved to the recovery area. The team quickly acknowledged this as an opportunity and identified the need for a versatile bed that could be used for surgery prep, the surgical procedure, and recovery. They found such a "bed" already on the market. With the new process, in many cases, patients are positioned on a bed that has been set up specific to type of procedure just before they arrive. This typically happens outside of the OR, eliminating several minutes of setup time in the OR itself. In addition, it eliminates the burden of staff lifting patients on to and off the OR table.

Another time-consuming step in the process of setup was preparing the "back table," a sterile location for surgical instruments that is essentially the sur-gical technician's workspace. Every procedure requires different tools and thus a different setup. In the old system, a surgical technician would come in after the OR had been cleaned from the previous patient. The technician might have looked over the instruments in the hallway outside the room, but he or she was unable to open them from their sterile containers and set them up due to the risk of contamination. Dunphy says the team wondered whether it might be possible to have a safe anteroom adjacent to but separate from each OR where all the prep work would take place. This would free up an additional and significant piece of internal setup time. This was a key part of VMPS: continuing to find ways to eliminate wasted room time by moving anything that didn't need to be done in the room to other areas.

Chapman says that when she is describing this idea to OR nurses outside of Virginia Mason she is often met with a guffaw followed by "You can't do that!" In fact, however, you can, and they did—although it was not easy. There was a good deal of discussion between the Virginia Mason team and the Washington State Department of Health (DOH) over the design. It was nothing like what the DOH had ever seen before. The DOH asked a lot of questions and the team had answers for all of them. Ultimately, the DOH approved this aspect of the design. The reaction of nurses to the changes at Virginia Mason demonstrates some of the deep mental valleys ingrained in the industry.

Breakthrough

In the new process, sterile instruments are set up in a dedicated room—prepared and laid out exactly as they would be in the OR. The setup area has its own air flow and air exchanges entirely separate from the adjacent OR to prevent contamination. When the OR has been cleaned, the table is rolled in and ready right away. "This allowed us to externalize certain setup activities that were once thought to have to happen in the operating room," says Bishop. "Through parallel processing and standard work, we minimized case turnover time and facilitated much smoother flow."

The journey didn't end there, though. Once all possible work has been externalized, it was important to reduce the cycle time for the remaining internal setup. One area that had to remain in the OR was connecting the leads on the patient to the equipment in the OR. Traditionally, an assortment of cables and machinery would have to be disconnected and reconnected when moving the patient from one location to another. The whole process couldn't be externalized because you couldn't get the patient connected if they weren't there in the room. However, the team identified a product on the market—affectionately called the "brick"—that allowed the patient to move with a sort of plug-and-play simplicity. Leads were connected to the brick, instead of the machine directly. The brick could be removed from the machine in surgery prep and could travel with the patient and plug into compatible machines in the OR and the recovery area. This saved six minutes of internal setup time per patient—a huge gain. "Put yourself in the shoes of the patient," says Bishop. "How uncomfortable is it for complete strangers to be constantly pulling your gown in every direction to take off and put on these leads? Now we put them on once and take them off once."

"The anesthesia and nursing team's work is very intense during case turn-over," says Dr. Rupp. "The elimination of the six minutes of moving patient from gurney to OR table, hooking up the monitors, and getting baseline vital signs was a huge gain for all. The six minutes saved at the beginning of the case are saved again at the end of the case during the transfer of care to the recovery room. The most amazing thing to me is that, as a provider, you don't have to know anything about VMPS to capture those twelve minutes! They are hard-wired into the system by the design."

Obligatory follow-up measurements revealed that setup reduction had created substantial gains for the OR. By using the tools of VMPS, the OR created a win–win for patients and Virginia Mason. Results from June 2009 indicate that patients wait less and have a better experience, and Virginia Mason can use the ORs for more cases per day by reducing the nonbillable turnover time.

Metric	Before	After	Improvement
Number of cases per room	5 per day	7-plus per day	40%
Number of cases for four rooms	100 per week	140 per week	40%
Case turnover time *Patient A out to Patient B in*	Over 30 minutes	Less than 15 minutes	50%
Surgery Prep Time *Setup to Suture*	106 minutes	85 minutes	20%

Data reported as of June 2009

As the 3P team worked on improving the process elements—which made the staff more productive and utilized resources more effectively—they simultaneously examined the process through the lens of the patient in an effort to address the four elements identified by the customer. The 3P facilitated communications, expectations, and knowledge of where the patient was at any point in the process, thereby helping family members better understand what was going on with their loved one. A newly created, customized day-of-surgery guide was provided to the patient and family at check-in. It is a very brief pamphlet that nonetheless covers the essentials of the day, helps them understand what lies ahead, and highlights expected surgery times and major process milestones.

Patients said that they felt separated from their families too early in the process. The team kept this in mind when they created the surgery prep rooms. Just after check-in, a patient care technician greets the patient and family members and guides them to the room. By taking them directly to the room, they have eliminated a handoff with a transporter—another concern for patients.

Patients also wanted privacy, and the 3P team included this in the design. "You enter the surgery prep areas and it is literally a room," says Dunphy. "It's private, so no more curtain separation, no more listening to your neighbor's clinical needs, no more feeling as if you are exposed to all who wander within earshot."

When the OR is ready, the patient is wheeled from the surgery prep room just across the hall to the OR eight to ten feet away. No longer is there a lengthy trip down a hallway where the patient's anxiety mounts along the way. At this point, the patient must separate from his or her family, but care has been taken to create transparency for the family—another of the main customer concerns. An electronic system allows family members waiting outside the surgical area to follow the process of their loved one. Each patient is assigned a patient-specific code that identifies that patient only to family members. Family members can then monitor via an electronic board similar to an airline schedule board, confidentially watching for progress of their loved one throughout the surgical process. The electronic tracking requires no additional work by staff because it is driven off of the electronic clinical documentation system. As the RN documents the incision, for example, that is transmitted to the patient tracking board electronically as "surgery start" and is immediately visible to the patient's family.

Finally, when the surgery is complete, the patient is wheeled directly into the recovery area and into one of the private recovery bays. More often than not, the patient is greeted there by waiting family members. The design includes a designated family area right by the patient to encourage their participation, yet in a spot where they will not impede the clinician's movement.

Responding to patients' privacy concerns and the need to improve the nurses' workflow, the 3P team designed the recovery area very differently than the typical ward style. "We wanted to provide privacy and keep our RNs at the bedside where they could provide better surveillance," says Chapman. "This leads to better, safer care." The team came up with a design that avoided right angles. This design allowed for direct visual contact from the central nursing station to the entry of each patient space, adding an additional safety feature.

In recovery, as the patient becomes more aware, the nurse has the time and the environment free of distraction to work with the patient and family to facilitate the healing process once they get home.

With all of the focus on process and customer elements, the team wanted to be sure that the environment was also physically appealing. They designed a family waiting area that is a calming, living-room-style setting that does not feel particularly medical or institutional. There is Internet and TV access as well as comfortable chairs for people of all sizes. Chapman notes that "natural wood with warm colors and textures were carried throughout the facility—starting in the patient preparation room, the recovery room, and into the family waiting area. This reduces the clinical feel, promotes consistency of environment, and reduced anxiety associated with the clinical setting."

All of these customer elements led to some dramatic improvements for the patients:

■ Patient travel distance is down 82 percent.
■ Patient time in process (defined as check-in to discharge on day of surgery) is down 40 percent.

"Setup reduction is a really powerful technique," says Andrew Baylor of the KPO. "So often, people try and solve capacity issues by asking employees to work faster or harder or for longer hours without looking at their work from a system perspective. When they inevitably fail, we assume that they need more resources—more tools, more rooms, more people, more inventory. When we carefully study the work with a setup reduction lens, more often than not, you reveal tremendous amounts of untapped capacity."

Center for Hyperbaric Medicine

Medical Director Dr. Neil Hampson was worried. The weather forecast was for sustained forty-mile-an-hour winds with gusts to seventy miles an hour, pounding rain, and low temperatures. This combination meant downed trees and power lines, likely leading to days of power outages that force people to create heat any way they can. Some will use faulty generators; others will bring charcoal grills inside their homes. Both actions cause deaths every winter. Hampson knew that within hours, dozens of men, women, and children who were just trying to have a hot meal and stay warm would be rushed to his facility. Would his hyperbaric chamber save the lives of these victims?

Hyperbaric oxygen (HBO_2) therapy is the delivery of 100 percent oxygen to patients in an environment of increased pressure. It is performed in a hyperbaric chamber and is probably best known for treating divers with decompression sickness, the bends. HBO_2 raises blood oxygen levels fifteen to twenty times normal, resulting in significant increases in tissue oxygenation. The chamber is pressurized with air and the patients wear hoods to receive hyperbaric oxygen. Modern-day hyperbaric medicine effectively treats both emergency and routine conditions. Emergency treatments are for such disorders as decompression sickness, carbon monoxide (CO) poisoning, and severe soft tissue infections such as gas gangrene. These patients typically receive one to six treatments each lasting from two to eight hours. Routine conditions treated with HBO_2 include nonhealing wounds, such as refractory diabetic lower extremity wounds or tissue breakdown following radiation therapy for cancer. These patients often are given twenty to forty daily two-hour treatments spread over one to two months.

In 1969 Virginia Mason Hyperbarics was established as a research facility across a busy city street from the main hospital. It was equipped with a four-person chamber augmented a year later with a single-person chamber. It was a fine research facility, but, in 1980, when the research facility transitioned to a clinical facility without any change in design, location, or layout, there were challenges. The waiting room was two wooden chairs in a hallway; a public bathroom became the dressing room; and the assessment area, where patients had pretreatment assessments and exams, was as private as a furniture store. On arrival at the treatment chamber, patients climbed three steps, twisted through a small doorway, and sat on folding metal chairs where they huddled knee-to-knee for their two-hour treatment with an attendant and other equally uncomfortable patients. Some patients and staff actually suffered ergonomic ills from the chamber experience. Certainly, this was not patient-friendly advanced medical care.

In addition, federal regulations required hospitalized patients to be transported by ambulance from their hospital bed to the hyperbaric unit—literally across the street. Once across the street they climbed out of the ambulance and walked to the clinic, often in a cold Seattle rain, edging their way through people waiting on the same sidewalk for a bus. The department was not connected to the hospital oxygen supply, so even that had to be trucked in.

In spite of the suboptimal conditions, demand increased and required the unit to remain open twelve to fourteen hours per day staffed with a second per-diem shift. Even with two shifts, routine treatments often were delayed as much as eight weeks. Emergencies further disrupted long-awaited scheduled treatments. Patients on a stretcher occupied even more space. This outmoded service continued to bump along with ever increasing demand and ever more cramped facilities. It was work as usual, with increasing amounts of patchworked processes to meet the needs of patients.

In early 2002, Virginia Mason made the strategic decision to construct a new Center for Hyperbaric Medicine. It would not be just a new facility, but a potential "model line" service, designed and managed according to principles of the Virginia Mason Production System. Anticipated demand was eighteen to thirty-six patients per day, with eighty to one hundred emergency patients a year, some of whom might arrive by the dozens during winter storms. Under the consulting guidance of John Black and Associates, Dr. Hampson and his staff began their improvement efforts.

Hampson had his eyes on a twenty-four-person megachamber. The unit's nurse manager, Claude Wreford-Brown, preferred eight mono-chambers. Ordinarily this could have been debated endlessly until someone reluctantly relented, someone pulled rank, or someone else came up with a better idea. Instead, Hampson was asked to gather former patients and members of his staff to join hospital leadership in a 3P to define the best layout for the new hyperbaric facility.

The team built rudimentary models of the competing designs on large tables using plastic building blocks, sticky notes, paper tubes, and other items to lay out the relative size and location of exam rooms, pathways, support spaces, nursing stations, and everything else deemed necessary for patients and staff. They modeled how each design would function. It was obvious that neither design enabled smooth patient flow and the efficiencies they were looking for. Hampson and Wreford-Brown had to let go of previous conceptualizations and begin anew. Continued modeling and simulation led to an ideal design consisting of two eight-person chambers positioned end-to-end with a common entry chamber in the middle. Patients entered the large chambers through doors from the middle entry chamber or through doors at the far end of each large chamber.

The 3P team recommended staggered chamber start times so staff could handle the maximum eight patients in each chamber without creating rush hour crowding. Staggering the start of the two-hour routine treatments by an hour allowed the team to utilize smaller batches up to eight patients. Using the smaller batches, only half of the sixteen patients being treated were in the changing rooms and assessment stations at any one time, and the flow of patients entering a chamber did not conflict with the flow leaving the facility. This allowed six routine treatment sessions to be performed per eight-hour day with a total daily capacity of forty-eight patients.

If an emergency patient arrived when both large treatment chambers were in use, therapy began in the central entry chamber. Once the routine patients completed their treatments and exited the large chamber through an end door, the emergency patient was transferred to that large chamber for completion of his or her HBO$_2$ treatment.

Ask Why

Because it was impossible to stuff the Boeing-737-sized seventy-foot long, ten-foot-diameter chamber into the existing space, Hampson envisioned constructing a new building just east of the hospital tower. This new building would cost $2 million. Here, the tool of asking "why" five times came into play.

Administration asked, "Because we can easily move the hospital library, why can't we put the chamber there?"

"Because," the team responded, "the largest possible entry into that area is through the side of the building (an old basement parking garage) and it has only seven feet, three inches clearance below the hospital's main sewer pipe, not the ten feet needed."

"But why can't we find a way to bring the chamber in under the pipe?"

"Because it's too big."

"Why is it too big?"

"Because that's the way it's built."

"Why is it built that way?"

"That's how they've always built them."

"Why can't it be put together in another way?"

"Oh, okay. Let's build the chamber inside the hospital building with pieces no wider than seven feet that can be placed on their sides (like sideways Lifesaver candies) and slide them underneath the sewer pipe."

And that is precisely what was done. The 25,000-pound sections were pulled into the hospital under the sewer pipe, rotated upward, and fastened together into the new hyperbaric chamber. Using VMPS—asking why five times—saved $2 million.

There was a new chamber, new facilities, and money saved. What more needed to be done? The setting had to be patient friendly. They didn't like the old hyperbaric facility. To ensure they were provided value from their perspective, patients were included on the 3P design team and played a key role. They wanted the following:

- A lounge where relatives and friends can wait (Starbucks would be nice)
- Male and female locker rooms like a country club
- More private nursing stations
- Warm and friendly colors everywhere
- A comfortable waiting room
- A homier, less clinical, and less mechanical-looking chamber on the inside
- Ultracomfortable reclining chairs inside the chamber

Patient Focused

One patient added, "When I make my way from the clinic entrance to the chamber, I'd like to feel like a turtle going from the woods to the ocean." The staff complied. Near the entrance the floor looks like wet sand and becomes ocean blue near the chamber. The chamber is blue with fish painted on the far wall outside the chamber portholes, as might be seen from underwater. The ceiling is sky blue. Naturally, a "cabana," in nature's greens and browns, was designed as the waiting area, complete with artificial palm trees and a saltwater aquarium. Space design is such that the ceiling height increases near the chamber, thus shrinking its visual impact. All of this happened because Hampson and his crew were able to increase value from the patients' perspective by including them in the design process.

Most of the treatment process is equally patient friendly using VMPS tools. The principle of "pull" is utilized so patients can move through the system at their speed rather than the department's. Laminated *kanban* cards ensure a smooth flow. These cards display the patient's last name, facility and treatment numbers, and the current date. If the patient will need to see the doctor after the hyperbaric treatment, a large "X" is marked on the card. There is no need for the patient to find someone to check in. Patients just pick up their *kanban* card from the reception desk, post it, change into scrubs in the warmly designed, cheerful locker room, wander over to get vitals or other tests at the nursing station, and then relax in the cabana.

A white board on wheels is the movable visual cue. It is located outside the changing room and lists the next treatment time and the number of patients for that treatment. It has Velcro strips to hold the *kanban* cards. Any staff member can see in an instant which patients have arrived, which chamber will be used, the scheduled treatment time, and the need to meet with the patient to provide necessary services. Patients and the rolling white board move to the chamber simultaneously. Staff don't wait, and patients wait only as long as they wish by coming in a comfortable time-frame prior to treatment. Care is pulled by the patient, including using a call button when ready to be seen by a nurse.

After the treatment, the patient changes back to street clothes in the locker room, returns the *kanban* card, and leaves, or goes to an exam room, posts the *kanban* card on the door (which visually announces that he or she is ready to see the doctor), and goes inside. Patients learn how to use the *kanban* cards mostly from other patients who are returning for treatment. This pull system creates flow by minimizing staff intervention and maximizes patient control. All are able to independently manage their own course of treatment by pulling what is needed when it is needed.

Just before opening the new facility, the team suddenly was concerned about how to operate the place. They didn't want to continue the old ways of working in the brand new facility. They wanted to figure out who was going to do what, when. They conducted an RPIW to help create standard work for every staff member. Their first decision was to specify the work of nurses and doctors on laminated standard process description cards they could carry with them. Then other details like collection of copays by the receptionist were tackled. Standard work was seen as especially important to ensure any temporary or per diem staff working in the chamber could be successful members of the team.

Another important VMPS tool the team utilized was 5S (sort, simplify, sweep, standardize, self-discipline), a visual system designed to keep the workplace safe and organized. There is a place for everything, everything is in its place, there is rarely too much or too little, everyone knows how the system works, and everyone can tell in a glance if something is amiss. Here are some examples of how the team implemented 5S:

- Supplies and documents were *sorted* into necessary and unnecessary items. The necessary items are *simplified* by creating a place for everything and clearly labeling cabinets and drawers on the outside with their contents.
- There are two fully equipped carts that can be taken into either of the chambers, one for cleaning and one for restocking. This allows for quick and easy turnover of the chamber by allowing simplified *sweeping* through the chamber. Using these two carts reduces the number of trips to the cleaning and supply cabinets.
- Work is *standardized* among the operators by documenting the method and how they will hold each other accountable and maintain *self-discipline.*
- *Kanbans* signal when to restock. For example, ten bandages are in a labeled transparent jar with five of them and a *kanban* wrapped together. As soon as the loose five are gone, the *kanban* is used to order five more.

The hyperbaric department is no longer a patchwork of procedures. It is orchestrated with standard work. Searching time is almost eliminated, walking distance is minimized, and the chamber area is renowned throughout the hospital as the neatest area, as clean as an operating room.

The results of using VMPS to design and operate the hyperbaric facility have been spectacular. With the new facility:

- Treatment hours are up 18 percent.
- There is no second shift.
- Patient wait times have essentially disappeared.
- Emergencies are treated without disrupting routine patients.
- The usual twelve- to fourteen-hour days of operation were reduced to eight-hour days, a 42 percent reduction.
- The average number of patients per attendant has increased from 2.4 to 5.4.
- There are no more regular ambulance trips across the street, saving $55,000 a year.

- Financial margins per patient are up 145 percent. The more patient hours increase, the higher the margin per hour.
- Patient travel time in the new facility has been dramatically reduced.
- There are no more ergonomic problems.
- Patient satisfaction has skyrocketed.
- Staff satisfaction is up.

Hampson, the team, and the patients are pleased. "Today, entering our VM Hyperbaric Center is entering a health care environment unlike any most patients have ever experienced," says Hampson. "This center is now as peaceful and quiet as a library, as organized and uncluttered as a computer-server room, as spacious and attractive as the lobby of a five-star hotel, without patients or staff moving about aimlessly or frantically. Visitors often ask, 'Where is everyone?' They are here being treated in our hyperbaric chambers, our examination rooms, or in some other location out of the public eye. Patients and staff love it."

The team believes these gains will be maintained and improved. Their optimism comes from their commitment to *kaizen,* to continuous improvement. They have proven this through their use of *kaizen* and RPIWs and also by actively soliciting new ideas from staff and patients through the Everyday Lean Idea suggestion program. Everyone contributes and tests out ideas, sharing new ways of doing things and implementing those of value. Patients are told that during treatment, they can be quality control inspectors. Once a week, they're asked what improvements could be made. With the combined efforts of staff and patients, this program will continue to improve.

On Saturday, December 16, 2006, almost 400,000 Seattle-area utility customers were still enduring life without power, heat, electricity, or hot water. A twenty-six-year old man was found dead that morning with a generator running in his living room. The same day more than 100 other people were treated in local area hospitals after inhaling the fumes of generators or charcoal barbecues brought indoors. Virginia Mason alone treated seventy over four days. Without the VM Center for Hyperbaric Medicine dozens could have died, with many more suffering needlessly. The facility treated up to seventeen people simultaneously. During this crisis, and all of 2007, not one routinely scheduled patient was delayed due to emergency care.

Chapter Seven

Transforming Inpatient Care

For many years, Virginia Mason provided very good hospital care to countless patients, but seeing the world through the lens of the Virginia Mason Production System (VMPS) showed that there was significant room for improvement within the hospital. Applying VMPS has transformed in-patient hospital care at Virginia Mason. Hundreds of staff members—doctors, nurses, MAs, technicians, housekeepers, administrators, and many others—played significant roles in this work. This chapter looks at the transformation through the experiences of the nursing leaders who inspired many of the changes.

Not so long ago, hospitals were among the most revered institutions in American life. For generations, they were considered safe havens. The very best and brightest worked there, and the most prominent people in a community served on the board. The turnaround during the past decade or so in how hospitals are viewed both by health care professionals and the public is nothing less than astonishing. Hospitals are now widely considered to be dangerous places to be avoided if at all possible. A look at the popular media as well as professional journals suggests that hospitals are fall factories where infections rage, readmissions are common, and medication mistakes happen again and again. American hospitals are paid hundreds of billions of dollars each year and while they produce an epidemic of injuries, they are wasting tens of billions if not more.

In any hospital, nurses are the first line of defense, operating at the front lines where care is delivered. Virginia Mason was fortunate to have hundreds of great nurses, but the hospital system within which they worked did not serve the nurses' work at maximum efficiency. Thus, that system was the focus of a significant and sustained effort at Virginia Mason to improve the quality, safety, and efficiency of care.

Charleen Tachibana, RN, Senior Vice President, Hospital Administrator, and Chief Nursing Officer at Virginia Mason, was the executive who led the hospital improvement work. Tachibana started work as a nurse at Virginia Mason in 1977 and spent most of her nursing years in critical care, gradually rising through the ranks. She combined extensive frontline experience with intelligence and savvy that made her a strong leader and one of Gary Kaplan's most trusted lieutenants. She also possessed a fierce determination to apply VMPS principles and tools to improving nursing care within the medical center. In 2005, during a visit to the massive Boeing 737 facility in Renton, Washington, she noticed that the workers were always right there on the line and never seemed to have to go retrieve equipment or find supplies. She was struck by the contrast between that and the scene she was seeing day after day with nurses throughout the hospital.

In November, 2005, Tachibana sponsored a Rapid Process Improvement Workshop (RPIW) focused on nursing activity on a particular hospital floor. "I wanted to really focus on the question of how to keep the nurse on the line," she says. "How do you keep them there with the patient instead of always going somewhere else?" The RPIW measurements confirmed that nurses spent far too much time doing things other than caring for patients. Tachibana was aware of various studies—a major one was in progress at that time—indicating that nurses in the United States typically spent barely one third of their time with patients. Tachibana found this immensely frustrating, for she knew from experience that a nurse's real effectiveness was with patients—*right there at the bedside*.

Geographic Cells

Prior to the RPIW in 2005, nurses were assigned to rooms along a lengthy hallway and would spend a good deal of time walking to and from rooms or in search of supplies. With patients spread out along the hallway a nurse could never be in close proximity to all patients at once. Tachibana and her team changed that by creating geographic cells that physically position nurses only a few steps from each room. The impact was immediate. It placed nurses central to a cluster of rooms for which they were responsible. "They didn't have to be running up and down the hallway," says Tachibana. "They found that they could take any cluster of five patients because they saved so much time in the walking that the acuity differences among patients didn't matter as much." Geographic cells also improved coordination between nurses and patient care technicians.

With better coordination, staff members were readily available for patients, resulting in a marked decline in call lights.

Although geographic cells were a significant step forward, they did little to solve another problem keeping nurses away from patients. When Tachibana and her team continued observing and measuring, they saw that nurses were in a near perpetual search for supplies. The system was so chaotic and unreliable that when Tachibana was a nurse on the floor she recalls regularly running out of basic supplies and having to leave the medical center and travel a few blocks to the drug store to buy them. In the 1990s, a system was established that placed most supplies in a huge vending machine-like contraption. To get a supply or piece of equipment out of this mechanism a nurse would have to punch in a code, try to find the item among a series of randomly placed supplies, and then press a button to select the supply. This would initiate a supply order and add it to the patient's bill. Although the system theoretically improved the billing process, it added a huge amount of waste for the nursing staff. It wasn't uncommon to see a line of nurses or other floor staff waiting to get into the machine, often for nothing more than a bandage or needle. Rendering the whole process even more ridiculous was that changes in insurance rules meant only a few dozen of the hundreds of supplies were actually billable.

Even with the vending machine, says Tachibana, "We would have supply outages, so then we would have nurses stocking supplies in their locker because they'd say 'I'm never going to be caught again without having the Swan-Ganz catheter that I need.' There were all these workarounds to make sure the patient's needs were met." This system was no system at all, really. With the application of VMPS, the team began looking for an efficient way to make sure supplies were available when and where nurses needed them. First, they measured: What supplies were nurses leaving the patient's bedside to chase down? Were there twenty different supplies? Forty? In fact, after careful study the team discovered that the overwhelming majority of the time nurses left the patient to go and find one of seven supplies. The team went to a plastics manufacturer and had a custom-designed clear plastic container made to hold those seven supplies. The plastic containers—about a foot high and two feet long—are affixed to the wall of the patient's room near the bedside and contain the following:

- Prefilled saline syringes (no needles)
- Tape
- Specimen container
- Mouth swabs
- Male syringe caps
- Socks (slippers) or gait belt
- 5 cc syringes (no needles)

It was certainly not rocket science, but it was the first time—at VM, at least—that anyone had actually analyzed and measured what caused a nurse to leave the patient so often. Now they knew, and the new plastic bin was applied throughout the hospital with a simple system where it is refilled each day by nonclinical staff. A similar approach was applied to linens. The team utilized the same solution and have now standardized a backup set of linens—gown, sheet, and towel—in every room.

Report/Handoff

During the course of hospital improvement work, Tachibana and her colleagues were following VMPS procedures to observe and measure. As they did so, she saw a familiar sight: nurses huddled together during "report" at the start of a shift when outgoing nurses briefed incoming nurses on patient needs and care plans. By studying and measuring the existing process, Tachibana could see that nurses would typically spend anywhere from forty-five minutes to an hour—or even more sometimes—in the handoff process. This would typically take place in a conference room with the door closed and all the nurses tucked away—about as far removed from patients as it was possible to be and still be on the same floor.

"So that leaves no caregiver," she says, "meaning you stop taking admissions, you put everybody on hold, you don't answer needs at that point in time other than emergencies. There's no one out doing surveillance of patients, there are call lights going off all the time because people aren't out with the patients."

It also means that a nurse has been on duty for perhaps an hour or more and still not seen a single patient. From a patient perspective there is nothing value-added when a nurse is sitting in a conference room. During this report time call lights were going on all along the hallways. When the handoff process was finally over nurses were reacting—sometimes for another hour or more—until they had cleared all the call lights. As Tachibana observed during the RPIW preparation, she saw nurses frequently questioned by doctors or family members about the status of a particular patient. Almost invariably nurses replied that they did not know because they had not yet seen the patient.

"Sometimes this was two hours into a shift and they had not seen the patient," she says. "The quality of the handoff was very poor. The handoff is of no value if a nurse doesn't know anything about the patient at the end of the handoff."

Tachibana also observed that about an hour before the end of a shift nurses would often stop delivering care so they could do their documentation. Thus, nurses were unavailable to patients about an hour at the beginning and end of a shift. This made no sense, particularly in the context of a medical center where the patient came first. If the patient is at the top of the strategic plan how could you possibly have a system where the frontline caregivers were unavailable for portions of every shift?

Tachibana was joined in this work by a number of colleagues, including Rowena Ponischil, whom Tachibana had hired as a nurse manager. Ponischil had worked at another local hospital for twenty years, and she had believed for some time that the most efficient way to hand off between shifts was at the patient's bedside. After a thorough discussion involving Tachibana, Ponischil, and other team members, the decision was made to experiment with bedside handoffs. This would mean that the discussion about a patient would be shared with a patient. "The oncoming and the outgoing nurses go to the bedside with the patient," says Tachibana. "They do an introduction to the patient and a brief exchange of key points regarding the patient's care. They do a check on high-risk medications and other safety concerns."

The bedside handoff enables nurses to know the patient's baseline condition at the start of a shift—essential knowledge for a nurse to recognize change in a patient's condition. With a stroke patient, for example, says Ponischil, "If the patient deviates from that baseline, then we know her stroke is getting worse and that we need to get help. We also want to make sure we don't unnecessarily expend resources on something that's her baseline."

The result of this new process is that by the time handoff is completed, the nurse is not only not hidden away in the conference room, but has met with and spoken to every one of her patients, reviewed their plan of care, and set a solid start for her shift. All of this typically takes just about thirty minutes. "It takes less time and is much more focused," says Tachibana. "When you get a large group of nurses sitting together there are a lot of social components woven into it. There have been studies done looking at those handoffs and they found that something like forty seconds is actually spent talking about the patient's needs and that it's not always done in any kind of a meaningful way that actually passes good information. But when you're doing it in front of a patient, you're much more structured on what you're saying, you're much more thoughtful and focused on what you're saying because you've got your customer sitting right there. So we've gone from non-value-added time to extremely valuable time with the patient involved in our handoff process."

With a marked improvement in the quality of the handoff, the overall quality and safety of the care improved. Patients and families have responded very positively to the new method, with many families, in fact, making a point of participating directly in the handoff process. It gives them a sense of added confidence that all of the issues around their family member's case have been raised by the nurses, discussed, and passed along to the incoming shift nurse. "Family members add to the process and it's a huge confidence-builder for them," says Tachibana. "They'll say, 'Remember, this pain medication didn't work. Please don't give them this pain medication. Remember, that made Mom confused. Please don't do that.'"

Although the work has been quite successful, it was certainly not easy to implement. "We did the nurse-to-nurse handoff at the bedside and we would consider it a done deal and then we'd come back six months later and find it was not sustained," says Martha Purrier, RN. "We would lose the rigor of it and we found we were having to continue training. We'd look back and ask how did we train people in the first place? How thorough were we? Did we train them the right way?" After several months, a retrospective audit was conducted that identified variability with the implementation among different nursing units and shifts. It would take a great deal of focus and innovation to make this the way the work was completed with every patient, every time.

In-Room Documentation

During the RPIW process, the team found that nurses routinely broke away from the floor to complete their documentation in batches, which resulted in an additional thirty minutes to an hour off the floor away from patients. Nurses now use workstations on wheels (WOWs), which are easily maneuvered into patient rooms, enabling them to document whatever has been done to the patient at the time it is being done. The new system has nurses document in one-piece flow rather than batches.

Ponischil considers this a crucial breakthrough. When she was a frontline nurse she says she would squirrel away notes about patients and then do all of her documentation at the end of the shift. "Now we have computerized charting," she says, "so let's say you come on and you have four patients. You pull your four patients onto your screen and every hour something comes up telling you something is due—assessment, dressing change, pain medication. If an assessment is due, you click on it, the assessment form comes up, and you fill it out. It's really quite remarkable." This method not only eliminates the batch work at day's end, it also provides more timely, accurate information available electronically in real time to individuals on the patient care team.

Visual Work Environment

Toyota places significant emphasis on visual controls and visual management. "At Toyota and some of the other manufacturing companies that we visited, you could look at a factory floor and understand what was going on," says Tachibana.

"You look on a nursing floor and you can't figure out anything. You can't tell if they're ahead or behind. You can't tell anything, other than there's a lot of flurry happening here and it doesn't look calming, it doesn't look healing. Hospital hallways are also used for the movement of equipment and supplies along with the staff. Those hallways are also intended to be therapeutic corridors where patients walk and do their ambulation, but patients are always competing for space. When you put all of that stuff colliding together, who would want to come out of their room? You would look out the door and say, 'I'm not making my first attempt to walk in *that* maze.'"

The 5S method (sort, simplify, sweep, standardize, self-discipline) helped the team make the floor more visual and thus more readily understandable. Using 5S, the team established a designated place for everything ranging from thermometers to blood sugar measurement devices. Before the application of 5S, nurses would spend a good deal of time hunting for such items. Not only does this waste time, but it is a safety threat—when an important clinical tool is not readily available a patient could be at risk. Going through the steps of 5S to make sure there was a readily available place for everything saved tremendous amounts of time and reassured the staff that in a crisis they could find whatever they needed.

Another visual control is a board showing the status of all beds in the hospital at any given time—computerized and refreshed every fifteen seconds. The tool was not purchased off-the-shelf but was grown organically at Virginia Mason. Instead of going floor to floor or even room to room as used to be the custom, it is now possible to glance at a screen and know precisely how many beds are open and where. Electronic status boards are used to help staff prepare for a patient coming out of the recovery room. They also help to create a pull system so that patients are not pushed through the process. Instead, when a bed is ready the patients are pulled through the process, making it much more efficient and patient-centered.

"It used to be that a patient would go through the recovery stage and then we would start looking for a room," says Tachibana. "Now we know what floor they're going to, and, in fact, we know sometimes a week ahead of time as we look at those production schedules and the unit is watching that patient progressing closer and closer to the floor so they don't have the nurse at lunch when the patient is ready to come or they don't have the equipment ready. We've just streamlined the flow of a patient moving through as opposed to working in these silos where you wouldn't anticipate the patient is going to need a bed and figure out where that's going to be ahead of time and all these last-minute phone calls back and forth while the patient waits for hours."

Medical Emergency Teams

The changes enabling nurses to spend much more time with patients did not solve a nurse's problem when one of her five patients suddenly demanded an extraordinary degree of attention. Thus Virginia Mason instituted a system of Medical Emergency Teams (METs) to pitch in under difficult or uncertain circumstances. METs are common throughout health care, of course. Virginia Mason took the basic concept and created standard work to make a MET call more efficient and predictable. Applying VMPS, the MET process became more refined and standard work was clarified for each team member. For example, the critical care unit (CCU) nurse responding to a MET call assesses the situation using the SBAR method (Situation-Background-Assessment-Recommendation) to document the reason for the call. Other interventions developed auditory signals for MET calls through pagers and an overhead paging system.

Initially, Tachibana found nurses reluctant to call in the METs. "There is hesitancy inherent in nursing," she says. " 'Maybe I'm not seeing this the right way, maybe I'll give it little more time and see if the patient turns around.' Or they'll think, 'The doctor is here so it must be okay,' or 'I'm afraid to call the doctor because the doctor will yell at me because it will be seen as a statement to them that I don't trust what they told me.'"

Nurses were gun-shy in part because doctors sometimes reprimanded nurses who called in the teams. Ponischil says that some physicians resisted the teams because "It's a different group of caregivers who are going to mess around with their patients and possibly make decisions about their patients that they may not agree with. It was a lot of work to get the nurses comfortable with calling because there was such pushback from physicians. Not all the pushback has gone away, but now nurses are saying, 'You know, it's about the patient. We're going to do what's best for the patient.' And I say to the nurses, 'You know, for the most part, physicians are very accepting of this, but, once in a while you will get a physician who may question it. It's okay.' Someone who hasn't been looking at the patient for the past two days might say, 'Hey, did you think about this?' or 'This is what I'm seeing.'"

From the point of view of many physicians, MET calls were something very new and quite different than the way they had been trained and socialized. It was another powerful example of just how difficult change can be in health care. Many doctors were instinctively resistant to change because they had been taught "the best way" by men and women they looked up to (and in some cases idolized). During their education and training they had invested so much time and effort to master the best way that they often suspicious of anyone telling them there might be a better way to do something.

This was also another example of where the Virginia Mason physician compact played a foundational role. With the compact in place, there was a broad understanding that the patient came first and that change would be necessary to make that operational at all times. Over time, most doctors at Virginia Mason have come to accept and in many cases welcome, MET calls.

Nurses are urged to call a MET when they feel the need for an additional set of eyes or when they are pushed to the limit of their capacity and need more help. In fact, the new standard *requires* nurses to call in a MET any time they are worried about a patient. "It's not an option anymore," says Tachibana. "If the patient reaches a certain level it is an *expectation* to call. We want another set of eyes, a redundant system to make sure we haven't missed anything." Management is so insistent on enforcing this that nurses have been required to sign a statement saying they fully understand their obligation under certain conditions to call in the team.

Some of the most difficult cases are when a patient deteriorates, but does so almost imperceptibly over time. "It's like when your kids are growing up and when did it happen that all of a sudden they're taller than you?" says Ponischil. She recalls a particular case where a nurse was worried that a patient was not improving and wanted to call in a MET. The physician, however, said he had the situation under control and told the nurse *not* to place the call. The nurse knew this was a patient who never complained even when he was in pain, though. Now he said he was having trouble breathing and did not feel comfortable. Even though the doctor explicitly told the nurse not to call, she did so. The team quickly arrived, discovered the patient had a respiratory issue requiring intubation, and promptly transferred the patient to the CCU.

Shortly after the event, the nurse arrived at Ponischil's office in tears, shaken by the thought that if she had done what the doctor ordered something terrible might have happened to the patient. Ponischil reassured the nurse and called the physician. "I told him, 'I have a nurse crying in my office and you two need to talk.' And they did talk and they cleared the air and the physician said to her, 'Of course you did the right thing. I just wasn't seeing what you were seeing. Of course, it was right for you to call.'"

Tachibana and her team worried about these types of cases where the patient's deterioration was difficult to detect over time and they wanted to catch them before they reached an acute stage. Toward that end, they established broader, more detailed guidelines for nurses to call the team, such as when key metrics including blood pressure, heart rate, or respiratory rate move out of a certain range. In these instances, especially when physicians are tied up elsewhere, nurses call the MET team consisting of a respiratory therapist, a critical care nurse, and a hospitalist physician. The team arrives quickly and assesses the patient. In some instances they provide rapid treatment, in others they raise questions or make suggestions. It provides another check and there is a strong belief at Virginia Mason in successive checks—in getting a fresh set of eyes on the situation.

One result of instituting METs was that MET calls increased and avoidable codes decreased significantly. The reason? Teams got to the patient before cardiac arrest or other urgent trouble. "I'm confident we're saving lives by doing this work and we're making the nurses' work more fulfilling because you can't imagine what that felt like to be a nurse out on a floor and not be able to get someone's attention or not be able to get the help you needed for the patient," Tachibana says. "We used to have nurses driving home at the end of their shift feeling like total failures because they couldn't manage to get the help at the bedside. So those types of demoralizing kinds of shifts don't happen in the same way. It's not as though there aren't frustrations with some elements of care, but, boy, it's not that browbeating like it used to be."

Another layer of protection for patients came in the form of a clinical nurse leader. Tachibana and her team found that the care needs and coordination of certain complex patients—many of whom were in the hospital for stays of a week or longer—was somewhat beyond the skill set of less experienced nurses. This was especially apparent during nursing shortages when many new nurses, frequently recent graduates, were hired. Their training, commitment, and enthusiasm were excellent, but many did not yet have the ability to care for the most complex cases. Thus, she created a new role for nurses with particular abilities, often nurses with a great deal of experience coupled with an advanced degree of training. These clinical nurse leaders watch for care problems that might emerge in complex patients even as they watch for defects in the care system that need improvement. All of this helps the frontline nurse to remain near the patient's bedside.

Hourly Rounding: From Reactive to Proactive

Hospitals are places where the unexpected happens, but they are also places where the vast majority of a patient's needs can be anticipated. That, at least, was the firm belief that Tachibana and her team carried to the work. They knew that nursing care was at its best when it was proactive rather than reactive as was the case with hourly rounding. After the RPIW searching for ways to get nurses spending more time with patients, Tachibana and her team implemented a system of hourly nurse rounds as a way to get nurses to *anticipate* patient needs rather than *react* to them. She and her colleagues consider a call light to be a defect because it means the care team has failed to anticipate a patient's needs. Under ideal conditions, anticipating a patient's needs happens in a calm, predictable fashion. When nurses anticipate rather than react, they are less likely to be interrupted in the midst of caring for a patient.

These sorts of changes are particularly difficult because they often contradict cultural traditions in nursing. "A lot of nursing has historically been extremely reactive," Tachibana says. "We wait until the patient is done with recovery before we figure out what room they're going to. We wait until the sick call comes before we figure out where the staff member is going to come from. We wait until patients put on their call light, thinking they're not going to go to the bathroom. All these things could be anticipated. Patients are going to need to go to the bathroom at some time or they're going to have a question or need help getting comfortable in their bed. Some patients are more willing and able to ask for help. Others will hold back as long as possible because they might be embarrassed and they'll wait until they have such an urgency or such a need. To the extent that you can plan, you have more control over your work cycle and less chaos. You can help a patient just beginning to experience pain much easier than dealing with the worst pain of their life."

Tachibana, Ponischil, and their team prepared a choreography for rounds before training staff nurses. The training was carefully planned and done in a direct, hands-on fashion by Tachibana, Ponischil, and other senior leaders. "It's a series of steps starting with introducing yourself," says Ponischil. "Hi, Mrs. Smith, it's Rowena again. I'm here to check on you. Are you comfortable?' And the reason why we say, 'Are you *comfortable?*' rather than 'How are you doing?' or 'How are you?' or 'Are you okay?' is because if you say 'How are you?' even if they feel really bad, a lot of people will say 'I'm fine, I'm okay.' But 'Are you comfortable?' elicits a lot of remarks from patients, from the temperature of the room to their bed is uncomfortable to they're uncomfortable because they don't know the plan of care. So it runs the gamut.

"The next step is making sure they don't need to go to the bathroom. So if you're a patient and you are alert, oriented, able to get up, you know when you have to go to the bathroom. It's a reminder to you to make sure that you go to the bathroom and that you don't wait until the last minute so that you will have to rush and possibly trip. For a patient who is alert and oriented but doesn't know when they have to go, we remind them. 'You know, it's been a couple of hours since you've been to the bathroom—why don't we go now? I have time to take you.' For a patient who's not alert and oriented, doesn't know when they have to go, can't feel it, we say, 'Mrs. Smith, it's time to go to the bathroom.'"

Part of the checklist also includes making sure that everything a patient might need—personal items, telephone, tissues, water, and so on—is easily within reach. This is important for patient comfort and convenience, but also for safety, as many falls occur when patients struggle to reach for something outside their grasp. The checklist also requires that nurses make sure the bed setting is correct and that if there is a bed alarm (for patients who are not supposed to get up on their own) that it is working properly. Nurses then give patients an opportunity to ask for any other help they might need, says Ponischil. "I'm going to check on another patient now and I'll be back in about an hour. Is there anything I can do for you before I leave?" That offers patients an opportunity to bring up anything else that might be on their mind and also reassures them that the nurse will be returning. The final step, before leaving the patient's room, is for the nurse to sign a sheet on the door documenting that she completed all items according the checklist. It is a classic example of standard work and "very purposeful," says Ponischil. "It's very different than saying, 'Did you look in on the patient every hour?'"

None of this is meant to suggest that the changes were easy. Initially, some of these changes yielded dramatic results. But, over time, as was so often the case throughout Virginia Mason, leaders discovered that there was real difficulty in holding the gains. Kaizen Promotion Office (KPO) Director Martha Purrier, RN, and Dana Nelson-Peterson, RN, KPO Administrative Director, reexamined the hourly rounding process several times, changing the training content on a number of occasions. They kept going back and each time they found variation in the work they would adjust the training. After doggedly sticking with it, they saw that gains were holding much better over time. "Now we have solid content transferable to every patient situation," says Nelson-Peterson.

As difficult as it has been to both do and sustain the work, the results to date are undeniable: Prior to the changes nurses were spending approximately two thirds of their time *away* from patients. After the changes they were spending about 90 percent of their time *with* patients.

Knowing the Frontline Work

How could it be that such elemental changes—moving handoff to the bedside, clustering rooms under a nurse's watch, placing a few essential supplies in a patient room—make a meaningful difference in the time a clinician spends with a patient? Viewed another way, how did the system reach such a point where these sorts of changes could make such an enormous difference? And why weren't all of these changes made standard practice in American medicine long ago?

There might be many explanations but certainly one is that the historical reality in health care for decades was the virtual absence of systems thinking. In the late 1980s, Drs. Donald Berwick and Paul Batalden, two of the founders of the Institute for Health Care Improvement in Cambridge, Massachusetts, joined forces with Blanton Godfrey, PhD, chief of quality at Bell Labs, to conduct an important experiment. The National Demonstration Project was intended to determine whether industrial quality techniques advocated by W. Edwards Deming and others—techniques focused on *systems* rather than *individuals*—might be applied successfully in health care. The project brought together twenty-two leading U.S. hospitals and twenty-two major companies and organizations known for quality. Experienced quality experts from industry and academia were matched with the health care teams to tackle a series of challenges. Some of the projects met with a fair amount of success, others less so. The critical bit of learning, though, was the realization by the industry experts that people in health care—very smart, hard-working people—were largely clueless when it came to the concept of systems thinking. At one point in the process a physician was having difficulty under-standing the idea of a process in medicine and Blanton Godfrey said, "You're the MD and you do a beautiful diagnosis. But what if blood is drawn from the wrong patient? What if you cannot read the X-ray? What if the pharmacist doesn't put the right thing in the bottle? We're talking about managing a system!"

The absence of systems thinking was obvious to Virginia Mason leaders. "You focused on clinical care and you did that patient by patient, but you really didn't look systematically at how this system worked together," says Tachibana. "During the 1990s, we did this slash and burn in health care. What was slashed was management and then you didn't have onsite managers. I had a period of time as a frontline manager where I had multiple units, and there was no way that I could be physically present on any one of those units for a period of time long enough to really help change these kinds of processes. During this time, we saw a lot of management leaving the work site because those positions were eliminated. We went through an era where management was not considered particularly valuable. Now, the role of management has shifted, and I certainly think we've gotten clear here on what they're responsible for. But we've been very deliberate in the hospital setting to rebuild a leadership structure."

To get those leaders out onto the floor where they can see the work at its most granular is central to the Virginia Mason Production System. Managers must be on the *genba*, and they must understand the work as it is actually happening—not as it was designed. They must understand the problems at a macro and micro level and commit themselves to identifying and eliminating waste. And as simple as some of these steps appear—as simple as some of them *are*—it is folly to think that this sort of change is easy. It is demanding and requires a level of energetic, sustained leadership that is not at all common in health care. It takes time and follow-up and a fanatical attention to detail. Without all of these elements the change fades and the teams default to old habits.

Dramatic Change in Nurse Culture

All of the efforts to standardize care and provide the kind of rational systems that enable nurses to do what they do so well have helped change the nursing culture within Virginia Mason. Standards that were poorly designed are now more clearly outlined. There has also been a change from a kind of cowboy culture to one focused on teamwork. Formerly, there was both a lack of accountability and no clear sense of mission within the medical center. As a result of these elements nurses took any sort of criticism personally. Discussing a system problem was difficult to do without nurses feeling as though they were being blamed.

Another cultural shift involved convincing nurses to work as a team toward standard work (as opposed to the old cowboy culture). "We used to heavily reinforce the value of the person who could kind of swoop in and save the day, the one who did the exceptional things," says Tachibana. "No one followed standard work and the cowboys did great things in health care, but they were probably some of the most dangerous people, too, because they weren't following standards. They were multitasking, they were doing everything that led to bigger errors. We wanted to make everyone successful, so one of the things I did early on was meet a lot with nursing students, because if our system didn't make sense to a nursing student, it wasn't safe enough. You shouldn't have to be the *super* nurse to be a *good* nurse. Everybody should be able to be a good nurse, but we didn't have our system built that way."

While the Virginia Mason nursing culture was changing rapidly, the old culture held nurses firmly in its grasp at countless other provider organizations throughout the country. Change in nursing is happening, but its pace is often glacial and many organizations remain firmly rooted in the culture that Tachibana and her colleagues have worked so hard to change.

Clarity has become an important watchword in nursing at Virginia Mason. If there is a problem and its cause or solution is not clear, the leadership team makes it clear so that all nurses grasp it. And they have sought to create rational processes that eliminate the need for nurses to find ways to work around roadblocks. Before the VMPS work in nursing it was important to know who to call to get anything done because the formal system didn't work very well. Now, the process makes it possible for any nurse to get done whatever a patient might need.

The new system has also helped foster more collegial relationships between and among departments. Formerly, nurses and others throughout the medical center tended to operate within their silos with little understanding of what was going on in other areas and little if any empathy for people in those departments. Nurses felt constant strain in a system that was not patient-focused and that often did not allow the nurse to provide the best possible care. They would see glitches not as system failures but as the fault of another department or individual. Sometimes it would get personal. "There was a lot of finger pointing before," says Tachibana, "nurses finger pointing to pharmacy, 'Why can't you get the medications up here? What don't you get? These patients are in pain.'

Or, 'These patients need their antibiotic. What's wrong with you?' It was just so antagonistic because you didn't understand the interfaces or how these two systems flowed together. Once we were able to start working on some of those processes and they made the work life easier, there was much more respect. You understood each other's world because you're coming together in teams to resolve the problem."

Clarity of mission at Virginia Mason has helped advance cultural change within nursing. Nurses typically got into their profession with a passion to help the patient, and it has always been the work directly with patients that nurses have found rewarding. In the absence of systems and a focused mission, conflicts flare between and among departments, making the life of a nurse difficult and frustrating. Tachibana observes the cultural changes on the floor, and she sees the results there as well in satisfaction surveys among the nursing staff. "It's a total transformation," she says. "It starts with clarity of what we're about, what our vision is and where we're going. I can't say in my previous twenty years in this organization I was ever so clear on where we're going, what we're working on—*the patient first.*"

A more stable work environment has significantly helped the nursing staff. Historically, there was little if any predictability in terms of how many nurses would show up for a given shift, leaving supervisors on edge, worried about ending up short-staffed. They would often overcompensate and wind up over-staffed, wasting resources. Unpredictability meant days when all the nurses on a given floor were familiar with the peculiar traditions of that floor and other days when half the nurses would be new or floaters who knew nothing about the standard procedures on that floor.

Using VMPS, Virginia Mason created a production board of strategic staffing for the year that forecasts needs. Regularly updated, this system enables leaders to see how many nurses are on staff, how many are on medical leave or vacation, or how many are in the orientation process. The system allows managers to see how many are actually available to work caring for patients and has brought significant stability to the workforce. This is a transformational change from the practice of nurse managers frantically searching to cover a shift.

The difference between the Virginia Mason hospital nursing units of six and seven years ago versus today is astonishing. The units run far more efficiently and smoothly. The quality of care is markedly better and measurably safer. Staff and patient satisfaction scores have improved.

This work was not easy, though. Dana Nelson-Peterson and Martha Purrier, nurse leaders on the front lines of these initiatives, say that making the nursing cells stick took time and a great deal of effort. "We learned with the hospital group over the past five years that when you go back and you don't see what you expect to see, you ask why," says Nelson-Peterson. "Was it bad design? Lack of training? Where did we fail with this? If something is designed in the very best way to do something the staff will follow it—so why didn't they?"

In part, their success was a product of a constant effort to test and measure and find failure. When advances did not hold over time they would find out why and fix the problem. This was a wonderful example of *kaizen*—continuous incremental improvement. After years of work and thousands and thousands of incremental improvements, Virginia Mason has succeeded in dramatically increasing the amount of time nurses spend at the bedside with patients. They have tackled some of the toughest safety issues—including falls—and have made progress in every area they have taken on.

"Everything is kind of coming together," says Dana Nelson-Peterson. "It's hard work—hard to sustain cultural change"—which is why it is essential to keep going back and checking and working to get back on track when gains have not been sustained over time. Bedside handoff, she says, is a perfect example. "If we'd been happy with bedside handoff two years ago," she says, "we would never have had the breakthrough we have today."

Shorter Length of Stay

A beneficial result of all the work Tachibana and her team did within the hospital was a shorter length of stay for patients. VMPS methods enabled Tachibana and her team to identify and remove waste throughout the nursing process. As they did so, they drilled down into length of stay looking for possible waste of time that would keep patients in the hospital too long. In a system where the patient comes first, it was critical to determine whether processes within the medical center contributed to a longer hospital stay than necessary. The Virginia Mason average length of stay was four and a half days. Tachibana's team arbitrarily selected a stay of six days or longer for study and saw that a delay in starting adequate nutrition could delay the recovery process. Getting calories and nutrients into patients is critical to the quality and speed of their recovery. The team conducted a number of RPIWs and figured out ways to get better nutrition to patients more rapidly. The team also discovered that there were delays in getting patients mobilized—up on their feet and moving around to accelerate the pace of recovery. RPIWs helped accelerate mobilization, as well.

In all, by focusing on the elimination of waste, the team was able to reduce the average length of stay by nearly a half-day. This was hugely important, for it not only meant a shorter stay—and less risk—for all patients, but it also significantly increased the hospital capacity. This, in turn, has a powerful financial impact, and it has enabled Virginia Mason to increase revenue as a result of increased capacity.

Much of this foundational work in the hospital will be able to be executed in a more effective and efficient manner in a new hospital building that will soon be completed at Virginia Mason. Scheduled for June 2011, the first phase of occupancy will begin. It will be the first hospital in the country entirely planned and built using patient-centric principles to reduce waste, improve quality, and make a perfect health care experience possible. An unprecedented number of VMPS events—3Ps, RPIWs, and more—were used to translate a vision of the new hospital into reality. The building was designed in the VMPS collaborative fashion and included input from the front lines of care—the frontline providers and patients as well. With insights from team members and patients, the Virginia Mason team has taken a very different approach to an array of elements—from eliminating some waiting rooms to a much more patient-focused way for people and supplies to move through the medical center. Parallel corridors, for example, separate the flow of patients and providers, thus eliminating a problem where hospital floors were laid out along the lines of a hotel, with a single corridor serving all functions. Virginia Mason created separate zones for patients and providers. In the patient areas there is no clutter and few supplies. Treatment rooms are designed to bring services to the patient—similar to the approach used in the cancer center. In every way, the hospital places the patient first.

Chapter Eight

Better, Faster, More Affordable

In 2004, Dr. Robert Mecklenburg was a well-known diabetes specialist who held two prestigious positions at Virginia Mason: Chief of Medicine and member of the board of trustees. Mecklenburg had gone on the original journey to Japan with Gary Kaplan and the rest of the senior team, and he had been among the early enthusiastic adopters of the Virginia Mason Production System (VMPS). He had worked diligently to integrate the new methods into the medical center.

One day in August 2004, something happened that would fundamentally change the direction of Dr. Mecklenburg's career. That something was a visit from Dr. Donald Storey, the Senior Medical Director of the Aetna Aexcel Performance Networks. Dr. Storey, via Aetna, purchased care from Virginia Mason and other entities on behalf of companies such as Starbucks, Costco, Alaska Airlines, and quite a few others. To better serve these huge companies, Aetna had developed a select network of high-value providers in various medical specialties ranging from orthopedics to cardiology. Aetna selected providers for the network based on quality and cost. High-quality performers who charged reasonable fees would be included and providers with less than stellar quality or excessive costs would be excluded. Aetna was deeply committed to this approach, believing that measurement and transparency were powerful forces to improve quality and control costs.

In determining which providers to include within the network, Aetna had done an in-depth analysis on cost data comparing various provider organizations in greater Seattle. That day in August 2004, Dr. Storey sat down with Dr. Mecklenburg and delivered some disturbing news. Storey said the data showed Virginia Mason was more expensive than its major competitors in a variety of specialties, including gastroenterology, neurology, and cardiology. Because Aetna was representing the new network as exclusive to *high-quality* providers, Mecklenburg considered Virginia Mason's inclusion absolutely essential. Exclusion from the network would constitute a financial and reputational blow.

"Don said, 'I've got a problem here,'" recalls Dr. Mecklenburg. "He said, 'I think Virginia Mason is great, but it costs more to receive care here. And many of my clients are competing in a global economy, and they are really burdened by the cost of care.'"

Storey told Mecklenburg that unless something changed Aetna would have no choice but to let their contract with Virginia Mason expire. Storey had held similar meetings with several other provider organizations in Seattle and their responses—as was historically so often the case in discussions between health plans and providers—had been argumentative, even pugnacious. Of the larger provider organizations in Seattle, most made the Aetna standard in some specialty categories but not in others. "Most of them argued with me or rejected the data," Storey says. "'And besides,' they'd tell me, 'our patients are sicker.'" He laughs at the recollection: "Everybody's patients were sicker!"

Would Mecklenburg respond as other providers had? Perhaps in the old days he might have done so, but this was a new day at Virginia Mason and the old way of doing business was no longer good enough. He made an immediate decision to engage with Storey and to try and understand the matter from the point of view not only of Aetna, but of the companies they represented as well. Mecklenburg was surprised by Storey's message to him that day, particularly in light of the fact that around that time other health plans had told him that Virginia Mason was an efficient provider in these very areas. Storey said the data were not perfect and, in fact, providers had long been suspicious of the accuracy of health plan data. Yet Mecklenburg decided not to argue about the data. For one thing it seemed fairly accurate to him. For another, he says he knew "that no matter what the figures were, that we could take a great deal of costly waste out of the health care delivery system. So I did not care to spend any effort at all disputing Aetna's methods. We cost too much, period."

Mecklenburg asked Storey for a chance to think more about the issue and come up with an improvement plan, but, in the meantime, Mecklenburg asked Storey to keep Virginia Mason within the network. Storey wanted to agree but he needed to consult with his customers—benefit managers at the large companies. As the two men talked they agreed that it would make sense for Mecklenburg to speak with the benefit managers directly and make the case for Virginia Mason's commitment to change.

Identifying The Customer

A conference call was arranged for a few weeks later and the benefit managers from Starbucks, Costco, and Alaska Airlines, among others, were gathered with Don Storey at the Aetna offices. It so happened that Mecklenburg was attending a medical conference in San Francisco with Gary Kaplan and both men got on the call back to Seattle. David Dreis, MD, Medical Director, Clinical Outcomes at Virginia Mason, was sitting with the group at Aetna. The conversation quickly turned to the idea of being customer-focused, and there seemed to be some disagreement about who the customer really was.

"Who do you think the customer is?" Storey asked and Gary Kaplan said at Virginia Mason there was no doubt about it—the patient was customer. Says Storey: "At this point I hear what is damn near a scream from [former Starbucks benefits manager] Annette King saying, 'What about us—we're paying the bills!' And I'm looking at David Dreis and his eyes are practically bugged out of his head!" Annette King's comment was jarring in part because of its intensity and in part because it was followed by a chorus from the other benefits managers echoing her sentiments. But it was jarring as well, for it was an idea with which the physicians had never fully engaged before. "They had never thought about the people paying the bills being the customer," says Storey.

After the din died down there was "this moment of silence and I did not realize what an awakening that was for them until I talked with Bob Mecklenburg later," says Annette King. But nothing could have been more obvious to the benefits managers, who were, after all, paying 90 percent of the cost of care for their employees. For the doctors, the call was a powerful revelation. "They were very, very clear on this—that they were our customers, too," says Mecklenburg. "There was a lot of emotion in that call—four or five voices speaking as one."

When the call was over and Dr. Dreis had left, Storey and the benefit managers discussed the matter. They agreed that it was important to keep a prestigious institution such as Virginia Mason in the network while Mecklenburg and his colleagues worked on how to correct the situation.

Mecklenburg knew that his team—physicians and their administrative counterparts in eighteen different hospital departments—needed to hear about this, and he wanted them to hear it directly from Don Storey. That November, Storey made the steep climb from his downtown Seattle office up to the Virginia Mason campus. He stood before the eighteen section heads and their administrative partners and displayed costs comparing Virginia Mason to its competitors. "I said, 'We like you guys—you're good docs, but this is how you look to these employers,'" displaying numbers very much unfavorable to Virginia Mason. "You're costing more than these other groups. I like you guys fine, but they are my customers, and I have to serve them. We're going to need some sort of change here."

Storey's message hit the physicians hard. "This was shocking," says Dr. Andrew Friedman, section head of Physical Medicine and Rehabilitation. "At Virginia Mason we have always felt like we're on the cutting edge and we do good medicine. So here's Don saying, we might not include you in our network anymore because you're really not performing as well as we would like you to. I was kind of stunned." Storey's attitude was direct, though not confrontational. In fact, his message was "Can you work with me on this?" Mecklenburg had been right to bring him in, for when the bogeyman of an insurance company is at a distance it is easy for doctors to reflexively demonize it as callous and greedy. Dr. Storey was neither. He came across, in fact, as someone quite reasonably looking for high-quality, affordable care for his clients.

When Storey departed, the room fell silent. Typically at such gatherings, there would be a buzz in the air—much talking, exchanging ideas, and questions. Not this day. Most of the doctors in the room—perhaps all of them— had worked behind an invisible wall that protected them from the marketplace. Few, if any, had ever met with an insurance company representative. Fewer still harbored anything other than contempt for insurance companies. But in the silence that settled on the room there was a humbling and tacit admission that the health care landscape had changed. These doctors had just collided head-on with the marketplace, and it was not a good feeling.

Mecklenburg opened it up to discussion by asking what everybody wanted to do—though he had his own idea. He did not believe for a second that this situation would be resolved in the traditional brinksmanship negotiation between health plans and providers. More than that, he did not *want* it resolved that way. Mecklenburg knew that without significant change they would surely lose the Aetna business, and he was convinced that something different was needed here—namely a much greater awareness on the part of the doctors sitting before him of marketplace realities. The world was changing and isolation from those realities was no longer an option. Mecklenburg steered the group toward trying to set up a meeting with the benefit managers from companies Don Storey represented. There was some discussion and clear agreement that the solution lay with the Virginia Mason Production System. They would put together a plan to demonstrate that they could use VMPS to revamp their systems to provide high-quality, efficient care while controlling costs. Then they would seek a meeting to present their plan to the benefit managers.

This reaction was a sea change from the way business had been conducted in the past. Typically, confronted with this sort of threat from an insurer, the Virginia Mason response would have been, according to Mecklenburg: "We're the best, our patients are sicker, your data is flawed, and you need us more than we need you." But the new attitude was "With your help we will reduce cost and improve service and quality for you and your employees." This attitudinal shift was revolutionary.

The more Mecklenburg had been thinking about this, in fact, the more he saw it not as a crisis but as an opportunity; an enormously valuable opportunity to figure out exactly what the marketplace wanted in health care and then to devise a way to deliver precisely that. "It was the crisis we really *needed*," says Mecklenburg. "For two years we'd been applying what we learned from Toyota to internal processes at Virginia Mason. Don Storey was providing us with the opportunity to take the Virginia Mason Production System to the marketplace."

Mecklenburg spoke with Storey, who agreed to bring the employers to a meeting at Virginia Mason where the doctors would outline their improvement plans. Dr. Friedman was fascinated by this and had a sense something positive might emerge from it. He noticed that Storey's somewhat draconian message was wrapped in a softer rhetorical package and that Mecklenburg seemed oddly upbeat in the face of it. Friedman noticed something of a shared team spirit between Storey and Mecklenburg. "Here's Don Storey from an insurance company coming and saying, 'We may be cutting you off,' and yet here was this enthusiastic Bob Mecklenburg saying, 'Well, this is really great. This is an impetus for us to change.'"

In the meantime, Mecklenburg called Annette King and asked whether he could come by and see her. She was somewhat taken aback, for she generally only heard from providers when they were seeking higher payments. The chief of medicine at a major medical center calling to request a meeting for how he might better serve her employees—now *that* was unheard of. "He came to my office and he really wanted to engage with us, to work on these issues," she says. "I never had anybody come and say 'We want you to work with us on how we care for your employees.'" She later told the *Wall Street Journal* that she "couldn't believe a doctor was making an appointment with me and asking what I wanted."

It was at that private meeting that King told Mecklenburg she had a real issue with back pain among her employees and asked Mecklenburg to work on a plan to improve quality and reduce cost. Mecklenburg was surprised back pain was an issue at Starbucks, but the reality was that Starbucks employees were on their feet for many hours at a time. "I could hardly believe it," he says. "Who would imagine that back pain was anything to get very excited about, and yet there it was: Large numbers of affected employees and a very high aggregate cost."

"We Can Do Better"

It took a couple of months to pull the meeting together—largely to give the Virginia Mason team time to work on their presentation. In February 2005, benefits directors from several major companies including Starbucks and Alaska

Airlines—along with Don Storey and a couple of his Aetna colleagues—gathered with the doctors at Virginia Mason. Some preliminary work had been done before the meeting to target specific areas each employer wanted to see addressed; areas that were particularly costly for them. Starbucks, of course, had selected back pain, one company chose migraine headaches, another focused on cardiac conditions, and another was interested in gastro-esophageal reflux disease (GERD)—essentially severe acid reflux. The list was fascinating to Mecklenburg and his physician colleagues, who could readily see that rather than focusing on highly complex diseases, the employers were interested in common, nonurgent conditions that nonetheless caused discomfort and disability. The cost burdens for companies wasn't due to "the infrequent case of pancreatic cancer," says Mecklenburg. "It wasn't the exotic thyroid cancer that allowed me to use specialized training and experience to the maximum. It was back pain and headaches! When we looked at our own list of the most common conditions we treat, the striking thing is that most of these conditions are uncomplicated and most of us when we get sick get sick with uncomplicated conditions—the case of back pain from lifting a case of beer out of the trunk or the occasional headache. So the population is like that. Relatively few of us get ICU-type illnesses. We've all been sick, but almost all of our illnesses are those from which we recover pretty easily. We might need a little medical care, but we most often don't need a *lot* of care."

When the benefit managers gathered at a small Virginia Mason auditorium, the physicians were well-prepared. Doctors specializing in each of the four areas selected by the employers made presentations to the group analyzing the problem and proposing possible solutions. The basic theme was that in each area the team would apply VMPS to eliminate waste and provide value-added care *only*. The idea was that this would improve quality and cut costs. "The docs were saying, 'We can do better,'" says Mecklenburg, "and we are committed to do so.'"

Storey and the benefit managers were impressed with the thoroughness of the presentations and with the fact that the doctors clearly understood the nature of the problems faced by employers; that they were thinking in a new way and viewing the employers as customers. "The presentations were very well-received by the plan sponsors," says Storey.

This was a defining moment, for it represented a radical cultural shift for the physicians. Most doctors, of course, had never met any administrative official of a company paying them for care. And now here were the Virginia Mason doctors essentially tailoring their care plan to the company needs.

"As doctors we all had a clear idea of what we loved to do, the conditions we wished to treat," Mecklenburg says. "I had come from NIH [National Institutes of Health] as a subspecialist in reproductive endocrinology, and I loved evaluating and treating rare causes of infertility. When I arrived at Virginia Mason it became very clear within three days that what the community needed was care for the most common endocrine problem—Type 2 diabetes—with much less demand for reproductive endocrinology. I accepted that reality and have had a wonderful career treating thousands and thousands of people with diabetes and other common conditions while treating very few persons with rare reproductive problems."

Thus, rather than trying to align the marketplace with doctors' interests, the solution was to align providers with the interests of the marketplace. "Retailers tell you that you have to know your customer's need and then meet that need," he says. "With our usual approach to health care delivery it seemed to me that we had it backwards. We were determined to sell what we wanted to produce without understanding what our customers needed as their first priority."

Mecklenburg, Dr. Andrew Friedman, and their colleagues were beginning to understand that from a purely business perspective, Virginia Mason was a supplier to these companies. Starbucks, for example, had a great depth of understanding of the procurement process when it came to purchasing coffee beans, milk, paper cups, and so on.

"These items need to be of consistent high quality and to be delivered on time, in the right place, and in the right quantity—and at an affordable price," says Mecklenburg. "All our employers procured goods and services to produce their products and Virginia Mason was one of the largest suppliers for each of these employers. When you look at the cost structures of these companies, it is very clear that health care suppliers such as Virginia Mason were among their most important suppliers in terms of their cost in producing the products they sell in the marketplace. And you've heard this from Howard Schultz at Starbucks—that the cost of health care for Starbucks was nearly as much as the cost of coffee beans. And you've heard the same kind of observation on the cost of health care compared to the cost of steel from General Motors. That's what they were saying to us, that we are important suppliers, and 'What we need to procure from you is quality health care delivered without delays, because this is essential for us to maintain a healthy, productive workforce and to manage our direct and indirect costs of care.'"

Value Stream Reveals Huge Waste

After the presentations, Mecklenburg extended an invitation to the companies to join him and his colleagues in what Mecklenburg and Storey called "marketplace collaboratives." These gatherings were intended to bring together three key players—company, insurer, and medical center—to focus on that particular employer's concerns and map out solutions. Mecklenburg believed that to make progress he had to get the employers, Aetna, and his team sitting together in search of common ground. He had learned firsthand how valuable it was for Virginia Mason to include patients in the improvement process, and he believed the same principle applied to employers. Each marketplace collaborative included a benefits manager from the employer, a couple of providers, and a representative of the insurance company. In addition, Storey and Mecklenburg would both attend the sessions, as would a finance person from Virginia Mason. The approach was similar to a Rapid Process Improvement Workshop (RPIW) in that the team would examine the value stream to understand the reality of how care for a particular condition was administered. The idea was to hunt down waste and come up with a new approach that eliminated all non-value-added steps in favor of evidence-based medicine. Once the teams had determined the value stream they would focus on determining exactly what the evidence was for each step to show it added value in the process.

The collaborative model used five principles:

1. Focus on customers' highest costs.
2. Adopt customers' definition of quality.
3. Create evidence-based value streams.
4. Employ systems engineering tools to remove waste.
5. Use a cost-reduction business model.

The collaborative for Starbucks included Annette King, Drs. Friedman, and Mecklenburg, Storey, and several others. They had accomplished the first step of the collaborative process—identifying back pain as a high-cost issue to tackle—and now turned their attention to identifying a definition of quality care from the customer's point of view.

Transparency was the starting point. With each of the employers, the Virginia Mason team did an analysis of their issue and, in marketplace collaborative meetings, fully disclosed the clinical and financial details. To do so for back pain, for example, the Virginia Mason team mapped out a value stream revealing precisely what happened to typical back pain patients. At their best, value stream maps strip bare a process and reveal the truth. In this instance the truth was that the process was rife with waste and inefficiency. It took too long to answer the phone at the spine clinic when patients called. It took weeks—sometimes a month or more—for patients to get an appointment. In the meantime, while a patient waited, he or she was in pain, often with limited mobility and a reduced ability to work—nearly always with mounting anxiety or even depression in some cases. The value stream revealed the whole process in striking fashion.

During the meeting to explain their findings to Annette King and Dr. Storey, Dr. Friedman talked about the way back pain was treated at Virginia Mason. He explained that a patient might enter into the medical center from many different portals. "They might see a primary care physician, they might see a specialist in neurosurgery/neurology or physical medicine, and they would then have to wait for their visit," he explained. They might have an MRI and "then have another wait to review that scan, then they would have another wait in order to finally get into physical therapy, where they would work on some of this reactivation."

Annette King had never seen anything quite like it—a value stream detailing each step a patient followed in the back pain process—and she was astonished.

"You could see that it took a long time to get in and get seen and there were significant delays between each step in the treatment," she says. "And it took an unbelievable amount of time to finally resolve the condition and an incredible amount of money." She was particularly disturbed by the excessive use and high cost of MRI tests.

A key step in trying to untangle this mess was the decision by the Virginia Mason doctors to clearly define the difference between complicated and uncomplicated back pain. This was critically important because the treatments for these two categories were significantly different. Complicated back pain often required extensive treatment, imaging tests, and even surgery. Yet Friedman and his colleagues found that more than 80 percent of patients with back pain fell into the uncomplicated category where a $1,200 MRI (with a margin of about $450 going to Virginia Mason) provided little or no value to the diagnosis and treatment. This would mean a small minority of back patients would need an imaging test. Friedman pledged to King that by applying evidence-based medicine, they would dramatically reduce the use of MRI testing.

As Friedman walked King and Storey through the tangled details of the value stream, it wasn't just the MRI that had no value in treating uncomplicated back pain—*it was just about every other step in the process, as well.* "The value stream showed that 90 percent of what we did was no help at all," says Mecklenburg. "Does an appointment with an orthopedic surgeon, a neurologist, a neurosurgeon help for uncomplicated back pain? The evidence says no. Does an MRI help? No. As far as we could tell the only thing the evidence showed was worth anything was physical therapy."

During that first marketplace collaborative meeting, Annette King scanned the value stream, and it could not have been more obvious what to do. "If the only thing giving value is physical therapy then why don't we start with that?" she asked.

Same-Day Access

Also obvious in the value stream was the lengthy delay for patients to get an appointment with a provider. Dr. Friedman explained to King and the others that it would often take forty-five days to get patients to where they needed to be and

Friedman knew that this was not even close to the level of quality he wanted to deliver. "There are curves in medicine that show patients lose function over time," he says, "and those curves really start to go down to irrecoverable loss of function at somewhere around six weeks, and so we were getting people at the point where they might have lost enough in terms of social function, mood, physical fitness so that we were really going to have a hard time getting them back."

That's all Annette King needed to hear. "Andrew," she said, "I need you to see my employees right away, as soon as possible."

"How about the same day?" Mecklenburg offered—to Friedman's mild surprise. She loved that idea! She had experienced back pain herself and knew how frustrating it was to be unable to get an appointment in a timely manner. Starbucks employees who had terrible back pain had come to her after being told there was no appointment available for six weeks "and they would come to me and say 'Please, please help me.'" During the meeting she turned to Friedman and said, "Andrew, first thing, you've got to see that patient today. Today. Now. Not two weeks, not three weeks, not a week from now—*today*."

Thus, the first element within the new value stream was a same-day appointment. Dr. Friedman's plan was that each patient would be treated by a two-person team consisting of a physical therapist and a physician and that the team would seek to provide psychological reassurance as well as excellent quality diagnosis and treatment. Friedman emphasized the importance of the patient's psychological health. "There are three things that patients usually want when they come in," he says. "One is an accurate diagnosis, to know that they don't have cancer or something terrible. They also want pain relief. And they want to know how to get back to normal function."

Nearly all patients presenting with back pain are in some state of anxiety or even depression, he says. A young person might fear suffering debilitating pain for years to come, whereas a middle-aged athlete worries whether his or her running or swimming days might be over. "Or the older person who figures this is really the beginning of real debility and pain that might ultimately end in death," he says, "or this might be cancer that's affecting them. Those worries go along with physical symptoms. We think of back pain in sort of an anatomic, pathological perspective. But the determinant of how well a person does, whether they end up with chronic pain, whether they go back to work, and how much they suffer has been repeatedly shown to be a function of how much *fear* they have, how much limitation of activity they subject themselves to, what their coping style is like, how much depression they have. Those far overshadow any of the anatomic determinants of their outcome. There are exceptions, of course. If somebody has got a really crushed nerve root that's only going to get better with surgery, then that person needs to go on to surgery. We know that treatment will help them get better faster. But for many patients, a very important intervention is dealing rapidly and effectively with their fear and emotional distress. If somebody hurts their back on the job and their job is something that really demands a high level of physical activity, if they don't get back to that level of physical activity, their life falls apart. We really try to help with those aspects."

Friedman's plan was that the patient would arrive at the spine clinic and immediately meet with a physical therapist, who would take the patient history and conduct a preliminary physical examination. A physician would then join the discussion and review the history "from a medical perspective," says Friedman, and "get a handoff in front of the patient from the therapist. The therapist explains what's going on and the patient can say, 'Yeah, that's accurate, that's what is going on,' and then the doc is trained to detect disease. If we need to order medications to help with pain, or if we need to order any imaging studies to rule out more serious disease, we can do that right there. Then, ideally, we'll be back out of the room in twenty minutes with a plan that we've discussed with the patient and with the physical therapist that we all agree on and makes sense. Then the therapist has time to initiate the first physical therapy treatment and also reinforce what happened. That discussion in front of the patient demonstrates that we really do know what's going on, we see this all the time, we've got an answer for this, and we're going to get you started on a pathway right away."

Friedman found that the physical therapists were, in fact, highly skilled at communicating with patients. "Physical therapists are just as good at it as we are, as long as the patient knows and believes that this is associated with correct medical diagnosis and that we really do have an eye on what's going on with them," he says. "Many of the therapists have better personalities than the doctors. Some of them are excellent with the patients and so when we talk about skill–task alignment, spending time and answering questions and reassuring patients, that's not the exclusive role of the physician."

This plan impressed Annette King, for it was clear to her that the patient's physical and psychological needs were targeted, and she could also see that the patient would receive a total treatment of an hour and twenty minutes on the first visit—a significant amount of face-time with both therapist and doctor.

Marketplace Defines Quality

There were countless traditional measures of medical quality as Mecklenburg, in his role as Chief of Medicine, knew all too well. Again, though, he was in alien territory—seeing with a new set of eyes—and looking for a definition of quality that his colleagues in the marketplace collaborative would endorse. During a series of meetings through the spring of 2005, the collaboratives—each working separately—came to essentially the same definition of quality. There were differences in emphasis and differences according to the clinical area, of course, but the collective wisdom of the more than two dozen people participating in the collaboratives was that quality had five components:

- Same-day access
- Rapid return to function
- 100 percent patient satisfaction
- Evidence-based care
- Affordable cost for both providers and employers

Mecklenburg was impressed by the clarity with which the employers approached defining quality. He had invested considerable time and energy through the years working to make sure that Virginia Mason performed well on a variety of national measures, but as he reflected on measurement in the context of a marketplace collaborative, he realized that process outcomes didn't really get him much. "Do we have intensivists in the ICU 24/7? We do and that's great, but is that an outcome? No, it's a process measure," he says. "Computerized order entry, it's important but it's a process measure. Eye checks, foot checks, or A1C tests in patients with diabetes—all process measures that do not register the health and function of the patient. So there are many learned organizations, subspecialty organizations, government organizations that measure quality. We measure over 100 different quality indicators here at Virginia Mason and report them to more than twenty-five outside organizations. Most of these are process measures and may not relate to return to function. So we're saying, yes, the process measures are important, they're a means to an end. But what we really want to deliver to you is a functioning worker, a functioning employee, and that's the outcome we want. So the number one and number two quality measures defined by employers were same-day access and rapid return to function."

Rapid return to function was critical for businesses such as Starbucks, which had a nagging problem not only with absenteeism but with "presenteeism"—being present at work but unable to fully function due to a sore back, headache, or other unresolved medical issue.

The team within the marketplace collaborative identified patient satisfaction as the third quality indicator. "We can't prevent patients from having bad things happen to them," says Mecklenburg, "but the service part of their care and our ability to relate to them emotionally and to understand their needs and their fears and to deal with them and be sympathetic and compassionate with them, that's got to be there." And here was an area where retailers offered important lessons for the clinical team. "The folks from one of our main customers are saying, 'We've got the ethic of 100 percent satisfaction. We provide this for you. Can't you provide the same for our employees?'"

The fourth quality indicator was delivering care that benefits the patient while avoiding non-value-added care. Employers wanted Virginia Mason to do everything necessary for their workers, but nothing unnecessary. The way to eliminate unnecessary care was to make sure that care was based on "what works"—or evidence-based medicine, the approach that had eliminated non-value-added MRIs in early meetings of the collaboratives.

The fifth essential element defining quality care was lowering cost so that it was affordable for companies and their employees. By the spring of 2005, the Starbucks marketplace collaborative had made significant progress that would soon prove to cut costs significantly. Friedman and his team designed a screening mechanism to separate patients with complicated and uncomplicated back pain. When patients called the clinic in pain seeking an appointment they were asked a series of questions aimed at detecting something more complex than uncomplicated back pain. Red flag symptoms might include a weak leg, a preexisting cancer, fever, a fall, or poor bowel or bladder function. With just a few questions it would be clear which patients should go through a standard pathway focused on physical therapy and which patients needed more specialized intervention. Because all these back patients were no longer being funneled through the same small space, there were enough available clinicians to see *all* back patients *that day*—eliminating the huge waste of waiting thirty days or more for an appointment. "Anytime you have a six-week wait, you get a certain amount of dropouts, so people have an appointment and they don't show, so there we eliminated some of the waste of unused capacity that we had," says Friedman.

For Friedman and his team in physical medicine, this was a radical change in their work. Their specialty was chronic pain and they had tended to provide comprehensive services for a small number of patients requiring highly specialized care. Now they were shifting to a new model of using reliable systems to treat very large numbers of patients with fairly straightforward, generally uncomplicated conditions. Predictably, there was mixed reaction among the doctors and other providers on Friedman's team. Some saw it as a sensible approach to the shifting tides within health care, whereas others viewed it as an unappealing, standardized approach to care. A number of providers, including one physician, disliked this new direction enough to leave Virginia Mason.

Despite some internal turbulence, Friedman was able to make significant changes quite rapidly. Just three months after the meeting where the idea of same-day access had been raised, Friedman was able to report that it had, in fact, been achieved. He and his team had whittled down the waiting period for an appointment from an average of thirty-one days to same-day in just three months. The hardest part of this was convincing doctors—who loved the financial security of having lengthy backlogs for appointments—that no backlog at all was a good thing. To accommodate same-day appointments, it was necessary to plan open slots in the schedule every day. Careful review of demand for back pain services over time had shown Mecklenburg and Friedman that there was a significant and steady demand for this service. However, doctors looked at openings in their schedules and worried that it would mean reduced revenue for them. Right from the start, though, it was clear that the openings filled up quickly.

The other concern among doctors was cultural. Suddenly, physical therapists were adding significant value; they were, in fact, arguably adding greater value for many patients than the doctors. This skill–task alignment made perfect sense from a cost and efficiency standpoint, but it was hard for physicians nonetheless. Friedman's physical therapy team also proved to be exceptionally effective at helping patients get back into form quickly. Nationally, patients require an average of eleven PT sessions to solve their back problem. Regionally, in the northwest, that number was eight sessions. Friedman's team at Virginia Mason, however, was successful with just three and a half to four sessions per patient—with outcomes equal to or better than the places providing more sessions.

Whereas achieving same-day access and rapid return to function was a huge success right away, the effort to reduce MRIs that were not evidence-based for uncomplicated back pain initially flopped. Friedman and Mecklenburg emphasized to the doctors that the evidence was clear: There was no need to order an MRI on a patient without any red flag symptoms. The physicians ignored them, however. From the start, Mecklenburg had wanted to put a screen on the computer system that would make it possible for doctors to order an MRI for back pain only in clearly defined instances based on the evidence. Friedman thought that was going too far and persuaded Mecklenburg that if they explained it well enough to the physicians MRI usage would decline.

"Being the young, naive doctor I was back then, I did not like the idea of legislating what would be okay and not okay," says Friedman. "I just had never seen that done in our institution or in an institution that I'd been involved in so I thought if we go to the doctors and tell them, 'Look, if we limit MRIs to these criteria, we're going to do some gain sharing, and we're going to be able to take better care of our patients,' I thought that that would be enough to change behavior."

In fact, MRI usage did not budge. Mecklenburg and Friedman felt they had no alternative but to put the screen in place so that when a physician was attempting to order an MRI for back pain it was necessary to click on one of the evidence-based indications for the MRI listed on the screen. "If the doc can't declare an evidence-based indication for the test, the computer will not schedule the MRI," says Mecklenburg. "There are ways around it, but it's not easy—nor should it be." The new computer block did what no amount of physician education could do: The utilization rate for MRI ordered for back pain plummeted 31 percent almost overnight. One of the five planks in the quality platform was the elimination of waste and nowhere was this more obvious than with the reduction in unnecessary MRIs. Rather than a $1,200 MRI that provided little or no value added to the patient, there was a $150 physical therapy session that was pure value added. If there was any doubt about the effectiveness of the block it was erased by statistics comparing MRI usage ordered by Virginia Mason doctors versus doctors at other institutions referring patients to the Virginia Mason spine clinic. In a study of 200 sequential patients referred to the clinic, Virginia Mason doctors ordered an MRI in 8 percent of the cases, whereas physicians from outside the medical center ordered MRIs in 43 percent of their cases.

Home Run

As far as the benefits managers were concerned, Mecklenburg and his team had hit a home run with four of the five criteria on their list of what constitutes quality. The spine clinic provided same-day access and dramatically improved the speed at which they were returning patients to function. And, in the process, they had eliminated significant waste—particularly imaging tests that were not evidence-based, thus reducing cost.

The other criterion that needed to be dealt with was patient satisfaction. Friedman and Mecklenburg sought to establish a measurement system in the spine clinic, but they did not want a system that told them days or weeks after a visit how satisfied (or not) a patient had been. They wanted to track their ratings in real time, which would enable them to rapidly identify and fix problems.

Sometimes the low-tech solution is exactly the right one for a particular situation, and this was one of those cases. In the spine clinic, they created what was fondly referred to as the poker chip exit poll. They set out five Lucite tubes looking like tennis ball containers. Next to the tubes were poker chips of varying colors. The question posed to patients as they exited the clinic was simple: "Based on your experience today, would you recommend our spine clinic to a friend or relative?" Patients would select a poker chip and place it in a particular tube depending on their level of satisfaction. The dynamic quality of this rudimentary tool was that simply by looking at the tubes the level of patient satisfaction and the trend was clear. By watching the chips stack up during the course of a day, says Mecklenburg, "you could actually detect a deficiency within hours." In such a case the team was ready with several additional diagnostic questions probing any level of patient dissatisfaction—"Are you receiving full information about your condition?" or "Is your health care team addressing your emotional needs?"

"So you could make sure in real time that you were doing great," he says, "or if you weren't, you would see it right away and you could correct it right away and measure the effect of your intervention in group terms."

Mecklenburg and his colleagues created similar services for migraine headaches, breast nodules, and shoulder, knee, and hip pain. In each case, they worked collaboratively with a company or government entity. The migraine work created a clinical pathway where a nurse practitioner specializing in migraines follows standard practice to evaluate, treat, and educate patients. The clinic also provided patients with "rescue medications" so that patients would not need to make a time-consuming and financially wasteful visit to the emergency department. Because the migraine value stream revealed that MRI and CT scans added little or no value for most patients, the clinic installed evidence-based decision rules for scheduling imaging. Following these measures the utilization of MRI imaging of the brain decreased by 41 percent across the Virginia Mason enterprise. Emergency room visits for migraine decreased as well.

A marketplace collaborative with one national retailer focused on severe acid reflux. The team achieved a significant reduction in reliance on branded medicines, resulting in substantial cost savings. The team found, in fact, that if they projected their results on this company's employees nationally—and only performed half as well as they had in Seattle—it would yield an annual savings of $1.2 million on this one disease. Another marketplace collaborative focused on cardiac rhythm disturbances. A combination of increased use of generic medicines and the elimination of redundant tests yielded significant savings.

Financial Conundrum

There was a sense of triumph among the participants in the marketplace collaboratives. Drs. Mecklenburg, Friedman, and Storey—along with Annette King and the rest of the employers—had participated in something truly special in health care. They had demonstrated an ability to change medical processes with speed and agility—and do so in a way that was directly responsive to the concerns and demands of the marketplace. They had shown an ability to return workers to function far faster than ever before. It was a classic equation: Eliminate waste, deliver only value-added services, and the result equals improved quality at a lower cost. It was, in its way, the health care Holy Grail.

There remained an important question, however. For although it was clear that most of the participants seated at the marketplace collaborative table had realized significant gains, the question was what impact all of this had on Virginia Mason's financial profile. The financial conundrum was obvious: Significant financial improvement for Starbucks meant a sizable cut in revenue to Virginia Mason. The perversity of the financial incentives in American medicine were writ large on the back pain value stream in that very first Starbucks marketplace collaborative meeting. The value stream showed the many things that Virginia Mason was doing—most of which added little or no value for the patient—nonetheless resulted in hefty payments to the medical center. The richest of all possible ironies was that by providing top-quality value-added care, Virginia Mason had reduced its own revenues. "Cutting costs to satisfy employers but bankrupting the medical center made no sense," says Mecklenburg.

To her great credit, Annette King had recognized this from the start and urged Don Storey to get Aetna to pay Virginia Mason more for the quality of their work. "These guys can't be losing money on this," she told Storey. "I need this supplier—I want them to be a preferred supplier. We pay fair trade prices in our coffee business to support the supply chain," and she was asking Aetna to do the same. She would be happy, she told Storey, to share her gains with Virginia Mason.

At the first marketplace collaborative meeting, Andrew Friedman had touched on the financial issue. "I told them that 'the methods that we know are effective are not well compensated," he said, "and if we could realign some of the value with incentive, if we could get paid for the things that make sense, we could deliver a better product.' And I remember being impressed by the fact that they wanted that and so that was for me a very liberating feeling—because I always knew that this was the right thing to do and that somehow and in some way we could deliver that, but in medicine often you can't get to the right thing because there are too many barriers."

The Wall Street Journal examined the Virginia Mason–Aetna–Starbucks collaboration in a front-page article on January 12, 2007. The article highlighted the financial issue, describing it as "one of the most confounding elements in America's health-care crisis: a perverse system of payments that rewards doctors and hospitals not for how well they treat patients, but for how much they treat them."

Mecklenburg, again, saw an opportunity on the financial side. He argues that margins are related to revenue and cost of production and by manipulating either you impact margin. On the revenue side, you could try and extract more money from insurance companies—typically what providers do at contract time. The much more effective approach, Mecklenburg argues, is to reduce the cost of production—just as they had done with back pain, migraines, and so on.

"This is what the Virginia Mason Production System is all about," he says. "Reducing the cost of production so that it costs us less to produce an episode of back pain care and headache care and many other services. When we treat common back pain with physical therapists and a small amount of physician input compared to treating common back pain with physicians alone, we can see more patients, provide better access and higher patient satisfaction, produce care at a lower cost per patient, and generate margin at three times the rate we could with the previous model. So delivering health care efficiently and effectively makes financial sense for providers—just as producing a product efficiently and effectively would be good business in general."

Mecklenburg further argues that the revenue loss from a reduction in MRI testing is again offset by Virginia Mason's new ability to see more patients. His bottom line on the financial side is this: "The provider groups are worried that the revenue will drop as they start providing less low-value care. They immediately see the potential for loss of revenue. What we've shown here is revenue does go down for certain types of care, but with the ability to see more patients and the attractiveness of these products, the patient volume goes way up. Reducing the cost of production is very good for the producer, for the providers, and for the purchaser. So we can save millions of dollars for purchasers and still do fine financially."

He notes that even though Virginia Mason lost all that revenue from MRI exams on patients with uncomplicated back pain, some money was recovered when Aetna agreed to increase payments to Virginia Mason for physical therapy. With dramatically increased physical therapy volume and the price increase, suddenly real dollars were being generated. With a more efficient use of doctors' time, Virginia Mason nearly doubled its back pain volume in a single year.

A key to making this new approach work for Virginia Mason is to get the skill–task alignment right. Under the old system that had been way out of kilter, with highly paid surgeons sometimes seeing patients with uncomplicated back pain. The surgeons cost a great deal of money—four times the cost of a physical therapist—but added no value for the uncomplicated conditions that afflict most patients. When the skill–task alignment is done properly, Mecklenburg says, the cost of producing care drops by about 50 percent. An analysis at Virginia Mason puts the medical center's cost of a patient seeing a surgeon or other "proceduralist" at $4.00 per minute, compared to half that for a physician who is not a proceduralist. And the cost of a patient being seen by a nurse practitioner is $1.00 per minute. "Deploying all their valuable assets with the appropriate skill–task alignment, the section was able to reduce physician time with each patient to just what the patient needed," says Mecklenburg. "Reassurance and checks to verify that they did not have a threatening cause for their back pain—that was value-added for the patient. The patient received additional value-added time with the physical therapist. Many of these providers who are less costly have high skill level because they do common, uncomplicated things repeatedly."

Perverse Incentives

All in all, the back pain work for Starbucks was a singular success. At the end of one year, waiting time was cut from thirty-one days to same-day and 94 percent of patients were returned to work that day or the next. In addition, no prescription medications were needed in three quarters of the cases and patient satisfaction was through the roof. The marketplace collaboratives were a VMPS triumph, for they demonstrated in concrete ways that the elimination of waste improved quality—and did so dramatically. The startling revelations in the value-stream mapping of low back pain and other issues could have been marginalized as somehow aberrational. But Kaplan, Mecklenburg, and others saw it for what it was: a tangible manifestation of the massive waste in *all* the Virginia Mason processes.

The financial question continues to nag, however. The issue is whether the health care payment system can change to support and encourage the kind of work Virginia Mason accomplished. Andrew Friedman, for one, is frustrated that the approach his team has used to produce high-quality, low-cost care has not spread more rapidly. "The reason it doesn't happen this way is that the incentives aren't properly aligned," he says. "Changing the incentives would change behavior more rapidly. If we were paid for our outcomes and we could deliver that care in such a way that was most efficient, you have a lot of smart people who would be thinking about how to change the game very quickly."

Typically, of course, fee-for-service arrangements pay for quantity of care regardless of the quality. The system, in fact, pays fairly well for a great deal of substandard care that often provides no benefit to the patient. From a purely financial standpoint, physicians and hospitals are often better off providing unnecessary care with little or no value to the patient. Consider a situation where there are major, competing providers—say two major medical centers in one marketplace. One chooses the Virginia Mason path of high-value, low-cost care. The other continues on the traditional fee-for-service path. If the payment system remains static, the Virginia Mason model might go out of business while the competitor flourishes. The absurdity of this is obvious to all, yet progress toward payment reform is painfully slow in many places and nonexistent in others.

Mecklenburg says that when providers eliminate waste and produce reliable quality care, the cost declines. For that to work, he says, health plans must then pay for "high quality and rapid access, not poor quality, waits and delays. To the extent that health plans are paying for poor quality care or delayed care, cost to employers and patients and even the government stays high. Customers—both employers and patients—or you could expand this to CMS [Centers for Medicare & Medicaid Services] also—need to buy high-quality and rapid access and stop buying poor quality and poor access. If they persist in purchasing poor quality it will remain available in the marketplace and drive up cost."

It could be argued that this analysis described exactly what needed to happen with health care in the United States. Don Storey says the work at Virginia Mason means that "the genie is out of the bottle. If you have openness and transparency around data, you can create phenomenal improvements around efficiency and quality. You could really start taking out tons of waste. This shows you can do the right stuff for a lot less money and do it better. We know we can make health care better almost instantly."

Annette King expresses the hope that others across the country will want to study the model created in Seattle. "I wish that more employers would get more involved as we did here in Puget Sound," she says.

Mecklenburg is seeking to accomplish exactly that. In 2007, the Virginia Mason Center for Health Care Solutions was formed to expand and accelerate the work. Mecklenburg believes so strongly that there are meaningful lessons in the Virginia Mason marketplace collaborative experience for the broader health care system that he gave up his position as Chief of Medicine to become medical director of the center. "The problem is that we squander 50 percent of our health care dollars on medical care that does not improve the health and well-being of patients," he says. "Poor quality is the primary driver of excess cost. In the U.S. we produce, consume, and pay for a great deal of great medical care; the best medical care in the world is available in the U.S. when we do it right. But we don't always do it right. We also produce, consume, and pay for hundreds of millions of dollars of ineffective and low-quality care that takes money out of the system without returning commensurate value. It is this waste that drives the price of health care beyond our reach as a nation. We are all paying the tab."

Chapter Nine

Management Method

As we have seen in previous chapters, Virginia Mason is different from other health care organizations in many ways. The Virginia Mason path and means of navigation is different. The experience of being a patient or a staff member is different. And, importantly, the work of being a leader at Virginia Mason is different, as well—very different. The methods and tools certainly distinguish Virginia Mason. But at a deeper, more profound cultural level, it is the nature of leadership and all that goes with that—accountability, transparency, rigor—that differentiates Virginia Mason at the core.

Seeing Virginia Mason with Fresh Eyes

Newcomers to Virginia Mason, especially those with long experience at other medical centers, have a telling perspective. Kate Reed, RN, Jim Cote, and Michael Ondracek are all relatively new to their administrative roles at Virginia Mason. All three have extensive experience working at other major medical centers—including some of the most prestigious in the country. Ondracek came to Virginia Mason from a prominent medical center in the Pacific Northwest, and Reed and Cote came from Harvard teaching hospitals in Boston.

In light of their experiences elsewhere, what is their view of Virginia Mason? "Everybody in health care says the patient comes first," says Kate Reed. "The number one thing that is evident here at Virginia Mason is that we actually *do* put the patient first. We live it. It is central to everything we do." Certainly one of the most distinguishing aspects of Virginia Mason is its mission not only to be

149

the quality leader, but also to transform health care. That aspect of the mission, says Reed, indicates that at Virginia Mason this is "not just about a patient, a group of patients, or us at Virginia Mason. We want to rethink how health care is delivered, and I don't know of another provider organization that has made the visible commitment to fundamentally transform how we provide care. That, to me, is a unique differentiator."

Another difference is the management foundation on which the Virginia Mason journey is built. It is this management method that enables everything else; that enables Virginia Mason to put the patient first; that allows Virginia Mason to aspire to transform health care. Understanding Virginia Mason means fully grasping this central point. The management system has created alignment throughout the medical center that is rare in the industry. At Virginia Mason, one of the most striking differences—noticed immediately by newcomers—is that the executive leadership and the medical staff are aligned in pursuit of the organization's mission and goals. "Here everybody is focused on the patient and trying to transform health care *together*," says Reed. "The physicians aren't off over here with their own agenda and administration is over here with their agenda. *Everyone is doing it together.* Where that was really powerful for me early on was being able to participate in an RPIW and there were physicians on the team and medical assistants on the team and the roles all stay at the door and everybody is in there to improve quality and everyone's voice is equal at the table. That's just a completely different culture."

Reed, Cote, and Ondracek all credit the physician compact from back in 2001 as an essential element in the foundational structure at Virginia Mason. The compact clarified expectations and brought a strengthened sense of mission alignment. This alignment, they agree, can only happen in a culture where doctors set their egos aside in favor of a broader vision. Reed says that one of the hospitals where she worked in Boston had many world-class physicians "literally saving lives every day." But the culture of the institution, she says, would never allow the kind of mission alignment that exists at Virginia Mason. "Jim and I both experienced on a daily basis physicians who just refused to evolve," says Reed, "physicians who refused to collaborate, physicians whose attitude was, 'It's my way or the highway.'"

In her prior experience the quality improvement effort tended to be compartmentalized, but at Virginia Mason she says it is "pervasive. It is part of everybody's job, not just the Quality Department. It goes back to the alignment of executive leadership with the physicians. In a lot of places that have really strong distributed quality programs, the physicians aren't necessarily in the tent, so there's a lot of work being done on the processes *around* the physicians with some physicians involved. But when it gets down to the fact that we really need to change something about the way physicians behave or do their work in order to get a better outcome, then you're hitting a wall; you're hitting the third rail."

The Virginia Mason experience is a true learning journey. It is by digging deeper into the difficult moments—the mistakes and failures—that we find some of its most valuable lessons. An important example came in 2005 when the Virginia Mason Kaizen Promotion Office (KPO) staff conducted an audit of every Rapid Process Improvement Workshop (RPIW) ever done at Virginia Mason to determine whether previously calculated gains had been sustained. Over a six-month period, the audit dug into the details of an incredible 275 RPIWs. The audit results were less than stellar. There was no question that there had been some outstanding gains, but the audit found that in too many cases gains had not been maintained over time. The critical question was why? Why didn't more gains hold? What was the key to sustaining those advances?

Linda Hebish, Administrative Director of VMPS Implementation, says that one example is particularly instructive. In 2006, the KPO initiated a process to create a more efficient assembly line for sterilizing surgical instruments. The KPO team went into sterile processing and designed and then implemented a new sterilization assembly line. Initially, the approach seemed to work quite well, but it was not long before the new process began crumbling. "It failed because the KPO team went in and did it *to* them," says Hebish. "No one likes to be told what to do for their job when they've been doing it one way for a long time and they think they're doing it the right way and they think they're doing it the safest way. To have someone come in and say, 'No, you're not going to do it that way. Here's your new standard work. Do it *this* way.' There was a lot of resentment, but there were also people in the department who kept trying to do it the new way, but then leadership changed and things kind of regressed."

It was an important lesson that resonated throughout the medical center. "The lesson was to make sure you're engaged with the operational leaders and the staff and work with them," says Hebish. "The theory behind creating standard work is the people who do the work create the standards, so you don't have somebody come in there and hand you your standards—you help develop them."

Sarah Patterson spent a lot of time digging into the problem of sustaining improvements, and the more she thought about it the deeper she looked into the Virginia Mason management process within the medical center. By about 2007, Patterson had the sense that an important ingredient was missing from the work—an *essential* ingredient. The more she thought about it and discussed it with Gary Kaplan and other senior leaders the more convinced she grew that the missing ingredient was not a single item, but rather a dynamic mix that included healthy portions of leadership, discipline, accountability, and rigor—the elements that hold the *system* together.

There was a problem, however: There was no system in place to ensure that standard work was followed consistently by every part of the work unit or every staff member. There was no method for improving on standard work; no real recognition that standard work might not be able to remain standard work forever. If, over time, a defined bit of standard work becomes outdated, perhaps due to other changes in management or new clinical discoveries—for *any* reason—then the standards must evolve. That was not happening effectively enough and Patterson wondered what the process was for managing and guiding the evolution. "We would go back into areas where we had done a lot of work and start asking the question of what's the status now and find out, 'Well, no, we stopped using that standard work or we changed that standard work in this part of the work unit,' and we started to see that it didn't hold up."

Structure and Discipline

She examined the nature of leadership at Virginia Mason. "Visionary leaders like Gary are critical," she says. "But then there's the piece of this that is the structure and the discipline." That includes leaders at all levels throughout the organization committing to the discipline and the structure that will enable Virginia Mason to become a learning, improving organization. Patterson says it is not about relying on strong leaders who get things done by sheer force of will. Rather, effective leadership is about reliance on a well-constructed, continuously improving system that long outlives any leader, no matter how dynamic. She notes that there are numerous inspirational leaders within Virginia Mason, many of whom have one great idea after another, but that type of leadership without the framework of the system would not get Virginia Mason where it needs to be. "As a leadership team, we've made a commitment to a system that's bigger than all of us," says Patterson. "It's really about how the whole system holds together and every single leader is committed to and expected to follow the standards."

In many other places, she says, leadership is "all about your intellect as a leader, your brilliance, your ability to create a vision and there is that piece in what we're doing. The vision has to be communicated. But it has to be communicated by every single person in the company, not just by Gary or me. Everybody has to be communicating and in the same way or the whole thing starts to unravel into the fiefdoms that are so prevalent in health care."

In the early years of the Virginia Mason journey, the goal was to get as many people as possible in the organization involved in using VMPS tools and methods to eliminate waste and improve quality. Much time during the first three years was focused on training. During that period every executive within Virginia Mason submitted to the certification process and led improvement workshops. But there was a bump in that road when some executives failed to pass the course. Patterson says John Black deserves credit for calling the team on this. "John was saying, 'Look, if you guys really mean this, you're going to make the executive team accountable. This isn't just a one-day seminar on an interesting topic. This is serious.'"

It became abundantly clear in 2008 there was an urgent need for greater accountability. Thus, the team added sixty-day updates to the weekly Kaizen Activity report outs. "We thought it was first important to establish the accountability, so we set up these sixty-day report out expectations," she says. The new approach exposed accountability gaps and required those responsible for the work to make a public report on their progress. "That exposed issues related to accountability," says Patterson. "People would say, 'Well, I led the workshop, but I'm not the person actually responsible for the process.'" So who *was* responsible? Patterson would wonder. Who was coaching and teaching at the front lines? Wasn't that what leaders were supposed to do? Teach the standard work to employees—make absolutely rock solid certain that the staff understood the standard work—agreed with the standard work—implemented the standard work? Wasn't that what real leadership was all about?

Training within Industry

Then came a breakthrough: Patterson realized that during the course of their journey, Virginia Mason had missed an important piece of the Toyota approach. "We were so focused on the discipline of the tools that we had missed the people part of it—engaging your people," she says. "And Toyota has done a tremendous amount of work on preparing the people in their workforce for change, supporting them through change—all the critical aspects of change management."

Scores of teams at Virginia Mason had proven to be highly skilled and committed to conducting RPIWs in every area of the medical center. Most of those workshops proved successful at identifying waste and at designing new processes based on standard work. When workshops were completed, the next step was how to roll out the new process to the staff in a way that made sure everyone understood and was committed to sustaining the new approach. Too often, says Patterson, this step did not go nearly as well as the RPIW process itself. "We learned that we really didn't know how to train people very effectively," says Patterson. She said that sending out an e-mail to the staff explaining the process proved singularly ineffective. The same was true of conducting a detailed PowerPoint presentation at a staff meeting. Neither really worked.

"The question was how do you actually develop people in terms of their specific job, and Toyota says most of the development of their people comes through on-the-job training and coaching right at the front line as they're doing their work. She says a book entitled *Toyota Talent: Developing Your People the Toyota Way* by Jeffrey Liker and David Meier, is all about the people part of their strategy and became required reading for Virginia Mason leaders. A key element talked about in the book is the concept of Training Within Industry—the approach Charleen Tachibana and her team had used to train nurses on the hospital floor. Training Within Industry was a program originated by the U.S. government during World War II to train workers at the most granular level how to build ships, planes, and other wartime equipment. The trainers figured out that by breaking down the job into very specific steps and training workers in those steps that the workers were capable of performing at a very high level.

This was a discovery of enormous import in the Virginia Mason journey, for it caused a fundamental shift in how workers were then trained in new work as change was happening around them. "You don't just do a training session and let people go out and do it," Patterson says. "You actually are there with them as a leader, supervisor, and manager, observing and giving them feedback."

Standard Work: Hand Hygiene

There are numerous examples of using Training Within Industry to teach standard work at Virginia Mason, but one of the most tangible and visible, which applies throughout the medical center, involves hand hygiene. Studies had shown that hand hygiene is the single most important thing that health care workers can do to prevent infection. Yet hand hygiene is generally spotty and inconsistent. Countless patients each year are infected with germs conveyed by caregivers. The National Institutes of Health had been on the warpath about hand hygiene for many years with some success. At Virginia Mason, the goal is to make it standard work for every employee every time.

Thus, Training Within Industry. The Virginia Mason teaching approach started with a clearly stated premise. As teachers, supervisors, and KPO staff fanned out across the *genba* they would engage workers by saying, "This is the most important thing we can do to protect our patients." Invariably, that statement would capture the worker's attention. *The* most important thing you can do to protect our patients is not to contaminate them with harmful viruses or bacteria.

Martha Purrier, RN, Director of the KPO, found that right from the start staff members were enthusiastic about the training. Nursing assistants, housekeepers, and both new and experienced nurses found the method to be simple and easy to master. They were convinced by the use of a special glow light revealing bacteria—or their absence—that demonstrated the method's effectiveness. The method caught on quickly and soon Purrier had nurses and doctors—even surgeons—asking for training. "And I said, 'Surgeons, are you kidding me? You don't know how to wash your hands?' They said, 'Our staff in the clinic are all doing it a certain way and they're telling us we're doing it wrong.'"

The spread of the method was so complete and uniform that Virginia Mason employees who did not know each other would recognize one another outside the medical center by the way they sanitized their hands. One worker traveling home on a city bus was sanitizing her hands and another passenger said to her, "You must work at Virginia Mason. That's the way they do it there." Another staff member was in the restroom at a movie theater when the same thing happened. There was enough curiosity among other women in the restroom that they asked the Virginia Mason worker to teach them the method.

These anecdotes, says Kate Reed, tell a deeper cultural story about the commitment of Virginia Mason leaders and staff. "There are very few cultures where it would not just be accepted but *expected* that when we make that level of commitment, we are all in," she says. "It's not everybody except the docs. We're *all* in—our physician leadership, administrative leadership buys in and we're excited about it. Is it easy? No. Compliance is much better than other places but it's not what we want it to be."

World-Class Management

Patterson was very proud of this work because it reflected so well on Virginia Mason and its dedicated staff, but also because it spoke to the management foundation on which the work was constructed. What people tend to see when they observe the Virginia Mason Production System, she says, is the innovation and creativity that defines so much of the work. That's somewhat like looking at a well-made automobile and focusing on the great paint job. Patterson says the creativity and innovation are the exterior of the vehicles—the way it looks and catches the eye. Her real interest is underneath the vehicle—beneath innovation and creativity—for that is where success depends on building an immensely strong and reliable chassis.

The fundamentals to building the strongest possible chassis come from an approach brought to Virginia Mason by John Black called World Class Management—a method intended to get leaders involved directly in the daily work of steady incremental improvement. There are three essential components to World Class Management: management by policy, daily management, and cross-functional management.

Management by policy involves setting clear goals with universal input from the organization's stakeholders. It is the aspect of World Class Management designed to provide focus and direction to the work. It means committing to goals and then aligning the work to serve those goals. As straightforward as it sounds, it took a number of years before the Virginia Mason leadership fully grasped it. Previously, says Patterson, they would set goals that were almost like a to-do list for the year. "Resources were not identified for how we could reach the goals," she says. "Will it require the IT department, human resources? There weren't clear statements of aim—how will we know if we've been successful?"

Patterson wanted to build more discipline and rigor around the process, arguing that a company-wide priority should be thought through with great care and that the process should involve identifying the most important issues that need to be resolved and then developing a comprehensive plan of attack. "Until we as a company decide this is an area we need to focus on, that it is among the most important work and we know exactly what it's going to take to accomplish it, I don't think we have any business committing to it," she says. "Because then we commit to an amorphous, vaguely described body of work. Then we get into these conflicts between parts of the company saying, 'You want to do that, but I can't support you if IT doesn't have the resources because they've got 100 other things that are on their list.' It really becomes the communication and the commitment. So it is not just an individual leader who through the sheer force of their personality will bust through the silos. It's the organization committing to put the resources and the attention across the organization to this important work. There's a rigor to it and the last two years we've gotten better."

Management by policy involves reaching out broadly to workers throughout the organization in search of ideas and feedback. Patterson and her team held numerous "catch ball sessions" open to the entire staff. At these gatherings, Patterson and other leaders would outline the organization's highest priorities and ask for feedback. "We want it to be transparent to the whole organization how we set goals and it was fantastic," she says of these sessions. "We found it was a huge opportunity to make people knowledgeable about what we were working on. People said, 'I never knew we were working on all these great things.' And we would also show metrics that demonstrated progress in these areas."

The process now involves beginning to identify goals as early as May with the intent of setting a final list for the following year by November. Along with goals, the organization establishes KPO target sheets that guide the work of the KPO personnel for the year. This is an essential piece of the chassis, for it creates a sense of focus and reduces the possibility of the limited KPO staff being tugged in too many different directions. With limited resources, says Patterson, it is essential to direct KPO resources at the top improvement priorities.

Daily Management

Daily management, the second of the three World Class Management categories, is clearly all about managing the work day to day. Patterson views daily management as about "creating a visual workplace where you know what's really going on moment-to-moment. You know what the standard work is that's been defined, you know if it's being followed, you know the flow of patients. And if there are bottlenecks in that flow on an hour-to-hour basis, the leader, the supervisor can go in and say, 'Whoa, we've got a problem.'"

Daily management is focused on the leadership and frontline involvement of middle management. "This is where things really happen in an organization," says Patterson. "If you don't engage and get the alignment of middle management you're not going to go anywhere. Those are the people the frontline staff look to for day-to-day guidance. Every staff satisfaction survey I've read says staff member relationship with their immediate supervisor is key to whether they are satisfied with their job. Our middle management people really are the coaches and teachers for this whole management system. "When you have standard work, you can see the deviations from it," she says. "You can go in and say, 'Why are we an hour behind in terms of our patients? What's the issue? Well, it looks like the lab is backed up. Well, what do we need to do? What's the issue in the lab? Is it that they've got a machine that's down? Do they have a staff person who had to go home ill?' So the leader can then go in and focus in on how do I need to get that bottleneck broken up and improved so that we get back into the flow."

Standard work is key to that, because deviations can only be measured if standard work is defined. Patterson wants to go deeper in this area to help managers and supervisors see their roles as most effective on the front lines. "Daily management is really keeping the process healthy and flowing and supporting the workers," says Patterson. "And part of that is knowing what the standard work is and if there are deviations. Is someone in registration at Virginia Mason not gathering a piece of information that then affects people in the clinic because they can't check the patient in? It could be any number of things that end up creating those bottlenecks."

The daily management approach establishes clear expectations for middle managers. They are expected to have a reporting wall where that particular department or section's goals are clearly stated and measured on an ongoing basis. Managers use these reporting walls—typically located on a high-visibility hallway in the work space—as regular guides. At least weekly, and often more frequently, managers gather their team at the wall and review the metrics or some detail of their work plan, also posted on the wall. The specific, current goals they are focused on are prominently posted and progress—or lack of it—is measured. Whatever they are working on in that unit is posted and measured on that wall for everyone to see. These hallways scattered throughout the medical center and satellite clinics are where managers huddle with their teams to help make the work come alive; to teach and guide.

"Our job as executives is to focus the middle managers on this work of helping the staff understand standard work and then follow it," says Patterson. "It means talking with people about specifics from hand hygiene to hourly rounding. If you can't explain it very clearly and demonstrate it very clearly you cannot assume they know how to do it the right way."

Patterson says that seeing a manager rush onto the factory floor at Toyota in Japan when a worker needed help illustrated precisely how she wants managers throughout the medical center to act. "I remember timing how long it took from when the worker pulled the cord to when someone was at his or her side to help," says Sarah Patterson. "It was, at most, thirty seconds. This just astonished me. I have seen this same event happen almost every time I have visited Toyota—five times so far—and it is always within thirty seconds that someone is there."

Patterson asked the *sensei* who the person was who arrived in just thirty seconds each time, and she was told it was the supervisor or manager for that line. He noted that supervisors and managers were always on the line; that, in fact, they did not have offices elsewhere in the building. "I think we realized even on that first visit how profound a change this was for us as leaders and how we spend our time," she says. "It was very different than how we have viewed our roles and the roles of our managers and supervisors. It really made the concept of a 'servant leader' come to life. What if your job was to support your workers to deliver the highest quality product day in and day out and do it by being right there with them and understanding what their challenges were?"

Patterson says she wants Virginia Mason managers on the *genba* with the staff, and she believes that can only be accomplished "if you create the standard work and make it absolutely a part of a manager's role to monitor it. Rather than being in our offices and in meetings, we should be right there with our staff helping them to do the work." World Class Management is clear on what constitutes standard work for leaders within the daily management sphere. Key functions for daily management include the following:

■ Knowing the status of daily work
■ Knowing if planned work is completed on time
■ Understanding both upstream and downstream impact
■ Knowing that standard work is being followed
■ Knowing when to take action and what action to take

The third component of the World Class Management system is *cross-functional management*—working seamlessly on the patient's behalf across various departments. Patterson thinks of it as more cross-organizational. "To me that really means working on things as the patients see them," she says. "The patient doesn't see us as departments, yet we do our work as departments. And that gets in the way of a great patient experience."

Patterson cites orthopedics as an example. Cross-functional management means looking at the orthopedic patient's experience across the departments— from the clinic when the patient is initially seen to the hospital during an inpatient surgical procedure (or inpatient stay), to behind the scenes where the supply chain must provide exactly what the surgeons need when they need it.

World Class Management requires cultural adjustments, for it is contrary to the heroic nature of some work done by leaders in the past. "Many people in health care are in leadership positions because they are able to do amazing things that save the day," says Patterson. "We call them 'capes.' They're the ones who come in during a crisis and make a decision that saves the day. That has been our system in health care—to rely on people who do it all and they keep the system together; people who can manage in a crisis. But we don't want a crisis. We want systems and standard work to *prevent* a crisis. If there's a crisis, most often it's a failure of leadership." Success depends not on the actions of a charismatic, heroic individual, but on the system.

"The State of the Union Every Tuesday Morning"

When Patterson, Kaplan, and their colleagues were searching back in 2005 for ways to create more accountability for leaders in the organization, they established a Tuesday meeting at 7:00 a.m. where KPO leaders in charge of improvement work would report on that work in detail. It is known as Tuesday Standup, and it is a sacrosanct event at Virginia Mason. The routine is simple: Three different people report on work in the three divisional areas. Their metrics over time are posted on the hallway wall for all to see. Each presenter is given seven minutes—not seven and a half minutes. The meeting starts at 7:00 a.m.—not 7:05 a.m. It is run, every week, by the CEO, or, in his absence, by Patterson. It is a mandatory session for all Virginia Mason executives.

Throughout Virginia Mason, workers are accountable at a variety of levels all the way up through the administration, but the ultimate accountability, in a way, takes place at Tuesday Standup. In its first five years, the meeting was canceled twice—once for a holiday and another time for a snowstorm. Put another way, over a period of 260 weeks the meeting was held 258 times.

Its importance has steadily grown. It is a time when men and women who are leading the improvement work stand before the top three dozen leaders within the company—including the physician leaders of major medical departments—and report on their work. The executives who are in charge of the value streams and their physician counterparts are there. Once per quarter, Tuesday Standup is moved to an auditorium and broadcast out to the entire Virginia Mason community.

Valerie Ferris, Administrative Director in the KPO, has presented at Tuesday Standup many times through the years, and she considers it "sacred time" at Virginia Mason. "Standup is intended to create alignment between the work and executive leadership," she says. "It's a chance to share with leadership exactly what is happening and what the opportunities and barriers are. I've never had that experience working in any other health care organization where you have a direct conversation every week with executive leadership on the work. It has created transparency so they know exactly what is going on, and you have very honest conversations about what you are achieving or not achieving.

"It demands that when we are presenting at standup we have to be extremely focused. We may review work from the past week, for example, but it also has to be connected in context with how that work relates to our overall organizational goals. Every week we are challenged to bring up a barrier—something that is preventing us from more rapid improvement. Gary and Sarah want to know exactly what you have done to understand the barrier, and what help is needed from leadership to address it."

Barriers can include lack of resources or time, difficulties with implementation across the system, a lack of engagement from staff, multiple process owners causing challenges with implementation, lack of clarity, lack of testing before implementation, inadequate home team participation, or preparation for change, to name a few of the most common.

Not only does standup by its very nature create transparency and accountability, it also ensures that the entire executive leadership team of the medical center is deeply familiar with the frontline work. "Our leaders know what is going on in our organization," says Ferris. "They *really* know."

Although there is nothing punitive about this session, there is tension in the air, in part because the entire executive leadership team is listening, but also because at the end of the presentations Kaplan and Patterson ask questions to create a dialogue to achieve alignment. Standup is very serious business. It is a place where rhetoric, embellishment, or gilding the lily is stripped away. Speakers through the years who have appeared unprepared or who have attempted to substitute rhetoric for facts (there have not been many) have been instantly exposed under the sometimes harsh glare of the gathering. This is where the rubber meets the road at Virginia Mason, for this is the place and time when the ultimate question is asked: Are we progressing toward our targets? Is the work helping us advance toward our overall goals? If not, why not? What are the barriers to improvement? How can they be overcome? If we've identified a bottleneck, how do we open it up?

This thirty-minute weekly meeting speaks volumes about Virginia Mason. It demonstrates that leadership at the highest levels of the organization is engaged in the work at a detailed level. It shows that leaders *know* the work. It shows that leaders are familiar with the many specific improvement processes happening throughout the medical centers *kaizen* events, RPIWs, 3Ps. It shows that they follow the metrics from these events, and when the metrics slip the leaders ask why. It shows that the leaders are deeply committed to VMPS and continuing to use the method, without shortcuts or workarounds, to achieve improvement. It shows that Virginia Mason is on a learning journey.

Tuesday Standup is many things, including a commitment from the top to identify and remove barriers to progress. Often, this is the most difficult, even awkward, part of the event. Often it is difficult to pinpoint precisely what the barrier to progress might be in a complex area. Other times, those who own the improvement work know exactly what the barrier is, and it so happens it is their superior, or a colleague, or an executive in another department. These are the frank conversations that dial up the level of tension during the meetings. Tension rises a bit further if the barrier has been reported a number of times. Then the tone from Kaplan or Patterson is sharper: "We've been talking about this for six months. Why is this still a barrier?"

It is essential that difficult, awkward conversations take place within the confines of Tuesday Standup. It is supposed to be a safe space in which candor is required, but it is a challenge. It is very difficult to stand up in front of the entire leadership of the medical center and say something that is implicitly or explicitly critical of a colleague, friend, or manager. This happens rarely, though when it does, it is done in the best interest of the patient. It is, in fact, a manifestation of putting the patient first.

"Everybody Can Be a Leader"

Building leadership into all levels of the organization is not easy to do, but for many it has become a reality. Arni Verkler, a VMPS Specialist in the KPO, puts it this way: "My perception of being a leader is not necessarily having a big title. Everybody can be a leader. The staff can see you're there to help them improve their practice. That's where we started when I worked in General Internal Medicine. When I go to my *genba,* they're seeing me not just like I'm a leader telling them what they need to do, but I'm part of the leadership that is there for them to support them. Involving the staff in the process, you have that kind of humble attitude, and the staff can see that. They can sense that."

Verkler and other VMPS Specialists work hard to get to know staff at all levels, of course, but they place a special value on strong relations with workers at the front lines because VMPS Specialists know that to be effective they must enlist the cooperation of the frontline workers. Because many VMPS Specialists have experience in frontline staff positions, their credibility is enhanced. Before becoming VMPS Specialists they were nurses, managers, lawyers, audiologists, administrative assistants, and more. Their varied backgrounds not only enhance their credibility, but add important diversity of knowledge in KPO. This helps to ensure that the team looks at a problem from multiple angles to achieve the best result.

John Black and others were emphatic at the start of the Virginia Mason journey that leadership must come from the top down. Well along in the journey, however, the VMPS Specialists suggest that in an organic fashion, leadership is also now coming from the bottom up. "There's been an evolution in management as people who are managers and leaders of the organization learn more about VMPS," says Ana Anuradhika, KPO Specialist. "I think initially people who just start learning about it who are from traditional management backgrounds will use it as kind of a top-down thing where I'm going to impose this RPIW on you to meet my own agenda because this is what I think should happen as the manager. I feel when people start using it here, the more they understand it the more you can see managers transforming to being more from the bottom up—'Let's get ideas from the staff.'"

With a program called Everyday Lean Ideas, that is precisely what has been happening. The program is designed to tap into the problem-solving abilities of frontline staff who know the work at a granular level, understand problems quickly, and often have excellent ideas for solutions. Traditionally, however, when staff members had ideas they were funneled into a central administrative location and dealt with at some point. With the Everyday Lean Idea program, supervisors encourage staff to identify problems and suggest solutions. And to a significant extent, when solutions are proposed they are implemented quickly.

"Staff see the problems every day," says Jennifer Phillips, Director of the Virginia Mason Center for Innovation Program. "The idea is to empower and equip them to work on improvements. The message is that if things are in your control in your work area, we encourage staff to work on it; to fix it. And we ask what they need to do that and provide the support or materials they might require."

The program is targeted at relatively small problems that nonetheless interfere with providing the most efficient care possible. Whereas larger problems are addressed by tools such as RPIWs, smaller challenges within the control of a frontline worker or small team are ideal for the Everyday Lean Ideas approach. As an example, hospital staff members were having difficulty keeping other staff members aware when patients had fallen. Staff members coming on for a shift would sometimes not get word right away about a patient who had fallen or was at a higher risk for falling and thus required an added dimension of protection.

Staff members offered an idea to place red laminated stars attached to the fall alert flags outside the rooms of patients prone to falling. This visual cue made it instantly clear who was at additional risk. The idea worked so well on one floor that it was spread throughout the hospital. "We're trying to create a culture where staff have permission and the capability to just fix things and make it better—to make it part of their everyday work," says Phillips.

Leadership

What is the nature of leadership in an organization such as Virginia Mason? On a particular day in early 2010 two small examples are telling. In one case, Lynne Chafetz, Senior Vice President and Chief Legal Counsel, engaged in "executive rounding"—a process where all Virginia Mason executives spend some time each week in a particular department. Chafetz worked her way through the Cardiology Department, asking questions, listening, and offering encouragement. What was the medical center's head attorney doing in Cardiology? She was providing a form of executive surveillance. She was showing the flag. She was gathering information. More than anything, though, she was living the Virginia Mason culture—a culture that says that leaders are engaged at all levels.

On that same day, Gary Kaplan and Sarah Patterson made their way deep into the basement of the medical center to the Sterile Processing Department. They were accompanied by a half-dozen other senior executives, as well as a *sensei* in town that week from Japan. The leaders were there to see the result of intensive recent work in reorganizing the department. It had been a notoriously difficult task. Over a period of a couple of years various improvement efforts had been tried and overall improvement was minimal. One failed for the reason cited earlier by Linda Hebish—that the improvement was done *to* the staff rather than *with* them. However, a recent RPIW had produced a proposed new process and Kaplan, Patterson, and the others were in the basement to see it firsthand. The department leader explained that part of their problem was that the men and women cleaning the instruments too often had to get up from their workstations to go and find things. This was distracting and affected not only productivity, but quality as well. Now the team was proposing a new process design to solve that and other problems. Because it was a clean environment similar to an operating room, Kaplan, Patterson, and the others were required to don blue sterile coveralls and hats. They moved as a group through the department where lights glared and thousands of instruments used in surgical procedures each day were sterilized and repackaged to be ready for the next surgery. It was a complicated business to get the right set of tools to the right surgical location at the right time.

In a way, this is what being a leader at Virginia Mason is all about: Being there on the *genba* where the work is done. Showing workers with varying levels of education—among the lowest paid earners in the medical center—that what they do truly matters; that their work is valued and essential to the overall mission. Kaplan and Patterson focused on the work—a comment here, a few questions there. Mostly, they listened carefully. There was no pep talk, no histrionics. It was all about the work. All about getting better every day. All about providing that patient the finest possible surgical instruments—the finest care—and about showing the rest of the health care universe that there might be a better pathway ahead.

Chapter Ten

The Journey Continues

Will You Teach Us?

In June 2006, Dr. Gary Kaplan traveled from Seattle, Washington, to Newcastle upon Tyne, England, set on the North Sea coast 300 miles north of London, a sixteen-hour journey covering 6,000 miles. Dr. Kaplan's trip to Newcastle came at the invitation of physicians working within the Northeast region of Britain's National Health Service (NHS). NHS Northeast is a sprawling organization, one of the ten Strategic Health Authorities in Britain serving as administrative regions of the NHS. The group of physicians and health care leaders Kaplan was here to address were responsible for taking care of 2.5 million Britons in a geographic area running as far north as the Scottish border. The area included eight hospitals, mental health trusts, and a dozen primary care organizations.

Addressing leaders from throughout the Northeast at the University of Newcastle Medical School, Kaplan spoke about the basics—about the Toyota Production System as a management method; about adapting it to health care in the form of the Virginia Mason Production System. He talked about the dramatic difference it was making in quality and safety within his medical center and in the lives of patients. He told the story of Virginia Mason's journey with a focus on quality and safety and the elimination of waste. He talked about the physician compact, the idea of patient first, and the Virginia Mason strategic vision.

There was something special about this day, about this particular presentation, for during the course of it, Gary Kaplan's passion for his patients came to the fore. Yes, he was the CEO of a medical center—that was true—but on this day he was a doctor speaking to a room full of other doctors. They understood one another at a visceral level. There were obvious cultural differences, of course, but there were many more professional similarities that bound them together. They shared backgrounds, training, frustrations, and hopes. That Kaplan had practiced medicine on the front lines for his entire adult life—that he *still* practiced even as he worked as CEO—gave him important credibility with the English physicians.

To this particular audience, however, he was more than a CEO and more than a doctor: He was a visionary with the courage to find and follow a new and very different path, and he had followed it and stuck to it and the results were impressive. This struck a powerful chord with the caregivers in the audience, because it was what they wanted for their patients—a better, safer, more efficient system.

When Kaplan completed his remarks the audience—the physicians and administrators and others—rose to their feet and began a sustained level of applause that Gary Kaplan had rarely experienced in his life. Dr. Jack Silversin, a Cambridge, Massachusetts, consultant who had been working with the British group for a while, was stunned by this show of emotion. "When Gary finished his remarks he was given the most sustained round of applause I have ever heard in England," says Silversin, who originally introduced Kaplan to the NHS Northeast leaders. "Gary was being recognized for what he and others in his organization had done working at the coal face, as they say in England. More importantly, I think the applause said 'If he did it, so can we.' His message was affirming."

Dr. Stephen Singleton, Regional Director of Public Health and Medical Director of the NHS Northeast, found Kaplan's presentation compelling. By that point, the NHS had been working on a variety of improvement efforts for a couple of decades. Kaplan, though, was talking about something different—something deeper and more sustained. Initially, when Dr. Singleton looked at the Toyota-inspired methods, he worried that it might be "another improvement toolbox," but as he heard Gary Kaplan speak—and after engaging in lengthy discussions with him—Singleton saw that it was "how Virginia Mason was running the business top to bottom." After a series of discussions with Kaplan, Dr. Singleton and his NHS colleagues were deeply impressed; so impressed that they asked Kaplan and his team to teach them the Virginia Mason Production System. The folks at NHS were proposing an arrangement where they would invest time and money over a period of years to learn from the folks in Seattle.

If You Build It ...

Health care professionals from all over had started visiting Virginia Mason as soon as word got around about the medical center's use of the TPS—five years before Dr. Kaplan traveled to Newcastle upon Tyne. The visitors came in search of a new pathway to improvement. They came from different cities, states, and countries; from small, rural practices and large, urban medical centers—all in search of a new and better way.

Kaplan and his colleagues had barely returned from Japan in the summer of 2002 when the calls started coming in with questions and requests for visits. Curiosity about what was happening at Virginia Mason increased exponentially in December 2004 when Kaplan and Mike Rona made a presentation at the Institute for Health Care Improvement national forum (the same conference where Dr. Don Berwick announced the IHI 100,000 Lives Campaign—an effort to save 100,000 lives through the application of a specific set of quality and safety improvements). The Virginia Mason presentation created a buzz at the conference packed with a self-selected group of more than 5,000 health care professionals passionate about quality. Right away, calls from around the country and beyond streamed into Seattle. *"What is going on? How does the Toyota Production System relate to work in a medical center? What exactly are you folks up to?"*

"In those early days people were really, really curious," says Susie Creger, RN, the Kaizen Promotion Office (KPO) manager at that time. "Typically the first thing the callers would say was 'I understand you're implementing the Toyota Production System and we've heard about that in factories and in industry, but we just cannot figure out how you're doing that in health care and we want to know more.'" Linda Hebish would recount various aspects of the improvement work to callers, trying "to get them to understand that a process is a process whether you're in manufacturing or health care."

By 2005, rare was the day at Virginia Mason without a visiting team trying to understand the method. The KPO took responsibility for hosting visitors and Hebish, Creger, and others would seek to get as precise an understanding as possible about the potential visitors' interests. Many wanted an overview although there were groups that wanted to focus on specific areas such as primary care, safety, the supply chain, or the cancer center. In the early years the cancer center and hyperbaric medicine were the most tangible examples of the improvement work and thus nearly every group made stops in those areas. "We wanted to organize group visits around a quarterly seminar format so we could limit the stress the tours made on our staff and patients," says Creger. "It worked most of the time but sometimes people were coming to Seattle as part of a larger tour from China, Singapore, or Australia, for example, and it was hard to say no."

The team decided early on to charge a fee for visits in part to cover the time of the Virginia Mason staff conducting the visits, but also to make sure that anyone wishing to come was serious about the work. In the years following the presentation at the 2004 IHI national forum, as the work at Virginia Mason grew more robust and produced ever better results, news reports appeared on the *CBS Evening News,* in the *Wall Street Journal, Washington Post,* and more.

Typically, the day for visitors would begin in the auditorium where Hebish or Creger would provide a forty-five-minute overview of VMPS. Gary Kaplan would then come in and speak for fifteen minutes and then take questions for an additional fifteen minutes. Following that would be a presentation on the Virginia Mason patient safety work, and then a presentation on a specific area of interest to the visitors. If they had said in advance, for example, that their main interest was primary care, they might hear a presentation from Kim Pittenger about the work at the Virginia Mason Kirkland Clinic. Visitors would be guided on tours to two or three different areas of the medical center. Virginia Mason set a visitor limit of fifty people per day, and there were a number of cases where a single institution bought all fifty spaces.

Why this level of demand? There were many places across the United States and beyond where superb clinical and administrative leaders were forging change and improvement. There was great work being done at places such as Intermountain Health Care and Kaiser Permanente; at Cincinnati Children's and the Mayo Clinic; at Geisinger and ThedaCare and dozens of others. Nowhere else in the country, however—nowhere else in the world (according to a leading Japanese *sensei*)—had TPS been adapted in health care to the degree that it was at Virginia Mason. Thus, anyone seriously interested in seeing the Toyota principles applied rigorously in health care had to make the trek to Virginia Mason.

Role Model

There was a difference in order of magnitude between having visitors come to Seattle for a day or a few days versus agreeing to teach the NHS Northeast region over a period of years. Before Kaplan agreed to the arrangement, he conducted interviews with key NHS leaders. He wanted to make sure that the British were truly committed. He wanted to reflect and make sure he was comfortable that his team in Seattle was ready for such a massive undertaking. "My speculation," says Singleton, "is that Gary was getting a lot of interest in what VM was doing but until then he didn't want to talk it up too much. And the Northeast of England was far enough away to teach VMPS and how you do it, before teaching a high profile outfit in the U.S."

Deeper discussions led to additional visits, including trips to Seattle by NHS officials. The result was a contract for Virginia Mason to teach the NHS Northeast how to apply VMPS in the United Kingdom. Susie Creger traveled to Newcastle and conducted a day-long seminar focused on explaining VMPS tools. She and other Virginia Mason employees taught value-stream mapping, led *kaizen* events, and went to work on the *genba* in various NHS Northeast sites. The Virginia Mason team certified fifty-two NHS participants in VMPS that first year, and it was seen as such a landmark achievement that a black-tie evening was held to mark the occasion. The learning process involved eight to twelve clinicians and administrators from England coming to Seattle every month for a week at a time to learn, and a team from the NHS joined Kaplan and his colleagues on a working trip to Japan, for the first time in 2007.

Several times each year, Kaplan and colleague Diane Miller, executive director of the Virginia Mason Institute, travel to the United Kingdom to coach senior leaders, and other Virginia Mason personnel travel to the United Kingdom monthly to help lead improvement workshops. Customarily, the Virginia Mason team includes a clinician or administrator along with specialists from the KPO or others who have been trained in depth on the methodology. One of the constant challenges is impatience on the part of English clinicians and administrators for results—and with how difficult the work can be, particularly in terms of cultural changes. The Virginia Mason team coaches both patience and rigor.

"It's clearly developed well," says Dr. Singleton. "There's a genuine partnership involved here. Although they are teaching and we are learning the Virginia Mason Production System, we've given them a safe way to learn how to teach it. We're a big system, but not high profile in the states. And VMPS itself has been developing. We've learned a lot from each other in Seattle, here in the Northeast of England, and in Japan." There are obvious differences between the two health systems, yet they share a common language around quality, efficiency, and safety. Most important, they share the same ardent desire to improve.

Perhaps the most powerful aspect of the relationship is the model Virginia Mason provides for the NHS Northeast. "The best thing we've got," says Singleton, "is Virginia Mason as a role model saying, 'This is the way we run our organization. It's not this year's new improvement technique. This is actually the way we run our organization, and we are going to follow it to its conclusion.'"

Already, positive results are evident in NHS Northeast. Dr. Singleton says that one of the mental health trusts within the Northeast region (which serves more than 1 million people) conducted a Rapid Process Improvement Workshop (RPIW) on a single ward to improve efficiency, and it worked so well it was spread to seven additional wards. The result was increased capacity in existing space significant enough to cancel a $1.5 million expansion. News of this sort of progress spread quickly and provided important credibility for VMPS work.

Dr. Singleton says other health care provider organizations—including some areas within the NHS—are engaged in what he terms "lean light." In contrast, he believes he and his colleagues are learning a "pure version" of TPS from the Virginia Mason teachers. He says when he and his colleagues talk with academics who have a deep understanding of the work, "we speak the same language."

Not everyone in the NHS speaks that language, however, or wishes to. Dr. Singleton and his associates recognize that there is a certain inevitability to the pushback. "More people want it to fail than to succeed," he says. However, Singleton and his colleagues believe it will work, and they know that Kaplan and his team faced similar pushback and persevered. They intend to do the same. An essential part of the learning process for the British is to understand the failures their counterparts in Seattle have experienced.

"This is really, really important," says Singleton. "One of the best things is that the people at VM have shared their failures with us. They don't hide anything and talk only about the good stuff. They are quite honest about the fact that some things have not worked—that is really refreshing and has really helped us knowing that it's hard and sometimes does not go well." Says Kaplan, "Part of our job is to ensure we have the results but also to tear down the barriers and to celebrate failure as well as success. Failing is part of change, it's part of innovation, it's part of being willing to go to a different place. It's what you do and learn after you fail that's most important."

Singleton has various ways to measure progress in the broad scheme of things. In the overall arc of history, he says, "Toyota is sixty years ahead of us, and Virginia Mason is a few steps ahead of us." He says he and his colleagues in Britain have accomplished enough to see some important results and also "to see how hard it is." He has pride in the work and the journey, recognizing that there are few others out there who have followed this path—who are, as he says, "trudging through the snow."

The Virginia Mason Institute

There is no shortage of ambition at Virginia Mason. The medical center's original vision—formulated back when Kaplan took over in 2000—was "to be the quality leader." But within a few years Kaplan and his colleagues realized they were building a storehouse of knowledge and experience with potential application far beyond Seattle. It was then that the mission broadened "to be the quality leader *and transform health care*" throughout the United States and beyond (emphasis added).

The work itself at Virginia Mason would be the foundation for transformation, but it was clear to Kaplan and his leadership team that a vehicle was needed to teach the method in the United Kingdom and elsewhere. Thus was born the Virginia Mason Institute in October 2008. Creation of the Institute allows the internal Virginia Mason KPO—which was bearing the brunt of the visiting traffic—to stay focused on internal improvement. This is pivotal, because it is the improvement work that is the rationale for the Institute.

"And that is essential to the mission to transform health care," says Kaplan. "The single biggest thing we've got to transform health care is our own experience and our own results."

Diane Miller uses an agricultural metaphor, saying that the Virginia Mason Institute harvests the ideas, experiences, and work of Virginia Mason to share with the world. "It's classroom and hands-on work, all about patient care, all about putting the patient first," says Susie Creger. "It's about strategically looking at it and putting a structure in place so that others can sustain their own improvement work."

Because the Virginia Mason Institute depends on work at VM, all Institute faculty members are drawn from the medical center, where they are actively working even as they teach. All faculty have extensive firsthand experience with the methods and tools of VMPS and all have firsthand experience learning the methods on the factory floor in Japan as well. Although a few faculty members are assigned half-time or full-time to the Institute, most are drawn into projects on a case-by-case basis, depending on the particular expertise required. It is essential that Institute faculty members are actively engaged in improvement work within the medical center, for it means their teaching is practical, drawn from real-world challenges and solutions, and based on current experience. Dr. Henry Otero, for example, who played such a pivotal role in the redesign of the cancer center, serves half-time on the Institute faculty while also practicing in the Oncology Department.

Diane Miller recognized from the day she became the Institute's first leader that the key to its success rests within the medical center itself. At the outset she received assurances from Sarah Patterson that the pursuit of improvement would continue "because the success of the Institute is *totally* dependent on Virginia Mason's success," says Miller. "So if we're not making progress, we'll have nothing to share with other people."

Miller estimates that about half of the visitors to Virginia Mason "have begun to embark on this work in some fashion and they really are kind of lost about what does that really look like and what will it take for us to really continue this work. So they come to talk with executives, exchange information, and see it on the shop floor." The Institute runs many custom visits for organizations interested in a highly targeted aspect of the work—the OR facility design, for example. An organization planning on building a new hospital might come and ask "How are you applying these principles as you build a different kind of hospital and what does that look like? How are you doing it?"

On a practical level, the Institute provides income that can help Virginia Mason. On a different level, the Institute enables the Virginia Mason team to share knowledge with others on a quality improvement and transformation journey and, as such, it is an important source of pride for the entire Virginia Mason team.

"Accountable Outside Our Own Walls"

At the deepest level, however, the Institute serves as an ongoing challenge to Virginia Mason to *sustain* the work. If they are committed to teach, then they must be committed to learning and improvement. Anything less than a full commitment to *kaizen*—continuous incremental improvement—would make them less than fully qualified as teachers. Worse, perhaps, it would reveal a lack of commitment to the essential nature of the journey. "The Institute," says Kaplan, "helps us sustain our work by forcing us to be accountable outside our own walls—to others."

There are clearly limits to what the Institute can accomplish and its existence does not mean to suggest that VMPS is the only available means to improvement. That is certainly not the case and Dr. Kaplan is careful to point that out wherever he goes. However, health care organizations serious about transformation around quality and efficiency have little choice in this environment but to choose *a* way—some path that leads to a better place. The Virginia Mason Institute teaches VMPS, but within that it teaches leadership and a willingness to identify, understand, and confront the present state. It teaches many tools and ideas that can be used outside of VMPS itself. Whatever improvement path is chosen, the essential ingredient will have to be leadership, and that is what the Virginia Mason story is about in so many ways. "At the end of the day," says Kaplan, "as senior leaders that's what we do, we sponsor change," by whatever improvement method that works.

Through the years, many calls to Virginia Mason have come from quality improvement personnel or clinicians who feel a sense of urgency about change that is not shared by the leaders of their institutions. Linda Hebish says that many calls would begin with someone saying "I've been trying to get my executives to let me do this here. Can I bring them to Virginia Mason so you guys can convince them for me?" Hebish generally explains what a visit might or might not accomplish and is clear in saying that leadership from the top of an organization is essential to success with VMPS.

The volume of visits became challenging particularly when increasing feedback from the Virginia Mason front lines indicated that the visits were disruptive.

"We realized we had to be more careful in the patient care areas," says Creger. "We're here to take care of patients, not to tour visitors through the halls. We had too many people coming, and we were asking our managers and our front-line staff to stop their work and talk with these people." There was an inherent conflict. On one side, frontline workers at Virginia Mason did not want their work with patients interrupted, yet these same workers were often so enthusiastic about the improvements that they were eager to share what they had learned.

One of the most revealing parts of any trip to Virginia Mason is when visitors are shown clinic or hospital floors. The cumulative nature of the work over a period approaching a decade—the hundreds of RPIWs, all the nursing work, facilities changes, and on and on—has created a health care system in flow. VMPS has eliminated much of the waste that creates chaos and makes hospital floors feel confused or disorganized. Susie Creger says when she takes groups on tours of the facility, they are struck by the calmness. "And people think, 'Well, they must not have many patients,' and they ask and I say, 'Oh, yeah, we're full.' And they say, 'Every room here is full?'"

Visitors often find it difficult to believe that a particular floor or section is full—every exam room occupied—because there is none of the typical chaos that goes with a busy section. "And then visitors see the waiting room is mostly empty," says Hebish, "and they think, 'Doesn't a full waiting room mean I'm a success—that I have a successful practice?' Breaking free of those old assumptions is an important part of the whole process. Guests eventually realize that it's not any one aspect of VMPS—not any one method or philosophy or tool. It's a cultural transformation—an entirely new and different way of thinking about, analyzing, measuring, and *doing* the work."

It is just that—the transformation of the Virginia Mason culture—that lies at the heart of the achievement. "We're being held to expectations and standards, and we are much more focused on outcomes, on things that are measurable," observes Charleen Tachibana. "The cultural change is about much more respect for people within the organization and the role of different individuals contributing to different parts of process—really a huge leap in respect for one another and what people do. We listen better to our colleagues. We understand the work they do as never before, and we *appreciate* the work that they do."

The Institute is the most tangible manifestation of the Virginia Mason effort to transform health care. Even as the Institute seeks to teach at a granular level, it also seeks to inspire at the broadest level. The most difficult change in health care is cultural. It is impossible to attend any health care conference on improvement without hearing at least one presenter—and usually more than that—utter the wisdom that "culture eats strategy for lunch."

The Obstacle of Arrogance

The improvement path is strewn with obstacles, many of them formidable. In health care, change is difficult almost by definition. Certainly an important lesson of the Virginia Mason experience is just how hard it is to improve—how much work, determination, and time it takes. In the Virginia Mason story, the difficulty encountered has been (and continues to be) part and parcel of a committed effort to change and improve. For many other health care organizations in the United States, an initial obstacle to improvement is the unwillingness or inability—for whatever reason—to commit to an improvement pathway.

Among the many obstacles to improvement, there are two, in particular, that stand out. One is complacency—a sense among some in health care that things might not be perfect but that the current system is working well enough and to attempt any sort of sustained change would be overwhelming and disruptive. At many health care organizations there is little or no sense of urgency for change or, worse, a pro-forma impulse to change because it seems to be what others are doing as the storm outside gathers.

The other obstacle, perhaps more deeply rooted, is a sense of arrogance or hubris that has been embedded within the DNA of American medicine for generations. Arrogance is particularly corrosive, for it has allowed many well-intentioned people to believe that the U.S. health care system is the finest anywhere. But as the *New York Times* observed, "the truth is that this country lags well behind other advanced nations in delivering timely and effective care ... [and] a growing body of evidence" indicates "the United States is a laggard not a leader in providing good medical care."

The question of whether the United States has the finest clinicians should not be confused with whether the nation has the best health care *system,* whether it delivers the highest quality care. Certainly the United States has some of the most accomplished physicians in a wide variety of medical specialties anywhere in the world. But brilliant clinicians do not a system make. A quality system is one that delivers superb care, safe care, efficient care, and affordable care. Applying this definition, it is clear that the belief that the United States has the best system in the world is little more than myth—and the myth of America's health care supremacy is far from benign.

Arrogance in American health care is the failure to recognize how serious the system problems really are and to act on that recognition. If you believe you are the best, it would be irrational to take on the kind of difficult change that leads to quality improvement. Thus, the culture of arrogance slows, suppresses, and resists change. Dr. Paul Batalden suggests that doctors tend to be "in love with what they were doing and to suggest that these smart people should do something different was an affront." Says Gary Kaplan, "People go into medicine because they want to be in a helping profession, but many also like the prestige and working in perhaps the most respected of professions. It fits the ego needs that most of us have."

This notion of arrogance within health care is not new, of course, having been studied for years by physicians and scholars. What is relatively new, though, is the idea that cultural arrogance in medicine is an obstacle—and perhaps a very serious obstacle—to improving quality, efficiency, and affordability. Columbia's Dr. Barron H. Lerner has written that "physicians actually enjoyed relatively little power until the early 20th century. Then, a series of scientific discoveries, most notably the germ theory of disease, enhanced … the 'cultural authority' of the medical profession. With improved tools like insulin, penicillin, and the polio vaccine, the reputation of doctors accelerated further over the coming decades." In one sense this growing prestige was positive, for it gave doctors a prominent enough role so that patients might listen more carefully to their guidance and abide by it. But there was a clear downside as well. "Rewarded in terms of money and prestige," Dr. Lerner writes, "some physicians became vain and arrogant, making extraordinary demands and openly misbehaving. Most notorious were certain surgeons who ran operating rooms like fiefs."

In its 1999 report, *To Err Is Human,* the IOM identified "authority gradient" as an obstacle to improvement in health care. Authority gradient describes the hierarchy in a given situation, and it has been the subject of increasing discussion in health care. In some situations, the authority gradient is extremely steep—the surgeon holds the power and no one else dares speak, for example. In other situations where input is welcomed by the senior surgeon, the gradient is more gradual—and thus others on the surgical team feel more comfortable speaking up. An intimidating boss creates a steep authority gradient, whereas a collegial boss creates a more gradual authority gradient.

Drs. Atul Gawande and Peter Pronovost have identified the authority gradient as an important element in preventing medical errors. Pronovost, a physician at Johns Hopkins Hospital in Baltimore, has been working to understand how best to improve patient safety for years, and his checklists for a variety of procedures are used in hospitals throughout the nation. Inspiration for checklists came originally from the aviation industry, where checklists have dramatically improved safety through the years. An essential element of the improvement in aviation was flattening the authority gradient—changing the culture to not only permit but encourage any crew member, regardless of rank, to speak up if anything on the checklist was amiss. A similar cultural shift is required in health care.

VMPS is built on a very gradual authority gradient that not only welcomes but encourages input from everyone in the organization. It goes so far, for example, as to empower and encourage every employee within the medical center to stop the line when a patient might be threatened in some way.

Is it possible the culture of arrogance also blinds the United States to important lessons from other countries? "The United States has been slow to learn from countries that have systematically adopted policies that curtail spending and enhance value," writes Karen Davis, President of the Commonwealth Fund. Charleen Tachibana says Virginia Mason was as guilty of arrogance as anyone back around 2000 before Gary Kaplan took over, but the cultural shift at the medical center from provider-centric to patient-focused does much to erode that arrogance. Now, she says, "we are much more humble." The difficulty of the work—the enormity of the undertaking at Virginia Mason—tends to make personnel within the medical center more humble than not, and it makes for constant vigilance on the part of Virginia Mason leaders.

The antidote to complacency and arrogance, says Dr. Kaplan, "is to understand the work—the as-is state, the current state. The first thing we did when we came home from the first trip to Japan was to require a value stream map in every major area of the medical center. When you see that—when you see the reality—you cannot be complacent. You cannot be arrogant. When you see the waste, spinning wheels, you see that ultimately the person who suffers is the patient. To me, that's the eye-opener. You go into it thinking 'We're good, we're high quality, we've got great people.' Then you map out the work. You go out on the *genba* with a clipboard and stopwatch and sketch pad and you see the reality and at that point how can anybody be complacent about this? How can you be arrogant about this?"

A Nonsystem

The Virginia Mason Production System is many things, but one of its greatest values is as a powerful antidote to complacency and arrogance. Anyone adopting the system would only do so with the recognition that the existing nonsystem does not work. Deciding to act on that notion conquers complacency. The fact that VMPS requires continuous improvement—the concept of *kaizen*—is the antithesis of arrogance or complacency. The empowerment of all individuals within an organization to stop the line, for example, or for the frontline workers to participate in quality improvement, is the antithesis of arrogance. An RPIW where employees from the chief of surgery to housekeeping gather as equals to analyze and improve is the antithesis of arrogance.

When an RPIW team convened to improve the cancer center it was a nurse—not one of the physicians or the department head—who said that they should bring all services to the patient. It was a front-line supervisor of a single department who suggested to the Chief of Medicine, Dr. Mecklenburg, that every employee in the medical center should get vaccinated for the flu.

VMPS is egalitarian at its core. The system itself and the way it is applied each day at Virginia Mason is the antithesis of arrogance. VMPS says improvement must be continuous and if that is required then it means, by definition, that the existing system is flawed; is not good enough. If you recognize as the underlying principle of your work that the existing system is flawed, then how is arrogance possible?

Certainly, viewed from the 30,000-foot level—from Washington where policymakers grapple with the various implications of reform—the system is broken. More urgently, however, those who know best can see that it is broken at the ground level—at the front lines where doctors and patients come together. Primary care can reasonably be called the front line in health care and practitioners there tell a compelling story. Dr. Kim Pittenger has been practicing as a primary care doctor now for twenty-eight years, nineteen years under the traditional system and nine under VMPS. And Pittenger's view is that the traditional system is no system at all. "I was trained in a craftsman school of developing my own style and techniques of getting things done the best way, and I've realized that that was a nonsystem that was attempting to organize and improve care in a highly complex environment that's unstable, that's not self-organizing," he says. "And if you want it to be organized and to quit making mistakes and if you want it not to take so much time that all you do is work, then you're going to have to adopt *a system.*

"It's not going to happen by virtue of craftsmanship methods. We are just not all that self-organizing, and we all don't have the time to look at our work and see with clear vision where the waste is and where we're about to hurt somebody. You have to have a structured system that does that and once that sets you up, your life improves and all day long you get thanked and all day long you do not live in fear of what you just forgot and what you've got to remember to do tomorrow. That's been the main thing that's happened to me and along the way we've got a cadre of doctors who've weathered this storm that's causing everyone to burn out and say medicine is no fun. And what VMPS has really done is preserve that eighteen to twenty minutes with the patient—and sometimes more—that is fun, that is creative, and that is the intellectual exercise we all wanted when we went to medical school."

Why is the American health care system not a system? How is it that an industry with so many of the smartest people in the world has been so chaotic for so long? Part of it is cultural, of course—the reflexive acceptance of the way things were done because iconic individuals said so. Part of it, as well, has been a lack of vision, a failure to see over the horizon that something better might be possible. "I don't think leaders felt empowered or had a method to improve," says Charleen Tachibana. "The way the hospital ran when I was a manager was I knew what happened in my unit, but I didn't have a clue what happened in anybody else's unit. In fact, I never even met with those managers, so we were running thirteen different hospitals all doing it our own way. Even within a unit you would do it differently on every shift, or you might do it differently on a weekend. There was no accountability to a standard. There were no standards. So someone has to help declare the standard, and then you have to make sure that everybody knows how to do it and actually does it and maintains it over time."

A Sense of Hope

Perhaps the most significant achievement on the journey thus far is sustaining the method. This singular achievement is about leadership at every level within the medical center. It is about leadership that inspires, demands, pushes, insists—leaders who are committed to the path and who will not yield; leadership that shows the way and enables all workers to be successful and to see the value of their work within VMPS. "If you don't have the leadership that we have holding each other accountable and constantly challenging each other—if you don't have that you can't replicate this," says Vice President Katerie Chapman. "You just can't do it."

The essential lesson of the Virginia Mason experience is that leadership and discipline are the foundational elements that sustain the work. "One of the things I'm most proud of is our ability to have stuck with it despite a lot of criticism, despite the lack of popularity and, frankly, just being blatantly laughed at out there," says Charleen Tachibana. "I think we've done a really good job becoming a learning organization, staying open to ideas and open to continuing to look at ourselves in terms of what's not right, where can we fix it. I think we've done a really good job of having a common knowledge base, common language around a process, and a system for improvement and changing our culture to form around that."

"It's about day-in and day-out focus on results," says Kaplan. "It's about leveraging VMPS as a management system across the entire enterprise. Rather than fixing asthma and applying those lessons to diabetes and then fixing it disease by disease, we're saying change the management system and leverage it across the entire organization."

That Virginia Mason is able to do this provides hope for others within the industry. "We *do* have hope to offer the rest of the industry and promise that this is working and that we can take it further," says Charleen Tachibana. "I think that getting out, offering hope, offering potential, helping others learn what we've learned but then sticking to it to continue to evolve here as well. We need to be diligent on both of those fronts.

"The culture has also changed in that we feel a tremendous sense of hope throughout the medical center about what could be; about the possibilities. Our ability to create a vision and to translate that to the front line, to the entire workforce, has created a huge sense of hopefulness. It's palpable throughout the organization. There's no more grieving for what used to be. There's so much energy and optimism and forward thinking."

The aspiration is that the hope spreads to others—to clinicians and administrators throughout the world of health care who have embarked on their own effort to transform the quality of care at their organization. The Virginia Mason example demonstrates that with VMPS: Patients spend more value-added time with clinicians; defects in care have been significantly reduced and in many cases eliminated; patients are safer; waste has been reduced throughout the care process and eliminated in many areas; patient and provider satisfaction is significantly increased; and the organization is on much stronger financial footing.

John Black, the former Boeing leader who helped guide Virginia Mason in the early days, has contracted to bring a group of leaders from a Florida hospital to Seattle to learn by conducting an RPIW. What makes this a particularly noteworthy event is that the Florida team will be doing this work on the *genba* at Virginia Mason. This involves others doing at Virginia Mason what the Virginia Mason team did on the factory floors in Japan at Hitachi and Mitsubishi "They'll be doing an RPIW in a specific area, applying the tools, doing the measurements and giving recommendations to us," says Linda Hebish. "And that's a huge transformation piece because there will not be people from the VM department on the team. The VM people will be available, but the department is going to be comfortable with outside eyes giving them recommendations. It's an incredible step for us."

That is not at all an exaggeration, says Dr. Kaplan. The idea that an outside health care organization is coming in to work on the Virginia Mason *genba* is a powerful signal that the Virginia Mason team is committed to transparency. And it demonstrates, says Kaplan, "that we have intentionally set ourselves up for continuous challenge to help us sustain our course."

The Journey Continues

What does the future hold for Virginia Mason? Given the enormity of the task, there are obvious concerns. "I worry that we end up resting on our laurels, that we lose the drive or that we get distracted," says Tachibana. "We have not done that a lot but there are distracting things out there and sometimes our own pride can be a bit distracting if we were to let that get a hold of us. The ability to sustain the discipline over a time, I think is going to be what makes or breaks it."

There is so much happening in a positive direction that there is far more reason for optimism than doubt. The culture will likely continue to evolve in constructive ways. The alignment of mission and goals across departments will continue to improve and it seems quite likely that clinical results will improve as well. The dramatic improvement in leadership at every level of the organization has already produced significant results and will likely continue to do so. So much of the work has become and will continue to become more rigorous and with intensified rigor comes acceleration in the process of transformation.

Improvements in communication throughout the medical center are helping to capture the hearts and minds of increasing numbers of staff members. Leadership and communication together are a powerful combination in connecting the dots for workers; being crystal clear about expectations and each team member's critical role in achieving the necessary results for patients.

Dr. Kaplan believes a foundational element essential to success in sustaining the work is "the commitment of the senior team. Without that nothing would happen." That commitment, he says, includes a "shared vision for where we want to go. Without that shared vision you're not going to get there." In 2008 and 2009, increases in *kaizen* activity were fueled by 110 certified RPIW leaders, ten certified 3P leaders, and hundreds of VMPS-trained managers.

The following graphic shows the progression of *kaizen* activity since the inception of VMPS. The dramatic drop of events in 2005 represents the months-long reflective period in which all previous RPIWs had been remeasured and major events had been temporarily halted. In 2009, the number of *kaizen* events increased significantly as the organization rolled out new requirements for managers to hold events in their respective areas.

"We've been able to get more explicit about what leaders have to do to lead a transformation, to lead a changing organization, to lead a *Lean* organization,"

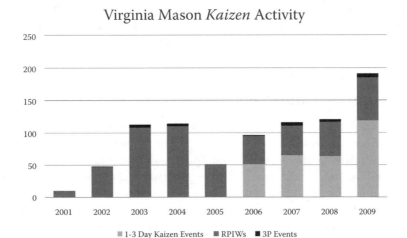

Virginia Mason *Kaizen* Activity

he says. "This is not a traditional way of leading—setting out the rules and policies we expect people to follow. It's a way of leading as a coach on the *genba*. It's being out there connecting dots, sharing the vision. When I say we have the commitment of senior leadership, I'm not just talking about leaders setting expectations or communicating. I'm saying that as a leader I am going to *do* the work, I'm going to learn the methods, be on the *genba,* lead the workshops. That's a huge message to send." A result of this type of leadership, says Kaplan, is a deeper understanding by frontline workers of the overall patient-focused mission. They buy into the idea of improving the quality and efficiency of care for every patient every time as never before. "It makes it much more an affair of the heart," he says.

"We're Just Getting Started"

As Dr. Kaplan looks around the health care landscape, he sees quite clearly that the system in which he and millions of others are working is "nowhere near as good as it should be." A defect rate of about 4 percent "would never be tolerated in any other industry," and he notes that for anyone harmed, the real defect rate is 100 percent. "We're asking people to do their best work in unreliable systems that are conspiring against them," he says. "And so that's what our work at Virginia Mason has been about, trying to create a reliable environment in which to work so that we can provide the patient with a defect-free product."

The critical first step in that process was recognizing that the patient had to come first in everything. Kaplan says that if you ask any of the 5,000 employees at Virginia Mason who is at the top of the strategic plan, every one of then—from chief of surgery to housekeeping—will tell you it's the patient. It is the patient who drives the Virginia Mason aspiration "to be the quality leader ... . What we really mean by that is if we could prove we were the quality leader, who would want to go anywhere else for health care, and who would want to work anywhere else? We can't prove it yet, but we're working hard at it."

Change is difficult, and particularly so in health care, where meaningful change nearly always requires cultural disruption. That is why Kaplan says that the Virginia Mason journey "at its core has been about change management." It means managing the change of a deeply ingrained culture—one where there is much too often the "lack of a shared vision. We have not taken the time in most of our health care organizations across the U.S. to actually focus on what is our common purpose, what are we trying to accomplish together?" There are also "misaligned expectations," especially among doctors who say, "What I signed up for is not what today's reality is all about."

There is a general "lack of urgency throughout health care," says Kaplan. "There's a lot of complacency out there." In part, that complacency is a result of ineffective leadership. An essential challenge to leadership is making change stick—which might well be the most difficult and underestimated part of the journey. "When the issue of holding the gains came up initially," says Kaplan, "a lot of people said, 'Well, you could create standard work and then you commoditize the physician. So you take any old doctor and plug him into the standard work. Well, that's not true. That's not what this is all about. What it's really about is taking great people and surrounding them with great systems. And when you take waste out you free up time, you create more value-added time: Value-added time with patients, because you eliminate all the non-value-added variation, value-added time with colleagues, value-added time with your family. Understanding this clearly helps us hold the gains."

Without strong leadership, of course, none of this is possible, and strong leaders, by definition, have courage. "This is really hard work, particularly these days," says Kaplan. "Feeling the urgency means understanding the magnitude of change that has to occur in our organization. And one of the challenges that I have is helping our team to have the kind of courage that's necessary to keep moving forward. Skeptics can become champions and knowing that has helped me develop the courage. There are a lot of people who are champions for our work who in the beginning thought we had lost our mind and basically said, 'Over my dead body,' and today they're some of our greatest champions.

"At Virginia Mason, we still have many challenges. We're almost ten years into a journey, and as far as I'm concerned, we are just getting started."

Source Notes

The Best Practice: How the New Quality Movement Is Transforming Medicine, was published in 2008 and contained a chapter about the innovative work at Virginia Mason. While writing *The Best Practice* I conducted a series of interviews in 2007 with a variety of physicians and administrators at Virginia Mason, including Dr. Gary Kaplan, Sarah Patterson, Dr. Robert Caplan, Dr. Robert Mecklenburg, Charleen Tachibana, Cathie Furman, and others. During the course of my work on that chapter, in addition to interviewing a number of people at Virginia Mason, I also interviewed others about Virginia Mason—including Dr. Don Berwick and Maureen Bisognano at the Institute for Health Care Improvement. In addition, I read a variety of articles and papers about Virginia Mason and the Toyota Production System (including the Harvard Business School study by Richard M. J. Bohmer and Erika M. Ferlins, published in January 2006). That work for *The Best Practice* equipped me with a foundational understanding of Virginia Mason, which I built upon in the course of writing this book. The great bulk of this book, however, relies on interviews I conducted with clinicians and administrators at Virginia Mason. For each chapter I sought out people within the organization who did the work at the front line or led the work, or both. The men and women who have been at the heart of this innovative journey are the ones who know the work and the story best.

Preface

The Preface relies on interviews with Dr. Kaplan and Sarah Patterson, Executive Vice President and COO, as well as Diane Miller, Executive Director of the Virginia Mason Institute; Linda Hebish, Administrative Director of the Kaizen Promotion Office; Andrew Baylor, Director, Hospital Kaizen Promotion

Office; Susie Creger, RN, a Kaizen Promotion Office manager; Val Ferris, KPO Administrative Director; Charleen Tachibana, RN, senior vice president, hospital administrator, and Chief Nursing Officer; Dr. Kim Pittenger; and Dr. Stephen Singleton, medical director of the National Health Service in the Northeast Region of England. The chapter also relies on the work of John Black, consultant and author (with David Miller) of *The Toyota Way to Health Care Excellence,* (2008, Health Administration Press, a division of the Foundation of the American College of Health Care Executives). It also relies on Black's book *A World Class Production System* (1998, Crisp Publications).

Chapter One

Chapter One relies on interviews with Gary Kaplan and Sarah Patterson as well as Drs. Robert Caplan, Joyce Lammert, Robert Mecklenburg, and Jack Silversin. It relies on *Why Hospitals Should Fly* by John Nance, as well as two of the defining studies by the Institute of Medicine of the National Academies—*To Err Is Human* (1999) and *Crossing the Quality Chasm* (2001). The chapter also relies on the work of John Black, consultant and author (with David Miller) of *The Toyota Way to Health Care Excellence* (2008, Health Administration Press, a division of the Foundation of the American College of Health Care Executives). It also relies on Black's book *A World Class Production System* (1998, Crisp Publications).

Chapter Two

The chapter relies on interviews with Gary Kaplan as well as interviews conducted in 2007 with Mike Rona, former Virginia Mason president. It relies on interviews with John Black; Art Byrne, CEO of Wiremold; and Drs. Donna Smith, Chief of Pediatrics; Robert Mecklenburg; and Fred Govier, Chief of Surgery. In addition, the chapter relies on Diane Miller; Sarah Patterson; Steve Schaefer, Vice President for Finance; Charleen Tachibana; and Ruth Anderson, former Senior Vice President of the Office of Process Improvement. The chapter draws from a *Seattle Times* article by Lisa Heyamoto, "Hospital on cost-cutting mission adds trip to Japan" (June 6, 2002), used with permission. The chapter draws on a series of letters written by Gary Kaplan and Mike Rona and sent from Japan back to the Virginia Mason community in Seattle as well as on John Black's book *The Toyota Way to Health Care Excellence.*

Chapter Three

The chapter relies on Dr. Andrew Jacobs, Chief Medical Officer, and Dr. Henry Otero, a specialist in Hematology/Oncology. It relies as well on Michaelle Wetteland, RN, Denise Dubuque, Sarah Patterson, John Black, and Gary Kaplan.

Chapter Four

This chapter relies on Cathie Furman, RN, Senior Vice President for Quality and Compliance; Gary Kaplan; Sarah Patterson; Lynne Chafetz, Senior Vice President and General Counsel to Virginia Mason; and Elizabeth Dunphy, RN. It relies also on Drs. Robert Mecklenburg, Robert Caplan, Joyce Lammert, and Daniel Hanson. The chapter draws from an article in the *Seattle Times* by Nick Perry and Carol M. Ostrom (November 25, 2004), as well as an article in *The Joint Commission Journal on Quality and Patient Safety* by Cathie Furman and Bob Caplan (July 2007, Vol. 33, No. 7).

Chapter Five

In this chapter I rely on Dr. Kim Pittenger, who was engaged in the work described here over a period of many years. In addition to a series of interviews I conducted with Dr. Pittenger, he provided detailed editorial guidance on events within the chapter and in some cases revised sections of the chapter that I had drafted so that they would more fully and accurately depict the ambulatory care innovations that are the focus of the chapter. In the course of helping me understand the work in this chapter, Dr. Pittenger relied on a number of his colleagues for important information and perspective including Drs. Brian McDonald, Mark Murray, Laurel Morrison, Ingrid Gerbino, Kim Leatham, Keith Dipboye, and Rich Furlong. In addition I relied on Dr. Joyce Lammert, and KPO Administrative Directors Cindy Rockfeld and John Eusek.

Chapter Six

In the section focused on creating a new ambulatory surgical experience, the chapter relies on Vice President Katerie Chapman and Dr. Steve Rupp, Medical Director for Perioperative Services and former Chief of Anesthesia. It also relies on Andrew Baylor, Robbi Bishop, and Liz Dunphy. In the section on the Center for Hyperbaric Medicine, I rely almost entirely on Dr. Neil Hampson, medical director of the center. I had interviewed Dr. Hampson in 2007 and toured his facility at that time. When I began the process of writing this book, Dr. Hampson had already drafted a section concerning the Center for Hyperbaric Medicine. Although I edited the section, I rely largely on his original draft.

Chapter Seven

The chapter relies on Charleen Tachibana; Rowena Ponischil, Nurse Manager; Martha Purrier, RN, KPO Director; and Dana Nelson-Peterson, RN, KPO Administrative Director. It draws from work done on the National Demonstration Project in the late 1980s by Drs. Donald Berwick and Paul Batalden, as well as Blanton Godfrey, PhD, formerly chief of quality at Bell Labs.

Chapter Eight

This chapter relies on a series of interviews with Dr. Robert Mecklenburg. I originally interviewed Dr. Mecklenburg in 2007 and conducted additional discussions with him for this book. The chapter relies as well on interviews with Gary Kaplan; Dr. Donald Storey, the Senior Medical Director of the Aetna Performance Networks; Dr. Andrew Friedman, head of Physical Medicine and Rehabilitation; and Annette King, former benefits manager at Starbucks. The article draws from *The Wall Street Journal* article on the Virginia Mason–Aetna–Starbucks collaboration (January 12, 2007).

Chapter Nine

The chapter relies substantially on Sarah Patterson. It relies as well on Gary Kaplan, Linda Hebish, Martha Purrier, Valerie Ferris, and VMPS specialists: Arni Verkler, Ana Anuradhika, Crystal McDermott, Amy London, Shawna Whipple, Gordon Sansaver, Erica Cumbee, Miwa Kudo, and Trudie Read. The chapter relies on Jennifer Phillips, Director of the Center for Virginia Mason Innovation Program; Lynne Chafetz; Kate Reed; Jim Cote; and Michael Ondracek.

Chapter Ten

The chapter relies on Gary Kaplan, Diane Miller, Jack Silversin, and Dr. Stephen Singleton. The chapter also relies on Linda Hebish, Susie Creger, Charleen

Tachibana, Katerie Chapman, Dr. Kim Pittenger, and Dr. Robert Mecklenburg. The chapter draws from the *New York Times* editorial "World's Best Medical Care?" (August 12, 2007). It also draws from the *Times* article by Dr. Barron H. Lerner of Columbia University entitled "Practicing Medicine Without a Swagger" (August 23, 2005). It draws from the Institute of Medicine study *To Err Is Human* (1999) and from the *New England Journal of Medicine* article by Karen Davis, PhD, President of the Commonwealth Fund, "Slowing the Growth of Health Care Costs—Learning from International Experience" (Vol. 359, No. 17, 1751–55, October 23, 2008). The chapter draws from two important books concerning safety: *Checklist* by Dr. Atul Gawande and *Safe Patients, Smart Hospitals: How One Doctor's Checklist Can Help Us Change Health Care from the Inside Out* by Peter Pronovost MD, PhD, and Eric Vohr (2010, Hudson Street Press).

Appendix

The section on spreading innovation in ambulatory care to General Internal Medicine (GIM) relies on Cindy Rockfeld, former director of GIM, Dr. Joyce Lammert and Dr. Julie Pattison, as well as John Eusek.

Glossary

3P: *Production Preparation Process*, a five-day event in which a team focuses on building a production system for a new plant, process or product

5S: a strategy that helps to keep our workplace safe and organized–it is a foundational element of the Virginia Mason Production System (VMPS). Includes Sort, Simplify, Sweep, Standardize, and Self-discipline.

Cycle time: the time required for one operator or machine to complete one cycle of work–it is measured with a stopwatch (includes the waste *within* the cycle and does not include waiting time before or after)

Defect: a mistake that is passed along to the next step in the process or to the customer

Everyday Lean Idea System (ELI): a formal method to capture staff ideas about removing waste in their work unit and develop them with their manager

External Setup: activities to prepare for the next process that can occur *while the current process is still running*

Final Report Out: a report given to the organization that includes a formal method for presentation that is intended to inform people of the work and inspire future improvements

Genba: where the work actually happens

Home Team: the workers that are not part of the improvement team, but whose work is affected by the changes–they are encouraged to participate by providing real-time ideas and honest feedback during planning, the event, and implementation

Inspection: searching for defects completed by comparing to a known standard

Internal Setup: activities to prepare for the next process that must occur *while the current process is stopped*

Jidoka: a method to increase productivity by implementing intelligent automation and defect elimination strategies

Kaizen Activity: events intended to meet one or more improvement targets in a value stream

Kaizen Event: a one- or two-day event focused on a particular process in which people who do the work are empowered to eliminate waste and reduce the burden of work

Kaizen: continuous incremental improvement

Kanban: a tool to effectively implement just-in-time and pull production–they are a visual cue that processes must begin

KPO: *Kaizen Promotion Office*, the department responsible for the deployment and application of the Virginia Mason Production System tools, methods, and concepts

Lead Time: the entire time required to provide a product or service, from request to completion–it is measured with a stopwatch (includes waits between cycles and "off hours" and weekends)

Lean: a general term describing methods similar to the Toyota Production System

Mistake: an inadvertent error

Mistake-proofing: a method that aims to prevent defects

Process Owner: a member of an improvement event planning team who will prepare the entire department for the event, assist in goal setting, ensure staff are informed of changes during week, and be accountable for implementation and follow-up

Product-Quantity (PQ) Analysis: a method that allows you to categorize your demand into specific families of products or services–after the PQ Analysis data may be used to identify root cause, level load, or otherwise improve the process

Root Cause: the true underlying reason that a problem exists (as opposed to the result or superficial reason)

RPIW: *Rapid Process Improvement Workshop*, a five-day workshop focused on a particular process in which people who do the work are empowered to eliminate waste and reduce the burden of work

Self-discipline: maintains standards through training, empowerment, commitment and discipline

Sensei: a term used to show respect to someone who has achieved a certain level of mastery in a skill–at Virginia Mason, it specifically refers to the consultants (not necessarily Japanese) that are regarded as masters of all or part of the elements of the Virginia Mason Production System

Setup: the time spent preparing to provide the next product or service–it measures clock time, not labor time

Setup Reduction: a method to reduce or eliminate setup time to increase capacity and flexibility

Simplify: makes places for necessary items

Sort: separates necessary from unnecessary

Sponsor: a member of an improvement event planning team who will select the area of focus, influence and approve targets and goals, support the event leaders, remove barriers that the team encounters and champion the team

Standard Operations: a specific method of observation and analysis to determine and document the most efficient way to complete the work

Standard Work: an agreed upon, repeatable sequence of work assigned to a single operator at a pace that meets customer demand

Standardize: creates a standard agreement and communicates it to the team

Sweep: a form of inspection that ensures everything is returned to its proper place

Target Sheet: a document that show progress toward end of event targets

TPS: *Toyota Production System*, Toyota's specific application of *kaizen*

Value Stream Improvements: actions that focus on increasing value from the perspective of the customer by decreasing waste

Value Stream Map: a visual tool to help see and understand the flow of process, information, and material

Value Stream Mapping: a process of understanding and depicting the transformation of a patient or product, then identifying and implementing improvements necessary to add value

Value Stream: the entire set of activities that encompass the transformation of a patient or product from beginning to end

Visual Controls: methods, devices, or mechanisms to visually manage operations

VMPS Flows of Medicine: the fundamental components of any process that flow together to create the patient's experience–patients, providers, family and relationships, medications, supplies, equipment, information and process engineering

VMPS: *Virginia Mason Production System*, Virginia Mason's management method, based on the principles and practices of the Toyota Production System and lean

Waste: any task or item that does not add value from the perspective of the customer. Taiichi Ohno identified seven types, including time, processing, defects, inventory, motion, overproduction, and transportation.

Work-in-process (WIP): the actual (counted) number of products or customers that have entered the process but have not yet been completed

Appendix

There are countless examples where VMPS tools and principles were applied to eliminate waste and improve patient care. Here, we examine several applications of the VMPS that provide insight into a variety of challenges that the Virginia Mason team has faced in their journey.

The first example details how the application of VMPS to the medical center business functions in finance has eliminated an extraordinary amount of waste and improved the bottom line. VMPS proved quite effective in the complex tangle of billing and collecting that is the web-like financial side of health care. "VMPS is embedded in all we do," says Steve Schaefer, Virginia Mason Director of Patient Financial Services. "It is our management method. It defines who we are and how we think each day. It's our foundation in putting the patient first."

The second example examines the work that brought flow stations to orthopedic surgery where initial resistance from surgeons was overcome.

The final example details much of the work done at a downtown ambulatory care site—General Internal Medicine (GIM)—referenced in Chapter Five. This section is particularly revealing in showing how challenging it can be to spread innovation such as the type developed at the Virginia Mason Kirkland Clinic. It also shows how the leaders and clinicians at GIM found a way to transform their system, eliminate waste, knock down silos, and provide significantly better care to patients.

Applying VMPS to Business Functions

The enormous complexity of the financial side of the house at Virginia Mason was laid bare in a value stream map in 2002 that revealed a system plagued by a silo-mentality; where, as Steve Schaefer, Director of Patient Financial Services, put it, the various silos "had no idea what the upstream process or downstream process did or didn't do."

Schaefer approached the revenue cycle with a strategic perspective that allowed his team to attack root causes, starting at what Schaefer called the headwaters. He likened the patient financial services process to a river where oil dumped upstream polluted waters downstream. "If the water is impure—polluted for example by getting the wrong insurance information—life dwindles. Payment delays affect our economic health," he says. Every day, hundreds of people were touching some component of what would ultimately be a bill to an insurance company or patient and if any of those touches introduced a defect, "oil" would just start flowing downstream.

"One of the great things about *kaizen* is it shines a light on a part of the organization," says Schaefer. "When it shines a light on your area the natural tendency is to defensively shield your area/process from the corporate light." Accepting the scrutiny that came with the VMPS was a critical part of the struggle and required a different mindset—a different cultural approach. And that meant seeing the organization as "horizontally connected," says Schaefer. "If you don't get that this is the way everything works, you don't get VMPS. When people say 'This is my area and that's your area,' it creates process dysfunctions. And it's this myopia that will stop the VMPS approach from thriving in any organization."

In 2003, Schaefer traveled to Toyota in Japan on a study trip where he saw workers change jobs after every break, thus minimizing worker boredom and demonstrating the workers' multiple skills. Returning from Japan, Schaefer reexamined the entire revenue value stream of the people who reported to him. He realized he had eighteen unique departments with numerous silos and subsilos within silos. Seeing these departments along the value stream and thinking horizontally, Schaefer decided to make four areas along the value stream. He set up a system to reward employees for, as he put it, "going horizontal, for learning other jobs, so the left hand knows what the right hand is doing."

He and his management team created an HR staffing and compensation model that applied VMPS horizontally. Each of the four areas was given three tiers of compensation based on gaining proficiency in learning a new functional area along the value stream. Not only would this help create a more multiskilled workforce, but it would allow the management team to better correlate staffing supply with daily and weekly fluctuations in demand. Without adding any new full-time equivalents (FTEs) to the overall headcount (due to the elimination of waste and thus the lack of need to fill open positions due to attrition), Schaefer and the team developed a training department to facilitate this tiering.

Relentless Attack on Waste

The second revenue stream principle Schaefer identified—after starting at the headwaters—was to focus relentlessly on attacking waste. "Once we receive a payment," says Schaeffer, "we post it further downstream into accounts receivable where they handle billing. We went to the billing office and created a dual-pronged attack, upstream and downstream. This included payment posting, which was tailor-made for VMPS with lots of backlog and other issues in its flow of information." The team focused three RPIWs in 2003 and 2004 on improving the payment posting process by identifying, removing, and keeping out the waste.

"We stay focused on attacking waste because if we don't old habits reassert themselves once the spotlight moves to another area," says Schaefer. "We thought in 2004 that payment posting could be ideal for showing the power of VMPS. Supervisor Rene Kiefer went after it and his team was recognized as Virginia Mason's Team of the Year in 2004 because they got it and implemented it. They have been one of our earliest adopters of VMPS."

Schaefer believes coordinated *kaizen* work between payer and provider is essential to improved efficiency. Thus, his Virginia Mason team worked closely with the team from Premera Insurance. They traveled to Japan together in 2004 and subsequently made Lean one of the three core pillars of their future success. Schaefer's team collaborated with Premera and discovered the power of *kaizen* when provider and payer unite. Four joint RPIWs in 2005 and 2006 with Premera yielded significant results: From 2001 to 2006 Premera hospital billed days revenue outstanding (DRO) declined from sixty-three to nineteen days and Premera clinic DRO declined from forty-four to seventeen days.

Schaefer's alignment is demonstrated through a series of accountability meetings. Every Tuesday from 7:00 to 7:30 a.m., Virginia Mason holds a Kaizen Promotion Office (KPO) standup conducted by CEO Gary Kaplan. This is all about alignment, transparency, and eliminating silos. In similar fashion, every Thursday from 7:30 to 8:00 a.m., Patient Financial Services (PFS) leaders attend their own standup. Six department leaders give reports similar to the Tuesday KPO standup, but focused on PFS targets and progress. They address the entire Virginia Mason revenue stream. "Now areas that never talked to each other talk to each other," he says. "We're improving communication."

Every PFS department has a dashboard updated daily. "But it's really just a Model T," says Schaefer. "Think about a dashboard in your car that's updated only once a day, or worse, once a week. In the future our dashboards will be true dashboards like airline arrivals and departures, with screens updating constantly as to the real-time health of this process." Schaefer is exploring a program that will loop through computer software every five minutes and show the real-time health of accounts receivable.

The results of all this work over an eight-plus-year period are impressive: On DRO Virginia Mason ranks among the top 3 percent in the nation at twenty-nine days compared to more than forty or even fifty days at most places.

Credit balance has been reduced from 12 days in 2000 to 1.6 days at the end of 2009.

Schaefer envisions a future where accounts receivable will be essentially eliminated. "We want to create a system where the patient walks directly into the exam room and then, when leaving, checks out just like any consumer by handing us a card that we swipe regardless of the payer: Medicare, Medicaid, Premera, Aetna, Regence. And then like any ATM transaction, the card information goes out, adjudicates, comes back, and the patient settles the balance with a credit or debit card and, thus, there are no accounts receivable."

Over time, as he has pushed ahead with this work, five guidelines have emerged for Schaefer:

1. "Get out of your office and understand how your shop floor *really* works."
2. Ask why five times or more. "Don't stop until you get to the root cause."
3. Create a sense of urgency in everyone. "We've got our backs against the wall in health care, and we need a sense of urgency."
4. Maintain a broad horizontal orientation that sees flows across departments and other boundaries, not just a narrow myopic orientation.
5. "Never forget that the enemy is waste—not Finance, not the physicians, not IT, not HR, not fill-in-the-blank—*waste.*"

Bringing Flow Stations to Specialty Department

Initially, says Dr. Paul Benca, the introduction of VMPS generated some push-back and frustration, especially from orthopedic surgeons. "It was really foreign to them initially," he says. "'You're going to take car-making methodology and bring it to medicine? You're going to bring it to *surgery?*' But people quickly realized when they started reading and learning about it that there was a lot of application, and it was apropos to what we do."

Flow stations had been established with great success in primary care settings throughout Virginia Mason, but Orthopedics was the first specialty care area where flow stations were attempted. Just as implementing flow stations had been a challenge on the primary care side, so, too, was it a challenge on the specialty care side—particularly with surgeons. Benca and his colleagues participated in several RPIWs to prepare for changing the work around flow stations. Focusing initially on outpatient visits, they zeroed in on the value stream from the moment the patient called in for an appointment, moving through check-in, rooming, and so on—breaking the process down into each step. That original value stream, says Dr. Benca, revealed that their process "was chaos. We were wasting a lot of time. Most orthopedic patients are going to require X-rays and we do have X-ray right up in the clinic, but just doing the spaghetti charts, watching the flows, and figuring out where people were going and how much time was being wasted was really overwhelmingly eye-opening to all of us."

Benca and his colleagues first tackled the start of the chaotic process—when patients called in for appointments. They followed a similar path to Virginia Mason Kirkland in whittling down the scheduling backlog and then going to open access. "We now have wide-open schedules," says Benca. "We've also employed non-operative physicians who are specialized in musculoskeletal treatment but are not surgeons, so we're trying to use those as a first line of interaction with patients, especially if it's a generic problem like knee pain, hip pain, or ankle pain with no obvious trauma or fracture. A lot of what we see in Orthopedics, even though we're a surgical specialty, is nonoperative."

A problem nobody had thought much about emerged during an RPIW. Under the old system, patients sat in an open hallway where nurses and MAs would conduct brief interviews in which some personal information was discussed including weight, medical conditions, and what procedures patients needed. The RPIW led to a simple solution: One of the medical assistants (MAs) was given a private office where she did all of the surgical scheduling, meeting with patients, going through a brief interview and taking down various information—all in private. This approach solved the privacy issue and proved to be more efficient than having a variety of assistants do scheduling in a multitude of ways. It was so much more efficient, in fact, that it significantly reduced wait times for day of surgery appointments and increased surgical volume. "It used to be weeks and weeks to get in," says Benca, "and we decreased our wait time for appointments from several weeks down to a matter of days to a week. Work continues in the department with a goal of same day access for patients."

Efficient scheduling makes a major difference not only to patient satisfaction and quality of care, but also to the business side of orthopedics. "If you don't get a patient in promptly and your competitor can, you're going to lose that patient most times, so we've gotten our patients in the door," says Benca. "We've gotten it so that when we want to set something up, the process is very standard so that if the decision is made when you're in my office to have surgery, we will fill out the orders, and you will meet with the surgical scheduler, you'll have all your appointments made, it's one-stop shopping, and so you can leave here with everything in hand for all of your appointments with a surgical date figured out, including all your preparatory appointments."

When Benca and his colleagues, supported by staff from the KPO, tackled flow stations in Orthopedics, it was not easy. What proved to make an important difference in Orthopedics was that the head of the department was driving the change. One of his more important moves was to make sure that every RPIW—every discussion about the changes—included dissidents, naysayers, and skeptics. "That's one of the things you have to figure out is who is going to be your biggest opposition and include them in the process," says Benca. "I think there's an art to selecting the right people. If you pick the wrong team, you're not going to accomplish what you need to. So you need to have people who are willing to roll their sleeves up, people who are willing to make decisions, willing to enter the process, speak their minds, not shrink back into the corners, but you also need to have some people that will challenge you."

Benca found that having skeptics join in an RPIW enables them to participate in creating the value stream and value streams don't lie—they lay the process bare. "The RPIW tends to break down your resistance," he says. "It's set up that way. It's set up to get you involved. And I think when people feel like they have a say in it, all of a sudden it's not so difficult to make that change because they felt they were part of it."

Orthopedics presented a layout challenge to flow stations. Out front is a waiting and check-in area, then a series of exam rooms. Beyond the exam rooms is a hallway followed by X-ray and the cast room and, finally, deep into the rear of the space, are physician offices. An RPIW revealed that when doctors went back and forth to their offices between or during visits the cumulative waste of time throughout the day was significant.

During the initial testing phase of flow stations the Orthopedic doctors quickly saw that the new approach saved considerable time and Benca says "it became very easy for them to buy into it." A variety of RPIWs helped the orthopedic team make their process more efficient. When the patient's pathway is determined, the office is set up to provide everything that patient needs going forward without forcing the patient to return for repeated visits, as in the old days. "Whether going to a total joint class to learn more about it, meeting the anesthesiologist, getting an updated history and physical by your internist, whatever is necessary, that's all taken care of so that you don't have to keep coming back and forth," says Benca. "A lot of the preparatory process has been broken down into other RPIWs. The information booklet for a hip or knee replacement, how we schedule those cases—there have been a lot of outgrowths of these in other areas in the process, so the whole interaction between our scheduling office and the general operating room scheduling office has been looked at and worked on multiple times."

An important breakthrough came in an RPIW focused on scheduling. The problem was the rigidity of the schedule: Surgeons saw patients on Monday, operated on Tuesday, saw patients on Wednesday, operated on Thursday, and had Friday open. There was no variation. An RPIW clearly showed the waste of leaving Operating Rooms (ORs) idle Mondays, Wednesdays, and most Fridays. As a result, the orthopedic teams cracked open the old schedule and examined what might make sense to better serve patients and more evenly distribute the use of ORs.

Thus, there has been a sustained effort to level-load the schedule. Level-loading is optimal because it reduces the peaks and valleys of the work. The challenge is to balance what is level in the OR with what is level on the hospital units, the supply chain, the clinic, or any other department that provides service to orthopedic patients. What is leveled for one might not be leveled for the other. This is an ongoing challenge for Virginia Mason, and requires continued effort working toward the goal of an even schedule for everyone.

When Dr. Benca looks back on the work in Orthopedics since the onset of VMPS, he sees significant improvements. "I think the process is much more patient centered; you're going to get a more prompt response to whatever you need, whether it's making an appointment, getting a surgical date figured out, whatever it is," he says. "And hopefully we can do this much more quickly and more nimbly by using flexibility in how we schedule surgeries and how we use the surgeons. We can open up more time readily for the patients so people aren't having to wait three, four, five, six weeks to get a surgery scheduled."

General Internal Medicine: Spreading Innovation in Ambulatory Care

While Virginia Mason Kirkland was making impressive strides, the downtown Virginia Mason ambulatory care site—GIM—was lagging well behind. Some physicians thought GIM had a more challenging patient population, and to a certain extent this was true, particularly on the Family Practice side. Cindy Rockfeld took over as director of GIM in December 2003. "It was a very chaotic environment," says Rockfeld. "There was little sense of team medicine even though that concept is at the heart of what Virginia Mason aspires to be."

She also found that there was minimal skill–task alignment. "I remember one evening around 6:30 p.m., long after all the patients were gone, there were two nurses struggling to get their work done so they could go home. This was ninety minutes after the clinic had closed and when I offered to help, one of the nurses handed me an accordion file and asked me to file a large stack of paper in alphabetical order. I could not believe we were paying a highly trained clinical RN to work overtime to file paper. And I thought 'This is not what RNs are trained to do.'"

The more she saw of the clinic operations the more Cindy found comparable examples of wasted time and warped skill–task alignment. It was obvious to her that both nurses and MAs were working well below their skill levels. Nurses were not only filing, but also performing a variety of other tasks that wasted their valuable time and talents and meant they were spending very little time with patients, and MAs were doing little more than getting height and weight of patients.

When Rockfeld first arrived, there was a great deal of talk from administrators about the Virginia Mason Kirkland Clinic flow work, and she was urged to follow that lead. She was impressed by the advances at Kirkland, but she also knew that GIM was not even close to being ready for such a leap. "Everyone was talking about how we had to implement flow stations," says Rockfeld. "It was the buzz word. But it was clear that to make flow stations a long-term, sustainable solution, we had to fix our foundation." In practice, "fixing our foundation" meant breaking down silos. It meant level-loading the schedule so that patients could be accommodated with better flow and providers would have the exam rooms they needed. It meant changing the work being done by nurses and MAs; it meant real skill–task alignment. It was clear a great deal of work would have to be done before flow stations could be introduced.

Breaking Down Silos

GIM, which had its own floor in Buck Pavilion in the heart of the Virginia Mason campus, was home to twenty-five providers including twenty-one MDs (both full-time and part-time), two nurse practitioners, two physician assistants, nurses, MAs, and customer service representatives. When Rockfeld took over she found that GIM was functioning not as one team, but as five distinctly separate, silo-like pods that were so disconnected that providers from different pods did not share any resources—not educational material, staff, not even exam rooms. It was as though there was not one large GIM clinic but rather five small clinics with their own habits, practices, and rules. In an organization aspiring to become patient-focused, it was about as provider-focused as could possibly be.

One pod of six doctors, for example, would work every Monday and cram into the same group of ten exam rooms while another pod of providers would decide not to work on Mondays, thereby leaving an entire hallway of exam rooms empty. Ideally, every physician should be able to work out of three exam rooms simultaneously to achieve maximum efficiency. In this case, though, the doctors were squeezed into two and sometimes just one room. Every Monday, without fail, the first pod of physicians would complain that the space was inadequate or that their day was incredibly hectic. They never thought to use the empty exam rooms available on another hallway. Each exam room had its own stash of supplies and education materials based on the individual provider's needs. "Because exam rooms looked different and felt different, providers were reluctant to share rooms," says Rockfeld.

This inflexibility to use available space caused delays in patient care and lengthy stays in the crowded waiting area. Waits in excess of forty-five minutes were not at all uncommon. By the end of her first year as director of GIM, Rockfeld's frustration mounted. With increasing pressure to improve access and increase visit volumes by having providers see more patients per day, she realized the existing structure had to be scrapped.

In 2005, Dr. Joyce Lammert, the section head of the Virginia Mason Asthma and Allergy Clinic, joined GIM as physician leader, teaming up with Rockfeld. No sooner had Lammert arrived than she heard the chorus from administration that GIM needed to move forward with flow stations. "There was an assumption that because so much ground work had been done in Kirkland, it would be easy to replicate and adopt in GIM," says Lammert. Administrators "would say, 'It works.' But it doesn't actually, not until you get people engaged, and they figure it out for themselves."

In an environment that prized standard work and knew that variation led to errors and poor quality, Lammert says that GIM had "twenty-five providers with twenty-five different ways of doing everything." Things would fall through the cracks, patients would get lab results late, and doctors were stuck in their offices until 7:30 or 8:00 o'clock at night doing mounds of administrative paperwork.

Skill–Task Alignment

"We felt we needed to reorganize and get rid of the five silos, but we felt like we needed to get them to do it," says Lammert. The solution could not be imposed on the doctors—it had to come out of a process where physicians played a central role. In January 2005, Rockfeld enrolled in a seventeen-week Virginia Mason change management course focused on leading change within the organization. Although the course was in addition to her regular duties and demanded a great deal of work, she was engaged by it. The teachings were based on the work of Harvard Business School professor John Kotter and his book, *The Heart of Change.* Throughout the first half of 2005, Kotter's teachings guided Rockfeld and Lammert, as well, in their restructuring efforts. Rockfeld sought to respond to Kotter's call to increase urgency by using data and communicating clearly to staff and providers the nature of the day-to-day chaos within GIM as well as the less than exemplary provider and patient satisfaction levels. She worked with colleagues to build a guiding team of doctors, a nurse, and other staffers who put patients first. The guiding team defined the purpose of the restructuring as creating "a solid foundation for GIM to better serve our patients and increase provider and staff satisfaction by reducing stress and chaos in the working environment and allow us to provide services with more consistency and meet the challenges of the future."

The goals were to maximize room utilization, improve provider coverage, ensure a consistent level of staffing, ensure seamless access for patients, increase collaboration and communication among providers, and ensure sufficient staff training. Kotter emphasized the need to communicate for buy-in and Rockfeld made a sustained effort to communicate to all staff members—with special emphasis on reaching out to physicians, for she knew that if doctors did not embrace the changes they had no chance of sticking.

The essential structural change resulting from the reorganization broke down the silos and created one GIM section to achieve better provider coverage, less disruption and movement, a larger pool of RNs to support the team, and increased availability of appointments. Also, some providers agreed to change their schedules to increase the amount of flow through the clinic. This solved the problem of having ten providers squeezed into one hallway and no providers in another hallway. It thus accomplished "level-loading" of provider schedules.

This was the kind of short-term win Kotter views as essential for effective change. Because the process had been so deliberate and careful—soliciting input from staff and providers at every step of the way and having the ultimate recommendation come from the guiding team—the plan to function as one section was embraced. Restructuring improved exam room utilization, staff utilization, provider coverage, and access for new and existing patients. It also laid important groundwork for flow stations.

For all its positive elements, the reorganization could not possibly transform GIM overnight. Dr. Julie Pattison had been working there for ten years by this time, and she was just trying to keep her head down, avoid the turmoil and change, and take care of her patients. "I was basically trying to hide," she says. "So many things started dropping onto the primary care provider in the 1990s and early 2000s that I just felt like I was barely getting it done and providing good patient care. I didn't have time for anything else on my plate, and I was kind of drowning like every other primary care provider in the country."

"I think that the morale in primary care at that time was similar everywhere. In talking to our colleagues in the community, many doctors were stopping practice, or finding another job. I actually would have and was thinking 'What else can I do?' back around 2001, 2002, but I didn't really have any other skills. So it was still a very enjoyable job, even then, because you get to interact with patients. It's such a great privilege, but it just was very hard. Everybody was working very late hours. And then when other providers quit, then it's even harder. You would want to accommodate all their patients as well, so we would double book and triple book."

She was wary of VMPS and felt she had enough to do without adopting a whole new management method. Nonetheless, she was impressed with some of the changes Rockfeld and Lammert were making. "Cindy had a lot of energy and she really started to do the basics of just getting rid of some of the chaos," says Dr. Pattison.

However, during this transition period when there was more and more talk about applying VMPS, standard work, and evidence-based medicine, some doctors grew increasingly uncomfortable both with primary care in general and the whole direction of GIM in particular. Over a two-year period about eight doctors left. Two opened a small practice but a couple of others left medicine entirely. Morale at GIM, already low, was sinking. Lammert says the doctors felt victimized and talked about the administration as some sort of adversary.

In 2005, Dr. Lammert sat down with the GIM physicians and asked what bothered them the most. "There were a lot of different responses," says Dr. Pattison. "People complained that having to leave the room a lot wasted their time. They really hated the paperwork, filling out forms that a physician doesn't really need to fill out. But we didn't have a process for anybody else to fill it out. They had very complex patients that required more time than any insurance company would allot for you to see a patient—for example, patients with diabetes."

Lammert worked persistently to solve problems that most bothered her colleagues. When she received a series of complaints about the air conditioning system, she had it upgraded. She took all the complaints seriously and tried to respond to each one. Pattison says it was also important that Lammert began building a new leadership team and that she made a point of being out on the clinic floor seeing people, talking with staff, and listening to their concerns. "The VMPS model as our management method requires you to be accepting of the improvements that come out of the process and standardization," says Pattison. "That is a change for a lot of docs who have been independent for years and having things their own way. So a couple of the people probably left because of that. They resented the intrusion of somebody telling them how things could occur, even if it was outside of the exam room."

Uphill Battle

In the fall of 2005, after the GIM reorganization had gone live, John Eusek and Alenka Rudolph from the KPO began working with Lammert and Rockfeld to apply VMPS in greater depth. Eusek and Rudolph became an integral part of the GIM leadership team and attended all GIM leadership meetings to ensure alignment of GIM efforts with VMPS. Eusek had been focused on GIM only briefly when he noticed what he considered "this mass beehive of chaos. Physicians were coming thirty or forty feet from their office down the hall to see a patient and going the thirty or forty feet back and the MA would be chasing after them. And when there are twenty-five providers doing that, there's no continuity of anything."

Eusek would frequently see the waiting areas for GIM patients jam-packed. The more he studied GIM and talked to providers, the more he realized that it was not only chaotic and disorganized, but that morale was abysmal. Eusek, Rudolph, and their colleagues from the KPO would stay around well after the 5:00 p.m. close of the clinic and for hours they would see one doctor after another closeted in his or her office poring over stacks of paper. On top of all this, when the KPO team observed and measured in an effort to lay the ground-work for improvement, there was a growing resentment among the staff. Their fear, Eusek came to understand, was that the KPO would try to turn them into an automated, factory-like operation.

In spite of the extensive communication effort by Rockfeld and Lammert, GIM staffers were deeply suspicious of the VMPS approach and Eusek believes part of the problem lay with the KPO itself. He says it was a mistake not doing more to prepare the staff for the observation and measurement by VMPS special-ists—elements that are at the core of the VMPS model. At the start of the VMPS process the staff from the KPO talked with the chief of medicine and the section head and then essentially descended on GIM to observe and measure. "It was hard for the staff," says Eusek. "They had this sense we were spying on them."

At one point a physician instructed a VMPS specialist to leave his office, and the doctor said if the specialist returned, the doctor would quit. Senior people within Virginia Mason spoke with the doctor and explained that VMPS was the Virginia Mason way of doing business, and they were going to stick with it. The doctor ultimately left the organization.

Restructuring

As part of the restructure, Lammert and Rockfeld tackled one of the most difficult issues at GIM—confusion surrounding the perceived shortage of exam rooms. KPO played an important role in helping the team to apply 5S to the exam rooms (sort, simplify, sweep, standardize, self-discipline). Lammert and Rockfeld were patient. They had no intention of forcing anything down the providers' throats. For months leading up to the 5S, they asked the physicians and staff what they absolutely needed. Every provider had a voice in the 5S change and Rockfeld and Lammert didn't make a move until clear consensus among the staff was achieved.

Once that happened, they jumped. Rockfeld, Lammert, KPO, and GIM staff descended on the clinic on one weekend, rolled up their sleeves, and got the work done. "Joyce and I would make trips to Walmart for cheap supply bins and Office Depot for plastic storage units for the exam rooms," says Rockfeld. "With GIM staff and KPO, we all participated as a team making it happen. We vacuumed. We labeled. We did the pick and shovel work that needed to be done. By Monday, we had applied the 5S method to all fifty-two exam rooms."

"It didn't matter which exam room you were in," says Dr. Lammert. "Everything was labeled and placed in holders in the same order. You knew where everything was." As a result, any provider could use any one of the fifty-two rooms. Although the layout of each room differed, the same medical supplies were in the same general location in each room. Prior to the application of 5S, it was common for providers in an exam room to search in vain for the particular supply or piece of equipment. This would delay the visit while the doctor searched outside the room for whatever was needed. This often led to frustration among both doctor and patient.

Additionally, they applied 5S to all of the educational materials. Previously, it was not uncommon to see individual stashes of educational materials. "One time, while flipping through a file of educational materials given to patients, I noticed there was a photocopy of a handout from 1992," says Cindy Rockfeld. "I was mortified that we were giving these to patients." After the 5S, all of these materials were discarded and an electronic path to the most current literature for patients was made available.

The 5S process "required docs to change the way they think about their work," says Lammert. "As doctors, we're really trained to be autonomous and every doctor develops what they think they need to do the best job possible when, in fact, your way may *not* be the best way."

Introducing Flow Stations

Lammert and Rockfeld approached the issue of flow stations with a clear idea of what to do and, perhaps just as important, what not to do. They communicated clearly and often and forced nothing. There was no twisting of arms, no compulsion for the doctors to do anything.

Through trial and error, Virginia Mason learned strategies to help accelerate the work. "We always pick a champion," says John Eusek, "somebody that's really going to put their heart into it and see what happens. It has to be somebody fairly well organized, fairly efficient, and somebody that the rest of the physicians can look at and say, 'Gee, you know, this thing really works.' If you try to spread it to every one of them during the workshop, you're probably going to fail, because you get a lot of people who don't want to do it."

Lammert, Rockfeld, and the KPO team worked with Drs. Julie Pattison and Keith Dipboye as early adopters in creating a GIM flow station. It was only a matter of weeks before Pattison and Dipboye were moving nicely through the day, working side-by-side with their MAs and disposing of nonvisit care between patient visits. Says Dr. Lammert, "You can build flow stations all you want but if people aren't mentally ready it won't work. You have to think about your work differently."

Rockfeld says flow happened when doctors and MAs started to work in sync together. "The medical assistant, as 'flow manager,' would continuously feed and direct the work of the provider so that the work is completed throughout the day," she says. "The flow manager would complete the nonclinical tasks and leave all clinical work for the MD." In the flow station, the MA and provider work side by side, huddling throughout the day as the MA feeds the physician between-visit work. They're sitting or standing right next to one another and the MA is handing over a sheet of paper or directing the doctor's attention to the computer and an e-mail message. "They're communicating all the time," says Rockfeld. "And we've made it clear to the MAs that they are in charge of managing the flow for the entire day of all the patients. We emphasize that the communication between them and their provider is essential."

Dr. Pattison says the flow stations made a huge difference in eliminating chaos and reducing the nonvisit work that was so annoying to physicians. She used the flow station in the hallway so effectively that she found she had no need for an office and gave it up. More significantly, however, flow stations enabled doctors to provide higher quality care. Between the physician and the flow manager there is a greater level of vigilance than in the past and a much faster work flow. Test results no longer lie unread in a pile ominously beckoning the physician.

Not long after the early adopters began the flow station work there was something of a buzz around GIM. It became obvious that Pattison and Dipboye were leaving earlier than anyone else. In fact, they were leaving not long after their last appointment with all of their nonvisit work completed. Word got around and gradually other providers asked whether they, too, could try a flow station.

Like other physicians, under the new system, Dr. Pattison greatly appreciated the new work being taken on by the MAs. She would make suggestions for how the MA could work more effectively, and she would ask the MA for suggestions on how she could do the same. "And so we started really improving quickly," she says, "and we never would have any paperwork left to do."

Pattison says that, in a similar way, skills of nurses at GIM were also being underutilized. Nurses had been doing phone and clerical work and under the new system they became care managers for patients with chronic diseases. Working in a planned care group, nurses do standard work around care management with patients who have diabetes, heart failure, and many other ailments. Nurses see these patients in an appointment prior to the patient's doctor visit to provide education, check medicines, discuss depression issues, and handle a wide variety of other concerns. The idea is to cover a fair amount of ground so that during the doctor visit, the key clinical elements can be thoroughly explored.

The New GIM

GIM has been transformed. Instead of two packed waiting rooms with patients standing against the back walls there are a few patients scattered here and there, and they will wait for just a few moments before being called. The chaos of the hallways is gone. MAs are in exam rooms or at flow stations conducting valuable work. Doctors shuttle seamlessly from flow stations to exam rooms. "When you walk along the hallways," says Eusek, "it's just this deliberate motion, no chaos, nobody is scurrying around to find anything, doctors aren't running out of the exam rooms to find missing supplies."

At the beginning of 2007, barely 30 percent of GIM providers had achieved three-day access or less for an appointment, but by the end of the year 70 percent had reached that level. The changes resulted in a far more efficient operation. Also in 2007, GIM absorbed 4,000 new patients compared with 2,800 new patients the previous year. Instead of lab results being sent out to patients in two weeks, they now go out the same day as the test or the next day. A patient having labs done first thing in the morning would likely get results in the mail the following day. This not only meant better, more timely care for patients—along with much less anxiety—it also yielded a side benefit of significantly reducing telephone traffic into GIM from patients waiting for delayed lab results.

Under the new system, Virginia Mason is scoring very well on a variety of primary care-related measurements. Whereas many other providers measure whether their patients have scheduled a screening test or procedure, Virginia Mason measures whether patients are actually up to date on their tests. Eusek says that prior to VMPS, Virginia Mason primary care at GIM was at a rate of about 20 percent success in making sure patients were up to date on key screenings. Now, he says, it's above 80 percent.

The financial improvement was dramatic as well. GIM had lost money for three decades. In 2007, it achieved its first positive contribution margin ever. Although there are many factors that contributed to this financial improvement, the lesson here is critically important: *Focus at GIM was on eliminating waste and improving quality and efficiency. Never did the team target finances. The financial improvements resulted from a relentless focus on eliminating waste.*

From the start, inspired by VMPS, Rockfeld, Lammert, and other team members recognized clearly that the elimination of waste according to VMPS principles creates time—time for physicians to spend with patients, colleagues, and their own families. Perhaps the true measure of success was when the skeptics on the medical staff came to recognize this. Central to the success was the leadership provided by Lammert, Pattison, and Rockfeld, and also the critically important work from the KPO. "KPO became part of our leadership team," says Rockfeld. "They sat in every single meeting and became integrated in all of our efforts."

Sometime after all the work was done at GIM, Eusek was there with Paul Plsek, who had done some early work in the 1990s with Don Berwick and was one of the more insightful people in the country about this work. Eusek was in the hallway watching the interaction between doctors and MAs and for the first time he noticed that it was very quiet; that doctors and MAs did very little talking to one another. Eusek observed this for some time with a variety of doctor–MA teams. He could see what was happening but couldn't think of a term to describe it. He turned to Plsek and asked what he thought was going on. "And Paul said, 'It's situational awareness,'" recalls Eusek. "And I realized that if you use the flow station properly as a tool you're going to be doing a great job and you're going to get into flow, but the key to that is to have a real connection between the two people working there."

It used to be that Eusek was insistent that the same MAs work with doctors to establish that connection. But over time the skill level of the doctors and MAs in general working with one another meant that many different MAs could work with many different doctors. It was about the flow station system. The real success of GIM is that it is in flow—that, as Eusek puts it, information on the patient flows easily through the system to the people who need it when and where they need it, resulting in a high-quality, defect-free product. "If you are in flow you are anticipating rather than reacting," he says. "You control the process; the process doesn't control you. Flow is attributed to standard work. When you have standard work, you can really see the details particularly when someone is out of flow. If this happens, you can make immediate corrections because you can see what part of the standard work is not being followed."

The improvements realized at Kirkland and GIM spread to all Virginia Mason primary care sites, with various modifications in each location. "We realized, over time, that we can't do everything exactly the same at every site—that every site is a little different—but there are certain parts that do translate to every single site," says Julie Pattison. The concept of standard work is so foundational to Virginia Mason primary care that Pattison says, "It would be hard for me to think of something where we can't or haven't applied standard work." The resistance from some doctors toward standard work back when VMPS was in its early stages is largely a thing of the past.

A crucial result of the new system—of standard work, evidence-based care, and flow stations—is that doctors now get to spend more time with patients. With virtually all of the nonvisit care handled in a tightly defined flow system, doctors are much less likely than previously to have to chase down a chart or supply or staff member. "It's freed me up to actually spend a lot more time with patients on prevention," says Pattison, "or even just to spend more time establishing rapport, especially with a new patient. We've timed it, and I actually spend more minutes with a patient face-to-face and that's very valuable for their satisfaction, for my satisfaction. But that is also how patients might trust you to make a change in their health or to follow through on a recommendation."

Through the years of VMPS, physician satisfaction scores have steadily increased, including among primary care doctors. Flow, standard work, and predictability—the virtual absence of chaos—have improved physicians' outlooks. "Doctors know what to expect when they are starting their day," says Dr. Pattison. "They know what's going to happen. There will always be a patient who might be more ill than you think or some unexpected finding that will require extra workup, but they no longer are apprehensive about it, because they know that they will be able to pull in somebody to help them. There's a process for that now. And they'll be able to get through their day and enjoy their day and feel like they're providing great service to the patients.

"When we interview people to hire them for any job, we always emphasize the importance that everything here will be standardized, so we are recruiting to that expectation. The other thing that's different here is we work as a team. We're not hierarchical. Everybody's voice is just as important—the medical assistant, the housekeeper. Their voice, their input into the process that they are involved in, which is caring for patients, is just as important as the physicians. If that would bother a person, then this would not be the right place for you. Most importantly, the overall care for our patients is safer, more efficient, and thorough."

Acknowledgments

I have consistently found through the years that people in health care are extraordinarily generous with their time, ideas, and insights, and I have certainly benefitted from this attractive cultural generosity. In recent years I have had the good fortune to learn about a variety of aspects of health care quality improvement from some of the most dedicated professionals anywhere in the world. Scores of health care professionals, both clinicians and administrators, helped me reach the point where I was able to write this book.

At the Institute for Health Care Improvement (IHI) in Cambridge, Massachusetts, I am indebted to Jonathan Small, Jenna Ward, Dan Schummers, Markus Josephson, Madge Kaplan, Tom Nolan, Jim Conway, Vin Sahney, and Paul Batalden. At IHI I owe special thanks to Maureen Bisognano, who is a wonderful guide and tutor. I am grateful to Don Berwick, former CEO at IHI and now head of CMS, who is many things but most of all an inspiration.

At Atrius Health in Greater Boston, I have learned important lessons about improvement from work being done by many people, including Dr. Gene Lindsey, Dr. Zeev Neuwirth, and Tanya Chermak.

I play a modest role in the Trustee Insight program, run by the Massachusetts Hospital Association and Blue Cross Blue Shield of Massachusetts. The program welcomes trustees of Massachusetts hospitals to sessions where some of the leading minds in health care discuss a wide range of topics. The Trustee Insight program has featured an amazing lineup, including Dr. Jim Reinertsen, Jamie Orlikoff (a member of the Virginia Mason Board of Directors), Lee Carter and Dr. Fred Ryckman from Cincinnati Children's, Gary Kaplan, and others. The program presents some of the very finest talent anywhere, and I have benefitted from all the presenters.

For a number of years I have worked as a consultant at Blue Cross Blue Shield of Massachusetts, where I have sought to help with various aspects of the quality improvement effort. It is a privilege to engage with such a superb cast—a health care all-star team of people who work with intelligence, determination, and grace to improve the quality and efficiency of care—for everyone. I am deeply grateful to Deb Devaux, Andrew Dreyfus, Nancy Driscoll, Dr. John Fallon, Deanna Fulp, Patrick Gilligan, Ralph Martin, Jay McQuaide, Dana Safran, Audrey Shelto, John Schoenbaum, Fredi Shonkoff, and Bill Van Faasen.

Others who have helped me understand various aspects of the health care world include Dr. Robert Mandel of Blue Cross Blue Shield of Tennessee; Peter Meade, director of the Edward M. Kennedy Center for the Study of the United States Senate; consultants Jack Silversin and Mary Jane Kornacki; Art Byrne, former CEO of Wiremold; Sorrel King, President of the Josie King Foundation; the team at Cincinnati Children's Hospital Medical Center—Dr. Uma Kotagal, Lee Carter, Jim Anderson, and Drs. Fred Ryckman, Maria Britto, and Steve Meuthing; the leaders of the health care system in Jönköping County, Sweden, Göran Henriks, Sven Olof Karlsson (now retired), and Dr. Mats Bojestig; and George Halvorson, CEO at Kaiser.

John Black's books and ideas helped me better understand the Virginia Mason story. I am grateful to Dr. Stephen Singleton, Regional Director of Public Health and Medical Director of the National Health Service Northeast; Dr. Donald Storey, formerly of Aetna, now medical director at Premera; and Annette King, formerly benefits manager at Starbucks, now Principal in the consulting firm of Pembrook Solutions, LLC.

At Virginia Mason Medical Center, dozens of people helped make this book possible. I am grateful to Ruth Anderson, Ana Anuradhika, Chris Backous, Richelle Bagdasarian, Dr. Paul Benca, Robbi Bishop, Robert Brown, Dr. Bob Caplan, Lynne Chafetz, Katerie Chapman, Joan Ching, Dr. Ruth Conn, Darlene Corkrum, Jim Cote, Susie Creger, Erica Cumbee, Denise Dubuque, Liz Dunphy, John Eusek, Val Ferris, Dr. Andrew Friedman, Cathie Furman, Gigi Gempesaw, Dr. Fred Govier, Dr. Neil B. Hampson, Dr. Daniel Hanson, Dr. Andrew Jacobs, Miwa Kudo, Dr. Joyce Lammert, Amy London, Crystal McDermott, Chihiro Nakao, *sensei* consultant to VM of Shingijutsu USA, Dana Nelson-Peterson, Michael Ondracek, Dr. Henry Otero, Dr. Julie Pattison, Kathleen Paul, Jennifer Phillips, Rowena Ponischil, Martha Purrier, Trudie Read, Kate Reed, Cindy Rockfeld, Dr. Steve Rupp, Gordon Sansaver, Steve Schaefer, Dr. Donna Smith, Julie Sylvester, Charleen Tachibana, Suzanne Tyler, Arni Verkler, Michaelle Wetteland, Shawn Whipple, Patti Wilbur, Rudy Williams, and Claude Wreford-Brown.

Diane Miller, the executive director of the Virginia Mason Institute (VMI), leant the prestige and resources of VMI to the project. The Institute was founded in 2008 with a mission to provide education and training in the Virginia Mason Production System management method and further development of the Center for Health Care Solutions. It is my hope that this book will help VMI in that mission.

Linda Hebish played a central role in making this book come to life, and Andy Baylor deftly convened a wide variety of Virginia Mason Medical Center clinicians and administrators to help convey the most accurate and complete rendering of this story possible. Significant contributions to this book came from several Virginia Mason leaders whose passion and experience have helped break new ground in quality improvement in health care. Sarah Patterson, COO, is honing a management method that will help countless health care organizations throughout the world. Dr. Bob Mecklenburg is marrying the efficiency of health care to the demands of the marketplace and creating his own revolution in the process. Dr. Kim Pittenger wages an unrelenting—and successful—effort to improve the quality of care in that sacred space where caregivers meet patients each and every day. At Virginia Mason, my greatest debt of all is to Dr. Gary Kaplan, who has provided the vision and leadership for Virginia Mason during the past decade.

Finally, I am grateful to my family—my wife Anne Detmer, daughter Elizabeth, and son Charlie, for their nonstop help and support.

Index

A

Accountability, 153
  Tuesday Standup, 160
  weekly reports, 159–161
Acid reflux, 144
Adverse events, 64–65
Aetna Aexcel Performance Networks, 129–130,
  135–136
Agency for Health Care Research and Quality
  (AHRQ), 50
Alaska Airlines, 133–134
AMA. *see* American Medical Group
  Association (AMA)
Ambulatory care. *see also* Outpatient cancer
  service
  breakthrough, 79–80
  cancer service, 33–48
  creating new tool, 75–76
  emphasizing primary care, 69–70
  external setup, 87–90
  flow care station, 90–92
  inventing flow station, 77–79
  jidoka, 85–87
  mistake-proofing, 73–75
  primary care transformed, 83–85
  skill-task alignment, 80–83
  waiting time, 70–73
American Medical Group Association (AMA),
  5
Amicus, 8
Anesthesia cart redesign, 61
Anxiety and back pain, 138
Appointments
  backlogs in primary care clinic, 71

  GIM, 203
  same-day, 141–142
  waiting period, 141
Arrogance as obstacle, 174–176
Aso Iisuka Hospital, xiii
Authority gradient, 175
Automatic loom, 89

B

Back pain, 136–139
  complicated *vs.* uncomplicated, 137
  MRI, 142
  MRI *vs.* physical therapy costs, 143
  outcomes, 142
  same-day access, 137–139
  Starbucks, 133–134
  value stream, 137
Back tables, 99–100
Barriers, 160, 161
Benefits managers, 131–132
  costly complaints, 134
  engagement, 133
Boeing, 10
  TPS, 13–14

C

Cancer center redesign
  fishbone, 36–37
  nursing dissatisfaction, 43
  patient satisfaction, 43
  productivity and capacity, 43
  team, 36
Cancer patients, 35

Cancer service. *see* Outpatient cancer service
Care managers, 81, 88–89
CCU. *see* Critical care unit (CCU)
Center for Hyperbaric Medicine, 103–105
Chemotherapy, 43
Chlorhexidine, 58, 61
Clinical practice guidelines, 74
Clinicians. *see* Physician(s)
Computer block on procedures, 142–143
Cookbook medicine, 12
Cost
    back pain procedures, 143
    control of insurance, 141
    MRI, 137
    production cost reduction, 145–146
    VMPS reduction, 145–146
Credit balance, 192
Crew Resource Management (CRM), 7
Critical care unit (CCU), 18
CRM. *see* Crew Resource Management (CRM)
Cross-functional management, 158–159
Crossing the Quality Chasm (IOM), x, 2
Customer identification, 131–133

D

Daily management, 156–159
Daruma dolls, 26
Dashboard, 191
Day-of-surgery guide, 101–102
Days revenue outstanding (DRO), 191
Deep vein thrombosis (DVT), 66
Department of Health (DOH), 100
Depression and back pain, 138
Diabetes, 74
Diabetic planned care visits, 81–82
Disease management, xiv, 73
Doctors. *see* Physician(s)
DOH. *see* Department of Health (DOH)
DRO. *see* Days revenue outstanding (DRO)
DVT. *see* Deep vein thrombosis (DVT)

E

Electronic medical records, 85–86
Electronic status boards, 117
Emotional distress and back pain, 138–139
Engagement, 84–85

Error. *see also* Mistake proofing; Patient Safety
    Alerts (PSA)
    interventional radiology, 58
    medical epidemic, 50
    medication, 53–55
    physician, 53–55
    prevention, 50
Everyday Lean Ideas, 162
Evidence-based medicine, 141, 205

F

Falling patients, 65–66, 162–163
Family
    involvement, 97
    patient communication, 101–102
    waiting, 103
Fear and back pain, 138–139
Fee-for-service, 147
Financial conundrum, 144–146
Fishbone, 36–37
5S. *see* Sort, simplify, sweep, standardize,
    self-discipline (5 S)
Flow care station, 80, 84–85, 201
    ambulatory care, 90–92
    breakthrough, 78–79
    GIM, 201–203
    indirect care, 92
    invention, 77–79
    orthopedics, 192–195
    to specialty department, 192–195
Flow manager, 81
Flow production, 82–83
Floyd & Delores Jones Cancer Center, 41
Flu shots, 176
    nurses' unions, 57
    RPIW, 55–57
Frontline staff and problem-solving, 162
Furlong, Rich, 71, 86

G

Genba, 164, 181
    defined, xi
    sensei, 158
    supervisors proximity, 21
General internal medicine (GIM)
    appointments, 203
    evidence-based care, 205
    financial improvement, 203

flow stations, 201–203
  MA, 203, 204
  new, 203–205
  physician satisfaction, 205
  restructuring, 200–201
  5S, 201
  skill-task alignment, 195–196, 197–199
  spreading innovation to ambulatory care,
    195–196
  standardization, 204–205
  transformation, 203–205
  uphill battle, 199–200
  waiting, 200
  waste, 204
Genie Industries, 10, 13, 14
Geographic cells, 112–114
Gerbino, Ingrid, 81
GIM. *see* General internal medicine (GIM)
Group Practice Advisory Committee, 5

H

Hand hygiene, 154–155
Handoff, 114–116
Health care
  arrogance as obstacle, 174–176
  institutions *vs.* Virginia Mason, 149–150
Health Maintenance Module, 86
  mistake-proofing, 88
Health maintenance organizations (HMO), 89
Health screening, 73–74
Heart of Change (Kotter), 197
Hitachi air conditioning plant, 19–20
HMO. *see* Health maintenance organizations
    (HMO)
Hourly rounding, 120–122
Human resources (HR) staffing and
    compensation model, 190
Hyperbaric oxygen therapy
  defined, 103–104
  transformation, 103–109

I

IHI. *see* Institute for Health Care Improvement
    (IHI)
Incentives, 146–148
Indirect care, 92
Infusion center, 34
Inpatient care. *see* Transforming inpatient care

Institute for Health Care Improvement (IHI),
    122, 167
Institute of Medicine (IOM), x, 2, 50, 175
  waste, 11
Internal medicine. *see* General internal
    medicine (GIM)
Interventional radiology error, 58
IOM. *see* Institute of Medicine (IOM)

J

Japan trip, 15–27
  first trip, 17–20
  humbling experience, 22–23
  Kaplan and Rona letter home, 18–19
  leadership bonding, 25–26
  resistance, 27–29
  synchronous assembly line, 20–22
Jidoka, 85–87
Journey continues, 165–182
  accountable outside walls, 172–173
  arrogance as obstacle, 174–176
  beginning, 181–182
  future, 179–180
  hope, 178–179
  nonsystem, 176–178
  role model, 168–170
  sustainability, 172–173
  teaching, 165–166
  visitors, 167–168
  VMI, 170–172

K

Kaizen, xiv, 176, 190
  continous incremental improvement, 23–24
  primary care indirect care, 77–79
  Virginia Mason progression, 180
Kaizen Promotion Office (KPO), 28–29, 78,
    95, 167
  hourly rounding, 122
  RPIW audit, 151
  standup, 191
Kanban cards, 107
Kirkland Clinic
  financial turnaround, 83
  phone access, 83
  transformation, 83–85
KPO. *see* Kaizen Promotion Office (KPO)

L

Leadership
  bonding, 25–26
  building, 161–163
  certification, 29–30, 152–153
  changes, 30–31
  daily management, 157
  discipline, 152–153
  engagement, 161, 163–164
  Japan trip, 25–26
  shaping culture by behavior, 31
  structure, 152–153
  VMMC, x, xiv
Lean manufacturing, 10
Leapfrog Group, xv

M

MA. *see* Medical assistants (MA)
Magnetic resonance imaging (MRI), 144, 146
  back pain, 141–143
  cost, 137
Malpractice
  premiums decrease, 65
  suits for adverse events, 64–65
Management. *see also* Leadership
  all are leaders, 161–163
  change, 44
  changing course, 197
  computerized, xiv
  daily, 156–159
  dealing with benefits, 131–134
  discipline, 152–153
  disease, 73
  flow, 73
  fresh eyes, 149–152
  genba, xi
  leadership engagement, 163–164
  methods, 149–164
  middle, 157
  mission alignment, 150
  by policy, 155–156
  standard work with hand hygiene, 154–155
  structure, 152–153
  training within industry, 153–154
  VMMC framework, 5
  weekly reports, 159–161
  world-class management, 155–156

Marketplace
  defined quality, 139–143
  financial conundrum, 144–146
Mason, Virginia, 91
Matsushita, 88
Medical assistants (MA)
  answering telephone calls, 72
  flow manager, 81
  GIM, 203
  indirect care, 78–79
  physicians avoiding flow stations, 78–79
  privacy, 193
  scheduling, 193
  skill-task alignment, 80–83
Medical Emergency Teams (MET), 118–120
  nursing reluctance, 118
  physician reluctance, 118
Medical errors epidemic, 50
Medical Group Management Association, 5
Medical practice, 7
Medical records, electronic, 85–86
Medication error, 53–55
MET. *see* Medical Emergency Teams (MET)
Middle management, 157
Migraine, 144
Mission alignment and management, 150
Mistake proofing
  ambulatory care, 73–75
  Health Maintenance Module, 88
  primary care clinic, 73–75
  safety crusade, 61
MRI. *see* Magnetic resonance imaging (MRI)

N

Nagoya, Japan, 18–19
National Demonstration Project, 122
National Health Service (NHS), xvii,
    165–166, 169
National Quality Forum, 52
Newcastle trip, 165–166
NHS. *see* National Health Service (NHS)
Nurses
  care managers, 81, 88–89
  culture change, 123–126
  dissatisfaction, 43
  patient care, xiv
  patient interaction, 112–113
  reluctance, 118

report/bedside handoff, 114–116
safety crusade, 53
satisfaction, 47
unions, 57

O

Operating rooms (OR), 93–94
back tables, 99–100
beds, 99
brick, 100–101
design esthetics, 103
electronic tracking, 102
family involvement, 97
family waiting, 103
internal setup, 100–101
internal *vs.* external setup, 99
mental valleys, 99
non-value-added time, 98
3 P, 98–100
patient and family communication, 101–102
patient anxiety, 97–98
patient family separation, 102
privacy, 97, 102
productivity, 101
recovery, 102
results, 101
RPIW, 98–100
scheduling, 195–196
setup reduction, 97–102
surgical instruments, 99–100
table, 100–101
OR. *see* Operating rooms (OR)
Orthopedics
flow station, 192–195
privacy, 193
RPIW, 193–194
scheduling, 195
time, 195
Outcomes measurement, 140
Outpatient cancer service, 33–48
continuous improvement, 41–44
new space and new process, 39–41
patient's voice, 37–39
revealing value stream, 34–37
RPIW, 42–43
standardization, 44–46
success, 46–48

P

Patient(s)
anxiety, 97–98
cancer, 35
care and nurses, xiv
centered, 4
coordinated care, 35–36, 149–150
falls, 65–66, 162–163
and family communication, 101–102
focused, 106–109
input, 37–39
listening to, 96–98
nurse interaction, 112–113
3 P, 37–39
safety checklists, 175
satisfaction, 43, 91, 140, 143–144, 193
scheduling, 193
transforming procedural care in HBO,
106–109
voice, 37–39
wasted time, 35, 37
Patient Financial Services (PFS), 191
Patient Safety Alerts (PSA), xiv, 51, 52–53
DVT, 66
safety crusade, 50–52
system evolution, 63–68
Payment posting, 191
PCP. *see* Primary Care and Prevention (PCP)
Report
Peer pressure, 47
Perioperative services, 93–103
Perverse incentives, 146–148
PFS. *see* Patient Financial Services (PFS)
Phone
access, 72–73, 83
calls, 72
in rooms, 92
Physical therapy
back pain, 138–139
vs. physicians in value-added for back pain,
142
Physician(s)
attitude, 11–12, 76, 141
compact, 29, 150
driven, 3–4
error, 53–55
marketplace alignment, 135
opposition, 28–29

reluctance, 118
resistance and standardization, 76
satisfaction and GIM, 205
standardization, 11, 12, 45, 141
Physician-centered
   vs. patient centered medical practice, 7
   VMMC, 8–10
Physician Insurers Association of America
   (PIAA), 50
Postanesthesia care, 94
PQ. *see* Product Quality (PQ) analysis
Premera Insurance, 191
Preventive medicine, 73
Preventive test reminders, xiv
Primary care
   appointment backlogs, 71
   clinic, 69–75
   financial turnaround, 83–84
   indirect care, 77–79
   mistake-proofing, 73–75
   phone access, 72–73
   scheduling, 69–70
   transformation, 83–85
   wasted time, 69–70
Primary Care and Prevention (PCP) Report,
   75–76, 86
Privacy, 97, 102, 193
Problem-solving, 162
Process measurement, 140
Production preparation process (3 P), 36
   HBO transformation, 105
   medicine flows, 37
   new space and new process, 39–41
   OR, 98–100
   patient's voice, 37–39
   process, 96
Product Quality (PQ) analysis, 39–40
Professional liability insurance expenses, xiv
PSA. *see* Patient Safety Alerts (PSA)
Pushback, 17

Q

Quality incident reports (QIR), 50, 52
Quality of care, 1–2

R

Rapid Process Improvement Workshops
   (RPIW), 14, 19, 24, 29, 120
   audit, 151

diabetic planned care visits, 81–82
indirect care, 77–79
marketplace collaborative, 136
new space and new process, 39–41
NHS Northeast, 169
OR setup reduction, 98–100
orthopedics, 193–194
outpatient cancer service, 42–43
shorter length of stay, 126–127
transforming procedural care in HBO,
   107–108
VMI, 173
waste, 191
Registered nurse (RN), 81, 88–89
Report/bedside handoff, 114–116
Restructuring, 200–201
Revenue cycle and headwaters, 190
Revenue loss, 145–146
RFID cards, 91
RN. *see* Registered nurse (RN)
Role model, 168–170
Rounding, 120–122
RPIW. *see* Rapid Process Improvement
   Workshops (RPIW)

S

Safety crusade, 49–68
   culture of safety, 61–63
   flu shots, 55–57
   mistake proofing, 61
   nurse's courage, 53
   patient safety alerts, 50–52
   physician's courage, 53–55
   PSA system evolution, 63–68
Safety screen, 86–87
Same-day appointments, 141–142
Scheduling, 193
   MA, 193
   OR, 195–196
   primary care, 69–70
Schein, Edgar, 31
Screening
   health, 73–74
   safety, 86–87
Sensei, xiii, xvii, 22–23
   genba, 158
Shingo, Shigeo, 88
Shizuoka, Japan
   Hitachi air conditioning plant, 19–20

Silos, 196–197
Six Sigma, 10
Skepticism, 16–17
Skill-task alignment, 146
 general internal medicine, 197–199
 indirect care flow production, 82–83
Sort, simplify, sweep, standardize, self-
  discipline (5 S), 29
 transforming inpatient care, 117–118
 transforming procedural care in HBO, 108
Spine clinic, 143
Staff
 feedback, 156
 satisfaction, 91
Standardization, 204
 daily management, 157
 GIM, 204–205
 opposition, 28
 outpatient cancer service, 44–46
 physician attitude, 11–12, 141
 physicians, 45
 physician's resistance, 76
 5 S, 29, 108, 117–118
Starbucks
 absenteeism, 140
 cost control, 141
 employee back pain, 133–134
 marketplace collaborative, 136
 presenteeism, 140
 procurement process, 135
 rapid return to function, 140
 same-day access, 137–139
Stop the line, xiv, 20–21, 24
Surgery. *see also* Operating Rooms (OR);
  Orthopedics; Perioperative services
 induction area, 94
 instruments, 99–100
 instrument sterilization, 151
 OR setup reduction, 99–100
 prep rooms, 102
 redesign, 94–95
 waiting, 93–94

T

Teaching journey continues, 165–166
Teamwork, 7
Telephone. *see* Phone
Temple, Rosemary, 91
Tests and computerized reminders, 75–76

3P. *see* Production preparation process (3 P)
To Err Is Human (IOM), x, 2, 50, 175
Toyoda, Sakichi, 18, 21, 89
Toyota Motomachi production facility, 20–21
Toyota Museum, Nagoya, Japan, 18–19, 89
Toyota Production System (TPS), x–xi, 10
 Boeing, 13–14
 eliminate waste, 11–12
 introducing, 13
 mistake-proofing, 18
 setup reduction, 18
 success elements, xvii
 vendor collaboration, 24
 VMMC adaptation, xiii
Toyota Production System: Beyond Large-Scale
  Production (Ohno), 12
Toyota Talent: Developing Your People the
  Toyota Way (Liker and Meier), 154
Toyota Way to Health Care Excellence (Black),
  14, 29
TPS. *see* Toyota Production System (TPS)
Training people, 153–154
Transformation, ix–x
Transforming inpatient care, 111–127, 112–127
 electronic status boards, 117
 geographic cells, 112–114
 hourly rounding from reactive to
  proactive, 120–122
 in-room documentation, 116
 knowing frontline work, 122–123
 medical emergency teams, 118–120
 nurse patient interaction, 112–113
 nursing culture change, 123–126
 nursing report/bedside handoff, 114–116
 5 S, 117–118
 shorter length of stay, 126–127
 supplies, 113–114
 visual work environment, 116–117
Transforming procedural care in HBO,
  103–109
 asking why, 105–106
 Center for Hyperbaric Medicine, 103–105
 financial results, 109
 kanban cards, 107
 patient focused, 106–109
 productivity, 108–109
 results, 108–109
 RPIW, 107–108
 5 S, 108
 standardization, 108

Transforming procedural care in perioperative
        services, 93–103
    breakthrough, 100–103
    creating new ambulatory surgical
        experience, 93–94
    design challenge, 94–95
    listening to patients, 96–98
    setup reduction, 98–100
Transparency, 136, 147, 160
Tuesday Standup, 159–161
Type 2 diabetes, 74

U

United Kingdom National Health Service, xvii,
        165–166

V

Value-added care, 11, 142
Value stream, 6, 135–137
Vendor collaboration, 24
Virginia Mason Institute (VMI), xvii–xviii,
        171, 172–173
Virginia Mason Medical Center (VMMC)
    Aetna-Starbucks collaboration, 145
    description, 1
    financial woes, 1
    founding, 1
    fresh eyes, 149–152
    improved financial performance, xv–xvi
    innovative genes, 1
    leadership, x, xiv
    management framework, 5
    vs. other health care institutions, 149–150
    patient-centered, 4
    physician-centric, 8–10
    physician-driven, 3–4
    physician retreat, 8–9
    primary care clinic, 69–70
    progression, 180
    quality of care, 1–2

quality *vs.* finances, 4
    TPS adaptation, xiii
Virginia Mason Production System (VMPS),
        xi, xiii
    applied to business functions, 189–190
    effectiveness, xv
    error prevention, 50
    fused into electronic medical record system,
        86
    production cost reduction, 145–146
    pyramid, 4
    zero defects, 26
Visitors, 167–168
Visual cues for falling patients, 162–163
Visual work environment, 116–117
VMI. *see* Virginia Mason Institute (VMI)
VMMC. *see* Virginia Mason Medical Center
        (VMMC)
VMPS. *see* Virginia Mason Production System
        (VMPS)

W

Waiting
    ambulatory care, 70–73
    family, 103
    GIM, 200
    OR, 103
    period for appointments, 141
    for surgery, 93–94
Waiting rooms waste, 22–23
Washington State Department of Health, 100
Waste
    elimination, 10–12, 98–100, 113–114
    relentless attack, 190–192
Weekly reports accountability, 159–161
Why Hospitals Should Fly (Nance), 7
Wiremold, 13, 14, 15
Workstations on wheels (WOW), 116
World Class Production System (Black), 10
WOW. *see* Workstations on wheels (WOW)

About the Author

Charles Kenney is a former journalist who served as a reporter and editor at the *Boston Globe*. He has served on the faculty of the Institute for Healthcare Improvement National Forum on Quality Improvement in Health Care. He is the author of ten books including *The Best Practice: How the New Quality Movement Is Transforming Medicine*, which the *New York Times* described as "the first large-scale history of the quality movement." Senator Edward M. Kennedy called the book an "important contribution to the nation's ongoing struggle to make the best in modern health care available and affordable for all Americans." He lives in Boston and can be reached at charliekenney@gmail.com.